FOOTSO

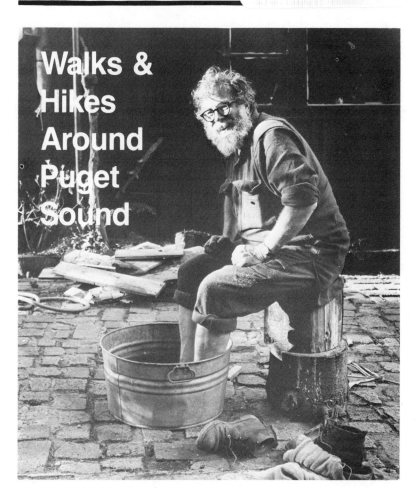

Walks &
Hikes
Around
Puget
Sound

By Harvey Manning/Photos by Vicky Spring
Maps by Gary Rands/The Mountaineers•Seattle

Carbon River • Puyallup River • Nisqually River •
Southern Frontier • Puget Sound Trail from
Tacoma to Olympia • Islands in the Sound •
Kitsap Peninsula • South Olympic Peninsula

THE MOUNTAINEERS

Organized 1906

To explore and study the mountains, forests, and watercourses of the Northwest;

To gather into permanent form the history and traditions of this region;

To preserve by the encouragement of protective legislation or otherwise the natural beauty of Northwest America;

To make explorations into these regions in fulfillment of the above purposes;

To encourage a spirit of good fellowship among all lovers of outdoor life.

First edition, April 1979
Copyright © 1979 by Harvey Manning. All rights reserved.
Published by
The Mountaineers
719 Pike Street
Seattle, Washington 98101

Manufactured in the United States of America

Distributed in Canada by Douglas & McIntyre Ltd.
1875 Welch Street, North Vancouver, B.C. V7P 1B7

Library of Congress Catalog Card No. 77-23727
ISBN 0-916890-81-3

Book design by Marge Mueller

Cover photo *(by Bob and Ira Spring): Mt. Rainier from old lookout site at Glacier View*

Title photo: *The author, Harvey Manning, after 3000 miles of walking for the Footsore series*

Photos on pages 37, 39, 93, 118, 120, 134, 161, 174, 219, 233 by Bob and Ira Spring

INTRODUCTION 4

As faithful **Footsore** fans know, this is a single book though in four volumes. The reader is referred to Introduction 1 for explanation of the data-coding system, Two-Hour Rule, Ten Essentials, and Trespassing Code; to Introduction 2 for the esthetics of tree farms and instructions on wallowing in snow; and to Introduction 3 for the technique of beachwalking.

A final time the reminder: most **Footsore** country is in such flux that a guidebook cannot give a moneyback guarantee. The bulk of this volume was surveyed in spring and fall of 1978; some trips were in late 1977 and a few earlier. If you wish to help the surveyor modernize future printings, or simply to tell him what kind of fool he is, please address corrections and comments c/o The Mountaineers.

Now to new business. Two items remain on the agenda.

MAPS

For civilized terrain the sketch maps in these pages suffice. In primitive regions they should be supplemented by U.S. Geological Survey maps, obtainable locally from map, mountain, and marine shops or by mail (write for a free state index map) from:

Branch of Distribution, Central Region
U.S. Geological Survey
Box 25286, Denver Federal Center
Denver, Colorado 80225

The maps noted in the chapter introductions are in the 1:24,000 (7½-minute) and 1:62,500 (15-minute) series that between them cover all **Footsore** country.

The new 1:100,000 sheets encompass larger areas and are useful for overview, yet have a surprising amount of fine detail. As of 1978 the Bellingham, Port Townsend, Seattle, Skykomish, and Snoqualmie Pass quadrangles are published, the remainder scheduled soon. Also at this scale are the new county maps, represented as of 1978 solely by King County.

The old 1:250,000 series covers even larger areas for even broader overviews but with minimal detail. The **Footsore** sheets are Victoria, Wenatchee, Seattle, Yakima, and Hoquiam.

Valuable variants of the USGS 15-minute sheets are published privately in the Green Trails series. Some GS information is deleted to improve clarity, other information is added. A hiker does well to carry both: the Green Trails for current status of roads and trails (updated every 2 years), the GS original for certain excised information (such as old logging roads) crucial to some **Footsore** routes.

Essential to the contentment of a **Footsore** pilgrim is a map of his entire world permitting ready identification of all visible works of God and man. As of early 1979 the best for the purpose is the pictorial landform map of the State of Washington drawn and published by Dee Molenaar and sold at mountain, map, book, and marine shops. However, in early 1980 Dee will publish a map even better for our purpose, **Puget Sound Country, Washington,** the indispensable companion of these volumes. Coverage will be from Cascades to Olympics, Canada to Chehalis — which is to say, precisely the **Footsore** world, beyond whose edges is the void. The map proper, plus two panoramas, one westward over Puget Sound to the Olympics, the other eastward to the Cascades, will let the traveler on a high vantage point read off mountain-front peaks and valleys up and down the length of Cascades and Olympics from Black and Bald Hills to Chuckanut Mountain, and sounds and canals and bays and straits and passages and inlets and coves, and cities and towns and freeways and pulpmills and nuclear power plants and Doomsday devices. In addition, the margin of the sheet will provide with maps, photos, and text a concise introduction to glacial geomorphology, explaining natural features and making every walk a class in Pleistocene history.

THE COMMERCIAL

If the surveyor, here at the end of the trolley line, may be permitted to step from third person to first, let me say I had no intention of walking these particular 3000-odd miles between Thanksgiving 1976 and Thanksgiving 1978. My plan was merely to spend several winter months revising Janice Krenmayr's **Footloose Around Puget Sound,** nationally-acclaimed classic and a favorite of mine since working with Janice to bring it to press in 1969.

The country had other ideas. Having suckered me in it wouldn't let me go until I'd satisfied three ambitions so old as to be half-forgotten: (1) Tracing the saltwater shore from Bellingham to the many ends of Puget Sound, and up and down the Kitsap Peninsula and across the northeast of the Olympic, and around all the islands (except the San Juans) readily accessible to boatless pedestrians. (2) Following rivers of the Cascades, Skagit to Deschutes, from saltwater to mountain front, or in one case to the glacier. (3) Surveying the mountain fronts that so neatly ring the cozy **Footsore** world — on the west the Olympics; on the east the Cascades; on the north the westward thrust of Cascades to saltwater and, in the wide opening-to-the-ocean westerly of that, the "San Juan Mountains"; on the south the thrust of the Cascades' outrigger Bald Hills west nearly to meet the Black Hills, the isolated upland in the gap between Cascades and Olympics; and in the center of the basin the "Pre-Olympic Mountains" whose most upstanding remnants, the Issaquah Alps and Green and Gold Mountains, are ruins of an ancient bridge from Cascades through Seattle and Bremerton to the Olympics.

When all that was done, lo, it seemed to me there was something more than merely a guidebook. What more? Whatever, you'll not find it in words — at least not in the technical-writer's prose here — but only where I found it — afoot in the length and breadth, ups and downs, of the **Footsore** world. If you do, it may be said of you, as of me by erstwhile associates:

". . . Beware! Beware!
His flashing eyes, his floating hair!
Weave a circle round him thrice,
And close your eyes with holy dread . . ."

You too will be a threat to the peace of tea parties and to orderly getting and spending, for you too will have fed on honey-dew and drunk the milk of Paradise — and you too will have witnessed the devastation wrought by the plague.

What plague? The one observed by Pogo. In the bubonic form it is symptomized by raging real-estate fever and buboes of laissez-faire subdivision. In the pneumonic form the contagion is in exhalations of engines on freeways, woods roads, trails.

The craven mountaineer scuttles off to his remote wilderness preserves and squats there in his sissy tent by his cute Svea cooking his freeze-dried chop suey and philosophizes, "Well, this is America, motorcyclists have rights too."

But to have lived through the ATV invasion of **Footsore** lands without fleeing, rather remaining to stubbornly resist, is to feel akin to the Indians, to empathize with Crazy Horse and the Ghost Dancers.

Shall we pedestrians submit to force and humbly shuffle off to wilderness reservations?

Or shall we say the hell with it and gallop down whooping and hollering and scalp the scoundrels?

Figuratively speaking, of course.

Harvey Manning
Cougar Mountain

ACKNOWLEDGMENTS 4

Information and assistance were graciously provided by R. Robert Burns and Linda Silvis, Olympic National Forest; Don R. Campbell, Mt. Baker-Snoqualmie National Forest; Temple A. Reynolds, National Park Service; Lt. Col. Donald G. Mitchell, 9th Infantry Division, U.S. Army; Willard B. Hesselbart, U.S. Fish and Wildlife Service; William A. Bush, Larry Chapman, Lanin E. Warriner, Mike James, Avery Winslow, and a bunch of nice folks whose names I didn't catch, Washington State Parks; Terry Patton, Jerry Kammenga, Mark Olander, Kenneth Solt, and John A. Kingsbury, Washington Department of Natural Resources; Daniel J. Evans and Pete Steilberg, Evergreen State College; Dale Cole, Steven G. Archie, and David Halme, University of Washington; Raymond E. Foley, Bremerton Parks and Recreation; Randy A. Hatfield, Kitsap County Parks; officials of cities and counties who didn't answer my letters but at least didn't have me arrested; Howard Millan, Jack Palmquist, and the fellow who drove from Vail to the reload in the winter night to let me out the locked gate, Weyerhaeuser Company; gypo loggers and brushpickers and oysterpickers and fishermen and birdwatchers and other prowlers of bushes and beaches met along the way; two pairs of Raichle Calawahs and one pair REI Wayfarer Deluxe; and a 1969 VW beetle that gave its miles from 77,436 to 114,059.

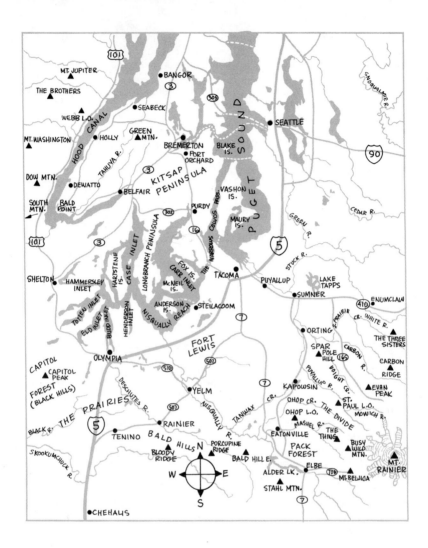

101
MT. JUPITER ▲
THE BROTHERS ▲
WEBB L.O. ▲
● BANGOR
3
305
MT. WASHINGTON ▲
● HOLLY
● SEABECK
GREEN MTN. ▲
HOOD CANAL
TAHUYA R.
DOW MTN. ▲
● DEWATTO
KITSAP PENINSULA
BREMERTON
● FORT ORCHARD
3
● BELFAIR
BLAKE IS.
● SEATTLE
SOUTH MTN. ▲
BALD POINT ▲
101
3
302
HARTSTENE IS.
CASE INLET
LONGBRANCH PENINSULA
PURDY ●
16
VASHON IS.
COLVOS PASS.
THE NARROWS
MAURY IS.
PUGET SOUND
CEDAR R.
GREEN R.
90
SNOQUALMIE R.
SHELTON ●
HAMMERSLEY INLET
TOTTEN INLET
ELD INLET
BUDD INLET
HENDERSON INLET
FOX IS.
CARR INLET
McNEIL IS.
ANDERSON REACH
NISQUALLY REACH
● STEILACOOM
TACOMA ●
● PUYALLUP
STUCK R.
5
● SUMNER
LAKE TAPPS
410
● ENUMCLAW
CR. WHITE R.
S. PRAIRIE
CAPITOL PEAK ▲
CAPITOL FOREST (BLACK HILLS)
OLYMPIA ●
FORT LEWIS
1
510
501
● ORTING
SPAR POLE HILL ▲
165
CARBON R.
THE THREE SISTERS ▲
CARBON RIDGE
THE PRAIRIES
DESCHUTES R.
YELM ●
7
● KAPOWSIN
PUYALLUP R.
VOIGHT CR.
OHOP CR. THE DIVIDE
ST. PAUL L.O.
MOWICH R.
EVAN PEAK ▲
5
501
NISQUALLY R.
TANWAX CR.
● RAINIER
OHOP L.O.
MASHEL R.
THE THING
BUSY WILD MTN. ▲
BLACK R.
● TENINO
BALD HILLS
BLOODY RIDGE
PORCUPINE RIDGE
● EATONVILLE
PACK FOREST
MT. RAINIER ▲
SKOOKUMCHUCK R.
N
W E
S
BALD HILL E. ▲
ALDER LK. ●
● ELBE
706
MT. BELJICA ▲
● CHEHALIS
STAHL MTN. ▲
7

CONTENTS 4

8

Carbon River below Crocker

CARBON RIVER

In 1881 Bailey Willis opened a tourists' horse trail to the Carbon River from the new coal-mining town of Wilkeson, and next year cut a way over the ridge to the Mowich, where (or perhaps on the North Fork Puyallup) he erected the cluster of log cabins grandly called Palace Camp. Prospectors later built a spur to Mowich Lake and Spray Park; a grindstone they left at the spur junction gave it the name of Grindstone Camp (at the head of Voight Creek?) and the spur the name of Grindstone Trail. When the railroad was extended to new mines farther up the Carbon, the Bailey Willis Trail became known as the Fairfax Trail, ultimately extended through Puyallup country to the Nisqually River.

Except for bits in the national park, the old trail system — here and throughout the Carbon province — has been obliterated by logging. Hikers long ago gave it up as a lost cause and herded into the park. However, the short hiking season there, the driving distance from cities, and the boots-boots-boots marching up and down, are reviving interest in the hinterland. Its time is coming — again.

If there's any smartness left in the world, the first of the Carbon subprovinces, the river itself, is sure to become not just locally but nationally famous. From saltwater of Puget Sound to glaciers of Rainier, a branch of the proposed Tacoma-to-Tahoma Trail, close to cities and walkable all the year, would go from pastures to wild gorges to icefields on the proposed Carbon River Parkway.

In the angle between the Carbon River and the White River (with its tributaries, the Clearwater River and Canyon Creek), is an enormous realm little known to walkers but immensely rich in low-to-high delights. At Wilkeson begins a long and roundabout but veritable buttress of Rainier, running from Gleason Hill to Carbon Ridge to Independence Ridge to Sluiskin Peaks to Old Desolate to Curtis Ridge to the summit icecap. Proposed here are (1) a Carbon-Clearwater Wilderness in Mt. Baker-Snoqualmie National Forest to preserve the pristine integrity of this buttress, and (2) a Carbon Ridge Trail starting at a "Hikers' Special" Metro bus stop in Wilkeson and extending the length of the buttress. From headwaters on Carbon Ridge flow South Prairie Creek (really a river) and its tributaries, Gale and Wilkeson Creeks. The high country, notably South Prairie Ridge and Three Sisters, has been scalped to the last twig, providing sublime panoramas of the lowlands, better than can be gotten from the park, and opening to boots in spring rather than midsummer. These ridges are suggested as bully routes for spurs to the Carbon Ridge Trail. However, the marvel is not the high country but the low, the deep and narrow and jungled white-water canyons, literally wilder than the interior of the Olympics or North Cascades. Wilderness thrusts out virtually to the outskirts of Buckley; by trading some lands with private owners and by obtaining easements, the Forest Service has the opportunity to establish a trail system starting at a Metro bus stop in Buckley and winding up the canyons through tree farms to the Carbon-Clearwater Wilderness and into Rainier Park.

On the other side of the Carbon is "Ptarmigan Ridge," so called here because it indeed is an extension of that ice-and-lava cleaver out through Tolmie and "Park Boundary Peaks" and down to Spar Pole and Microwave

Hills — a continuous buttress of Rainier from summit icecap to lowland plain. The outermost segment is in the Kapowsin Tree Farm, long beloved of walkers not only for open-in-winter, close-to-city, second-growth wildland forests, plus — nowadays — broad views from Second Wave clearcuts, but for the gate policy of St. Regis Paper. Except for a very few roads, and during only a portion of hunting season, the company's gates are firmly closed to public wheels (not feet) and the roads are zealously patrolled to convince bandito razzers that crime doesn't pay. Ah, the quiet! Deranged by motorcycle harassment? Come here for the cure.

USGS maps: Lake Tapps, Enumclaw, Wilkeson, Buckley, Orting, Sumner, Golden Lakes, Kapowsin

Carbon River Parkway Trail (Map — page 11)

Trails of the Carbon valley in Mount Rainier National Park are wildly nice, and lots of walkers know so. However, few realize a green-jungle white-water lane of lonesome wildness reaches out from the park nearly to suburbia. Confronted by this magnificent gift of nature, the rational response is to preserve it in a Carbon River Parkway, under national or state or county auspices, and build a foot-and-horse trail, open the whole year, through the gorgeous gorge and forest, over the colorful rocks and by the foaming cataracts, past the old coal mines and coke ovens and vanished villages.

But pedestrians needn't sit impatiently on their boots awaiting governmental action. Saving a hop, skip, or jump here and there, the entire route is walkable now. Indeed, via the Puyallup River (which see), it is not only possible but easy to hike the proposed Tacoma-to-Tahoma Trail from Commencement Bay to Carbon Glacier, saltwater shores to volcano icefields. That, folks, is a trip.

Carbon Mouth to Orting

Pent between gravel-forest precipice and dike, the Carbon wends its final miles to the confluence with the Puyallup in green lonesomeness, the walker scarcely aware Orting is near.

Drive Highway 162 to Orting and turn north on Calistoga Avenue, which becomes a gravel lane leading to the river. Park on the dike, elevation 180 feet.

Walk downstream on the dike or, when available, on bars of gravel and black volcanic sand tracked by deer and ducks, raccoons and herons. The dike is hedged by forest now and then broken by pastures. On the far side the river cuts the foot of a cliff of gravels and jungle rising as tall as 400 feet.

In 2¾ miles the dike ends and a gravel bar thrusts out to a tip between the Puyallup and Carbon Rivers, the former often yellow-green murky with rock milk while the latter is crystal clear — or, sometimes, brown with glacier mud. The presence of The Mountain is closely felt. A dandy spot for lunch.

Round trip 3½ miles, allow 2 hours
High point 180 feet, elevation gain minor
All year

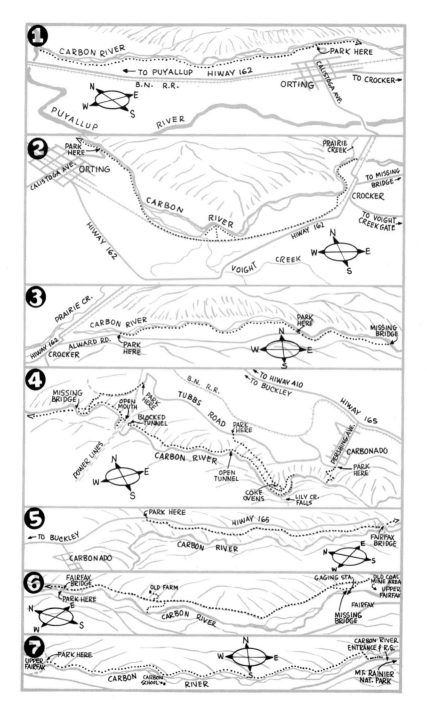

Carbon River near Orting

Orting to Crocker

The Trail follows gravel bars, dike, and railroad tracks as the route leaves the Big Valley of the Puyallup River (or, actually, of the Really Big River of Pleistocene times) for the Carbon's own cozier valley.

Park as before and walk upstream, admiring river and birds, wildwood wall, columnar basalt of the dike, and bullet-pocked concrete piers of some old mystery. Ahead rise Microwave and Spar Pole Hills and, farther along, the Park Boundary Peaks and Rainier itself.

In ¾ mile an easy-around stock fence halts razzers; footpath continues ¼ mile to the railroad. The river is joined by the alder-arched birdlane of Voight Creek.

The best part of the trip is a sidetrip. Dive off the tracks on a path through woods to river gravels. First walk the wild "island" downstream ¼ mile to the junction of Voight and Carbon, then upstream ¼ mile to a point where the tracks can be regained at 1½ miles from the start.

In the next 1 mile the walker is forced by river-near houses to stick to the tracks, which cut inland. But gravel bars and dikes resume for a final ½ mile to South Prairie Creek. The walk also can start here, parking by the Highway 162 and rail bridges.

Round trip 6 miles, allow 4 hours
High point 300 feet, elevation gain 120 feet

Crocker to Missing Bridge

Now begins the heart of the matter — the wild river, the solemn gorge.

From Orting drive Highway 162 south 1 mile to Crocker Grange Y and then east (left) 2 miles. Just before the railroad underpass turn east (right) on Alward Road, past a row of coke ovens. In ½ mile, where the road touches the river, park on the shoulder, elevation 330 feet.

In the forests live people who don't mind being occasionally wiped out; their floodplain habitations are hidden from a person walking gravels of the braided channels. The splendid stream brawls through the most exciting collection of boulders in any **Footsore** river: black and red Rainier andesite, iron-yellow Wilkeson sandstone, white granite, black coal, gray lignite chunks of petrified trees, gaudy clinkers from coke ovens, plus rusty artifacts from old towns. A scant 2 miles of ecstasy for a pretty-rocks fan leads to another contact with the road, where it ends. For a shorter walk park here, elevation 440 feet.

No houses now, because 300-foot walls of lush forest and outcropping sandstone press close to the river. And very shortly no wheels; muck ruts stop at a washout. Only feet continue into the utter wildness, following the ancient railroad grade cut in the jungle slopes. Fern-hung rock ribs jut into green pools. Black-sand beaches invite children to build castles and everybody to take off shoes and wade.

All too soon it's over, sob. In a scant 1 mile the rail grade runs out in the air; on the far side is the causeway-abutment of the missing bridge. So, turn back. But first descend to the abutment of quarried Wilkeson sandstone resting on an outcrop of the same rock. And having walked the grade upstream for the sake of trees and ferns and flowers, walk the gravels downstream for the sake of boulders and dippers.

Round trip (long version) 6 miles, allow 4 hours
High point 520 feet, elevation gain 200 feet

Missing Bridge to Blocked Tunnel

Gentlefolk will want to wait until the bridge is no longer missing, the Parkway Trail is built, before doing this short stretch. But brush beasts will find beauty here, now. And solitude. And the open end of the blocked tunnel.

Drive Highway 165 to Carbonado and turn right, into and through town, on Pershing Avenue. Just past Carbonado Tavern the road (now the Tubbs Road, though unsigned) bends sharp right along the canyon rim, joins another road from the right, and passes the sewage-treatment plant, swinging left and becoming narrow and gravel. At 2 miles from the tavern, where Tubbs Road crosses a wide powerline swath, turn left on the service-and-logging road to the gate. Park here, elevation 837 feet.

Or, if the gate is open, perhaps drive on. Follow the logging road as it veers rightward from the powerline and in a scant ½ mile reaches the canyon rim. The rail grade is 300 steep feet below. You can't miss it. No way down is dangerous if care is taken. Most, though, are mean and nasty medleys of thorns and logs and muck. The single neat way is the crest of an indistinct ridge, easily found from below (making the return a cinch) but requiring luck to find from above. The recommended procedure is to continue a couple hundred feet from where the logging road hits the rim, plunge over the brink, and look for the best. If fortune smiles, in several minutes you'll hit the grade precisely where it leaves the valley wall and strikes out across the floor on a causeway.

First walk downstream, out on the causeway to its end in rotting trestlework. Game traces lead easily to a wonderful wide gravel bar. Ah, solitude! Ah, pretty rocks and pools! Ah, dippers dipping, sandpipers peeping! Ah, picnicking, wading, napping! Ah, wilderness!

Now, upstream, resolutely cheerful as a gap in the grade puts you on game paths through a creek's brambles and slop; if only the deer were taller their routes would be more satisfactory. But soon the pain is rewarded by the open end of the blocked tunnel, the interior heaped with old rail ties. By clambering over the dry-rotting jackstraw a person might explore the Stygian depths. A happier tour is along the foot of the sandstone cliff to the river and upstream on a bar. The cliff overhangs 20-odd feet at the bottom, sheltering an alcove garden of maidenhair fern and dangling shrubs. Ah, charmingness!

When the river is very low, or the walker totally insane, the cliff corner can be rounded to the next segment of the route.

Round trip 2½ miles, allow 3 hours
High point 837 feet, elevation gain 400 feet

Blocked Tunnel to Carbonado

Here is the canyon climax — the narrowest chasm, the steepest walls. And here is the busiest walking, with not only trees and flowers and rocks, loud waters of the river and white ribbon of Lily Creek Falls, but coke ovens, an old mine, and railroad tunnels.

Drive to the Carbonado Tavern. For an optional overture, recommended only for the doughty, park here. Walk straight ahead by a half-hidden old brick building on the canyon rim, start down a road-trail that quickly ends, and pick a steep but safe way down down down to the wild wild river and the big big sandstone blocks. Wow. Now climb 470 vertical feet back to the rim. Whew. But it was worth it.

As above, drive Tubbs Road. At a scant 1 mile from Carbonado Tavern, spot a narrow road reverse-turning left, over the rim and down. Park here, elevation 1050 feet.

Walk the road past a slide that halts sporty four-wheelers (two-wheelers continue) to a switchback at ⅔ mile.

The missing bridge

Abandoned railroad tunnel below Carbonado

Sidetrip No. 1: Go straight off the end of the switchback, under a wondrous trog wall of sandstone, to a rail grade, which in ¼ mile ends at the mouth of the coal mine, long collapsed.

Back on the main trail, in ¼ mile begins a line of overgrown coke ovens. Everywhere hereabouts are concrete remnants of mysterious structures, relics of a considerable town, cokery, and mine, the terminus of the railroad.

Sidetrip No. 2: Descend a path upstream to a rail grade close by the river. Soon halt to enjoy Lily Creek Falls streaming whitely 300 feet down greenery, the sandstone cliff decorated with a large patch of corydalis in addition to the usual cedars, maples, moss, ferns. At a scant ¼ mile from the coke ovens, past a car-loading area and a clinker dump, the rail line ends at a sharp turn in the gorge where cataracts thunder through huge lumps of sandstone.

Back on the main trail, the route proceeds downstream on the riverside rail grade. In ⅓ mile is a stupendous overhanging cliff of Wilkeson sandstone; here, too, is a railroad tunnel 90 feet long with a 30-foot ceiling. The way goes on, passing a sidepath to partly-open mines, lovely gravel bars inviting picnics, and another egad cliff; among other joys, one suddenly realizes the motorcycles have been left behind. The trail dwindles and at 1 mile from the first tunnel ends where a rock rib juts out in the river. The railroad bored through the rib but a mudslide has covered the tunnel mouth.

Round trip (with sidetrips) 7 miles, allow 5 hours
High point 1050 feet, elevation gain 500 feet

Carbonado to Fairfax

Walk with ghosts along a wild river in a glory of a second-growth wilderness. Follow a long-abandoned railroad by a long-deserted farm in the middle of nowhere to a coal mine long swallowed by forest.

Drive Highway 165 past Carbonado ¾ mile. Look sharp just at the far end of a wide shoulder, just before a sign, "Speed Zone Ahead, 35 mph," and spot an obscure sideroad turning right, into the brush. Park on the shoulder, elevation 1209 feet.

Walk the green-tunnel sideroad following the railroad grade sliced in canyon cliffs; far below in lush forest is the river. At 2 miles the grade passes under the Fairfax Bridge (Highway 165). The walk thus far is a pleasant, peaceful stroll on a weekday. But never on Sunday or after school lets out.

For the shorter (and weekend) version, drive over the Fairfax Bridge to parking on the west side, elevation 1324 feet. Walk back across the bridge and skid down to the railroad.

The highway is across the valley, unseen and rarely heard; this is the wild side. At ¼ mile is a ghost — sandstone foundations of some unguessable structure; old maps show a mine downhill here. At 1 mile the ghosts throng — above the tracks, and also below, are fields of an abandoned homestead. Ascend the hill to concrete foundations of the house. Descend to pastures on a wide alluvial terrace. Beyond lichen-hung fruit trees find a rude path dropping to the river in an enchanted spot, canyon walls plunging to pools of glacier limeade. What went wrong in Shangri La? Aside from the train quitting and the house burning down?

The farm marks the onset of perfect peace. Grassy-overgrown and often log-blocked, the rail grade goes on, but no wheels intrude the forest of big firs and spruces and maples. And few boots — yet the walking is easy enough, if slow.

At 2 miles from the farm, 3 from Fairfax Bridge, the grade touches the river and the route leaves the grade, here blocked by slides and washouts. Game paths on flats beside the river lead in a short bit to the trip end.

Talk about ghosts! Wander the woods and ponder the "unnatural" look of the terrain. Suddenly, from the black earth of a mountain-beaver excavation, from clinkers enwrapped in tree roots, deduce these are the outlines of coal operation. In mind's eye strip away the half-century-old forest and see rail spurs and bunkers and buildings and machinery and waste-rock dumps of the Fairfax Mine.

Follow the main rail grade to pilings and concrete and sandstone blocks pushing into the river — another missing bridge. On the other side is a stream-gaging station. And, unseen, the hamlet of Fairfax, where in olden days tourists got off the Northern Pacific train and were conducted by pack train to The Mountain.

Round trip from near Carbonado 11 miles, allow 8 hours
High point 1350 feet, elevation gain 300 feet

Round trip from Fairfax Bridge 7 miles, allow 5 hours

Fairfax to National Park

The final segment is noted mainly for completeness, since it'll not be a popular walk until the Parkway Trail is built. The ultimate route should stay on the wild side of the river, not crossing to Fairfax; at present, however,the brush is too much.

Drive Highway 165 a long ½ mile past the Fairfax Bridge to the Y and take the left, toward the Carbon River entrance to Rainier National Park. In 3 miles, shortly after passing a couple of roadside homes and the clearing where the school stood until a decade or so ago, and just after crossing Evans Creek, is a Y with no signs; go left, switchbacking downhill ¾ mile to a valley-bottom T. The cluster of houses here is the center of Upper Fairfax. Unfortunately, the inhabitants don't take kindly to prowling strangers, even if they are harmless history nuts, so drive on, right, past a two-storey brown house that was the railroad station, and shortly cross the Carbon River. Park out of the way on a shoulder, elevation 1400 feet.

Proceed upstream from the bridge, partly on woodland paths, partly on river gravels; just here the river bed widens out to a "valley train" of braided channels that continue to the Carbon Glacier. In 4 miles the river can be crossed on the road 1811 bridge to the park boundary. In some 8 more miles on park roads and trails is the terminus of the Carbon River Parkway Trail, the snout of the Carbon Glacier.

History is thick hereabouts. The railroad continued 2 miles past Upper Fairfax to the hamlet of Carbon, which then had a school and a ranger station. From there the "incline" of a logging railroad went 1500 vertical feet up the south valley wall to a logging camp. On the north valley wall, 150 feet above the river, was the enigmatic Cliff House. At various times there were several logging railroads, on both sides of the valley, and three lumber mills. Before that were the coal mines and coke ovens, still to be seen, as are the old cemetery and logging camps moldering in second-growth forests. And in just about the beginning there were Bailey Willis and his trail.

Round trip to road 1811 bridge 8 miles, allow 7 hours
High point 1700 feet, elevation gain 300 feet
All year

Fairfax Bridge over Carbon River

Abandoned logging road up Gleason Hill

Gleason Hill (Map — page 21)

If there are any justice and wisdom in the world, someday there'll be a trail from Wilkeson along Gleason Hill to Carbon Ridge and Rainier National Park. A lonesome footroad permits sampling of the woodsy wilds now. The snow-line-probing is particularly recommended.

Drive to Upper Fairfax and cross the Carbon River bridge (see Carbon River Parkway Trail — Fairfax to National Park). Park here, elevation 1400 feet.

Uphill to the left a bit is the narrow track of the ancient Fairfax CCC Road, now closed to vehicles. The road angles gently uphill, downvalley, then contours, revealing itself as an old logging railroad from Wilkeson. In winter there are views through the mostly-alder forest to the Carbon valley and Ptarmigan Ridge. In spring there are flowers. Creeks are pretty. Watch for deer — and elk.

In 2½ miles, at 1850 feet, is a Y. The road straight ahead leads via the "Mud Run," beloved of local sports, to the vicinity of Wilkeson. Take the right, uphill, and ascend moderately, switchbacking, trending upvalley, to the ridge-crest plateau at 2300 feet. Where spurs go left, keep right, staying near the edge of the steep slope down to the Carbon. Part of the cab of a Model A truck is passed; watchful walkers will spot, at three other places, three other pieces.

In 1¾ miles, at 2350 feet, is a Y. Trip's end is near. Walk both forks. All around are moldering remains of an enormous logging camp and sizable sawmill of the 1930s. The right fork leads ¼ mile to heaps of weathered mill-ends, piles of rotten sawdust, collapsed buildings, rusting machinery. The left leads ¼ mile to a ridgetop clearing, more heaps of silvered mill-ends, and a large elk pasture at the head of South Fork Gale Creek. From here the proposed trail would climb Burnt Mountain, whose heights are visible above, and follow Carbon Ridge onward to Old Baldy, Pitcher, and Summit Lake, and then round Bearhead and Independence to enter Rainier Park.

Round trip 10 miles, allow 6 hours
High point 2350 feet, elevation gain 1000 feet
February-December

Wilkeson Creek (Map — page 22)

Because highways and byways take other routes to Wilkeson, since the trains stopped running the valley of Wilkeson Creek has been as purely innocent a second-growth wildland as could be wished, the grade traveled by only the occasional fisherman pushing through the bushes. Peace!

From Orting or Buckley drive Highway 152 to the hamlet of South Prairie,

whose most magnificent edifice,the Masonic Temple, was erected in 1914. Park anywhere in town, elevation 420 feet.

Walk east on the railroad, a branch line mainly used to park broken freight cars. A bridge crosses South Prairie Creek, really a river rising among outer buttresses of Rainier. A gypo's collection of rusting trucks amazes. Sheep and horses entertain. At 1 mile from town a rusting, fading sign announces "Cascade Junction," and the abandoned branch line to Wilkeson turns right — into a daunting thicket. Be brave and take the plunge. In a few strides is a bridge recrossing South Prairie Creek just a bit above its confluence with Wilkeson Creek. Local folks obviously come here in season to swim in the cool pool.

At ½ mile from Cascade Junction the line touches the bank (riprapped with — what else? — Wilkeson sandstone) of Wilkeson Creek. Here at a bend in the stream, secure from civilization in a splendid forest starring enormous cottonwoods, is a fitting spot to sit and watch spawning salmon, or dippers, or whatever other traffic is on the water avenue.

The survey assault thrust some distance farther but ultimately was hurled back by nettles-salmonberries-burdock. However, the grade is intact — in fact, ties and rails are still in place — and an armed band rather easily could slash a path the 3 miles from the Fitting Spot to Johns Road, on the outskirts of Wilkeson.

Round trip to Fitting Spot 3 miles, allow 2 hours
High point 650 feet, elevation gain 230 feet
All year

Wilkeson (Map — page 25)

In 1869, inventorying the booty heisted 5 years earlier in the Northern Pacific Land Grant, railroad surveyors found sandstone and coal on a tributary

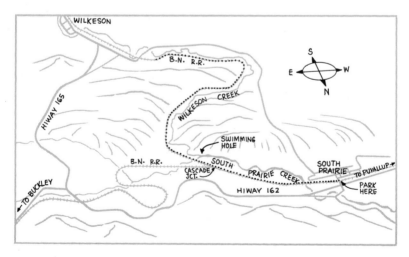

Abandoned railroad line to Wilkeson at Cascade Junction

of the Carbon River. From the company treasurer the resulting town took its name, Wilkeson. The place reeks of history, a century of artifacts lurking in the bushes. And it's pretty, too.

From Highway 410 at Buckley drive Highway 165 to Wilkeson. For the full tour park near the timber arch welcoming you to town, elevation 780 feet.

Muse through the cemetery; there's another off the highway on Johns Road. Poke into side streets for the 19th century architecture, including the

A coke oven

handsome building signed "Holy Trinity Orthodox Church in America 1900."
At the far edge of town turn left onto Railroad Avenue, past the striking
Wilkeson-sandstone school.

Where Railroad Avenue turns left over rusty tracks a sideroad goes right;
park here for an alternate start. The sideroad forks; do both. The low road, left,
goes by the coke ovens, beehive-like mounds of brick, their age shown by the
size of the trees atop them. The high road, right, climbs a black-soiled hill one
abruptly realizes was not erected by nature but rather is a 100-foot heap of

waste rock; look down to Wilkeson Creek, which long ago was pushed to the side of its wide valley floor to make room for mine, railroad, and town.

The main attraction of the town nowadays is the quarry, off-limits to visitors unless prior arrangements are made. However, there is no objection to walkers politely following the road of Wilkeson Cut Stone Company ¼ mile from Railroad Avenue to the fringe of the stone-cutting works. The quarry can be glimpsed, far up the hill. Overhead cables bring monster slabs down to the shed where gangsaws patiently cut into the stone at the rate of 4 inches an hour. The first use of the stone was by the railroad, for fill and riprap, widely distributed around the region. In 1886 the first stone was taken out for construction — of a church in Tacoma. A man named Walker quarried blocks from 1911 on, taking them to Tacoma by rail for splitting. In 1915 the present plant was built, the machinery pretty much devised on the spot by self-taught engineers; with minor modifications it continues, a time-warp trip to early days of the Industrial Revolution.

Across Railroad Avenue from the quarry entrance a sideroad switchbacks off the main road, up the hillside, into the canyon of Wilkeson Creek; the black slope on the far side was the location of one of the several coal mines in town.

The remainder of the tour, to Snell Lake, offers history of a more familiar sort — logging. Ascend the sideroad, usually closed to public vehicles, climbing steeply along the stupendous, gorgeously-forested gorge of Wilkeson Creek. At ½ mile from Railroad Avenue is Decision Junction — do you wish to go to the lake the easy way or the interesting way?

Assuming the latter, take the switchback left, to the gorge rim and a gravel mine. Continue into superb big-fir second-growth on the scarp edge to ¾ mile from the junction. Turn right on a narrow, soon undrivable old road into mossy-ferny woods. The track climbs a bit, then drops to become a corduroy road over a black-mucky skunk-cabbage bottom. So far so good, but now for a little while the way is very interesting, over and under logs. But at 1½ miles from the junction the trail becomes suddenly excellent. Here a path leads out on logs to a floating peninsula of peat in marsh-ringed, lily-padded, moody little Snell Lake. Enjoy ruminations in peace, because the excellent trail leads quickly to good road; turn right a short bit to the junction, and so home.

Total tour 7 miles, allow 5 hours
High point 1160 feet, elevation gain 400 feet
All year

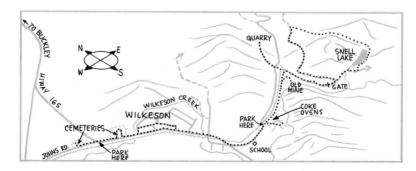

South Prairie Ridge (Map — page 26)

See four of Rainier's great valleys — White, Carbon, Puyallup, and Nisqually. See four large cities — Bremerton, Olympia, Tacoma, and Seattle. And glaciers and buttresses of The Mountain, and towns and farms, lakes and Puget Sound, all from a marvelous clearcut desolation.

From Highway 410 west of Buckley drive Highway 165 to Wilkeson. At the far end of town turn left on Railroad Avenue (probably unsigned, but readily identifiable by the rusty railroad tracks) past school and quarry. Stick with the obvious main road switchbacking up from the valley to a broad plateau ridge. At 5¼ miles from Highway 165 is a Y at 1950 feet. The left is road 1810; take the right, road 194. The road resumes climbing, making a giant switchback onto the end of South Prairie Ridge. At 4 miles from the Y pass a narrow, rough road climbing left to the now-towerless, now-viewless site of O'Farrell Lookout; a few yards beyond are a quarry and a Y at 3089 feet.

This trip comes in a whole mess of versions, including a swell snowline-prober. For that, maybe park at the 1950-foot Y, walking the 4 miles of splendid narrow footroad in 30-foot second-growth, with many little creeks in season, and windows out to lowlands. Or, park at the 3089-foot Y and walk either of the forks, in steadily shorter trees, by constantly more windows.

Beyond this Y are two basic trips, left and right.

South Prairie Ridge

Go left at the Y on road 194, swinging around ridges and valleys, up and up, 1½ miles to a Y at 3534 feet. Go right on 194 for 1 mile to a 3840-foot saddle in a spur ridge. Park here, if not before, because shortly the way emerges from early 1950s second-growth into a mid-1960s skinning and views become continuous pow zowie.

Walk 194 as it ascends 1 scant mile to a 4050-foot saddle in the main crest of South Prairie Ridge. Off left, at 4144 feet, was Carbon Ridge Lookout, now towerless but still big-view. However, views are everywhere on the embarrassingly-naked ridge, so at the Y in the saddle go right, contouring around the head of a little valley past Peak 4679 to a pass at 1 mile from the saddle. At the Y just beyond, stay left, continuing to ascend the nose of a spur. At ½ mile from the pass, upon rounding the nose, leave the road and turn left up the spur crest

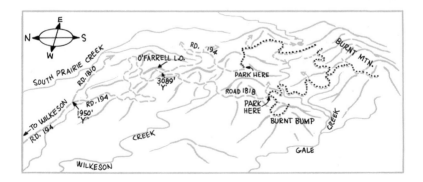

Enumclaw plain from near Burnt Bump

on a cat track. In a scant ½ mile, about 3 miles from the 3840-foot saddle, is the ridge summit, 4640 feet.

From amid the stumps of the timber-mining operation (centuries will pass before another forest regrows here) look down to ponds at the head of South Prairie Creek, over to Three Sisters, out to the White valley. To the south, hiding behind virgin-timbered Burnt Mountain, is Rainier. The big picture is in the other direction, out over the lowlands — for that, see the ravings below.

An interesting extension of the trip is onward and upward to the top of Burnt. Bits of old trail are found in the forest — and the potential can be seen of the trail proposed to run the length of Carbon Ridge from Gleason Hill to the national park.

Round trip 6 miles, allow 4 hours
High point 4640 feet, elevation gain 800 feet
June-November

27

Burnt Bump and Gale Grandstand

Go right at the 3089-foot Y on road 1818 for 2½ miles to a triple fork in a saddle at 3125 feet. Park here, if not before. Two choices.

First, take the right fork and ascend a steep, rough track, going right at a Y, and in a long ½ mile attain the scalped summit of Burnt Bump, 3360 feet. Zounds! This bump on a spur thrusting out in headwater valleys of Gale Creek is positively the best bump, the finest viewpoint, around. Rotate and see: naked brown barrens of South Prairie Ridge, virgin greens of Burnt Mountain, great white glaciers of Rainier, Gleason Hill, Carbon valley, Ptarmigan Ridge from Park Boundary Peaks to Spar Pole Hill, Puyallup valley and Ohop valley and The Divide, Mashel and Nisqually valleys, Bald Hills and Olympia and Black Hills, the full length of the Big Valley from Orting to Renton, Tacoma and Puget Sound, Olympics and Bremerton, Lake Tapps and Enumclaw and Buckley, Issaquah Alps and Seattle, Lake Washington and Elliott Bay, Three Fingers and Index.

Second, take the middle fork, rough and narrow, driven only by rare sports. Views don't get better but provide endless variations on the theme from big-sky clearcuts of the 1950s to 1970s, and there's a gaggle of lovely streams. At 2 miles is one of these; just beyond, on a shoulder at 3500 feet, is a Y. Two choices. Do both.

First, the right, which swings on around a valley ½ mile to a lovely-rushing branch of Gale Creek. Of the many spurs in this small-shrub terrain, the main one climbs past an odd marsh-bowl cirquelet and in ¾ mile from the creek ends at 3800 feet on the very end of Burnt Mountain, directly above Gleason Hill and the Carbon valley.

Second, the left, a rude track which climbs and traverses left over the creek to end on a shoulder at 3800 feet. Turn right, steeply uphill, and follow cat tracks to a higher road at 4100 feet. Turn right ¼ mile and at 4120 feet, where the road continues ahead, switchback left up to the spur crest. At the Y there, go right, to the road end atop the spur at 4400 feet, about 1¾ miles from the triple fork. This viewpoint is just a spit below the crest of South Prairie Ridge.

Various round trips 1-10 miles, allow 1-7 hours
High points 3360 to 4440 feet, elevation gains 250 to 2000 feet
May-November

Pitcher Ridge and the Forks of South Prairie Creek (Map — page 30)

The footings of Rainier are hidden from Seattle by Carbon Ridge, whose peaks are, reading west to east, Burnt Mountain, Old Baldy, "Old Nameless," and — highest and most prominent — the half-horn of 5933-foot Pitcher Mountain, which everybody sees and nobody ever heard of. Draining the north slopes of all these peaks is a stream nobody ever heard of — South Prairie Creek. There's a lot of great fooling around up high on the sky-naked 1970s-clearcut ridges, and down in the cool green woods by the cold white waterfalls. No single long tramp, but a bunch of neat little walks.

The East Fork of South Prairie Creek near confluence with South Fork

Drive from Wilkeson 5¼ miles to the 1950-foot Y (see South Prairie Ridge). Go left on road 1810, in 1½ miles dropping to cross South Fork South Prairie Creek; the heart sings to see the place, but save it for end of day and drive on. In 1 mile is a Y, maybe unsigned. Road 1810 goes left, but for the first walks go right on 1819, up the South Fork valley. In 2½ miles, at 3100 feet, is a Y beside the creek.

Walk 1 (views)

Take the road crossing the creek and winding up the steep slope in on-going clearcuts. At 1½ miles, 4400 feet, a rock knob juts, a fine viewpoint to Three Sisters one way and South Prairie Ridge the other, plus vistas out to the White River, Enumclaw, and all.

Round trip 3 miles, allow 2 hours
High point 4400 feet, elevation gain 1300 feet
May-November

Walk 2 (wilderness edge)

Take the road switchbacking up left a short bit to a Y, and there take the

29

switchback right, up the valley. Slides block the road. Virgin forest is entered. The creek becomes a continuous cataract. In a scant 1 mile, at 3600 feet, the road crosses the creek to one final clearcut. Don't cross. Step into the virgin green, beside the creek, and sit in the moss, the shadows, the peace. Here is wilderness edge, and if loggers go any farther upstream somebody ought to be nominated for hanging. A mile away and 1500 feet above is the saddle between Pitcher and Old Nameless. The most that ever should be done to this little headwaters vale is to put a little trail in it, up to that saddle to intersect the proposed Carbon Ridge Trail.

Round trip 2 miles, allow 1½ hours
High point 3600 feet, elevation gain 500 feet

Walk 3 (more views)

Drive back down the valley to the Y and take road 1810 a long 2 miles, to where the meager Three Sisters road proceeds straight, up the East Fork South Prairie valley. Switchback right on big wide (unsigned) road 1847 and climb some 2¼ miles to a Y near the ridge crest at 3300 feet. Park — the road roughens and views begin. Take the left, up the naked crest, in views to Three Sisters one way and South Prairie Ridge the other, and out to Enumclaw and Lake Tapps and the Big Valley and Olympics. Also see a goodly chunk of Rainier rising above Carbon Ridge. In a long 1½ miles the road ends at 4200 feet. The summit of Pitcher is hidden, though only a long mile distant, an easy trip for experienced off-trail ramblers, as is the secret cirque lake in the side of the peak. A spur trail could feed the proposed Carbon Ridge Trail.

Round trip 3 miles, allow 2 hours
High point 4200 feet, elevation gain 1100 feet

Walk 4 (cooling fevered brows)

Now to satisfy the heart's desire. Drive back to the bridge over the South Fork and park, elevation 1650 feet. A fishermen's trail goes an unsurveyed but

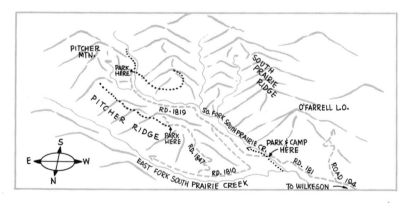

surely delicious distance upstream. Ah, but downstream! Through the road-side camps, then the walk-in camps, then to this gravel bar and that pool, the path just keeps poking along, often rude and slow but always easy and safe and always near the stream and steadily a joy. The trees are big — apparently, amazingly virgin — and mossy and ferny. In a scant ½ mile, oh joy, oh rapture, the confluence. Foaming down a sloping slab in a 12-foot falls to a pool, the East Fork bubbles and babbles to join the South Fork.

Downstream? That's no creek, that's a river. And that's a jungle, there, sirs. As you sit a long afternoon hour, cooling and rejoicing, ponder. This creek-river that nobody knows, draining a country that nobody (but loggers) knows, runs some 16 miles from here to join the Carbon River. The first half of the course is just touched by man's works, at two points, ever so briefly, and the second half is a blend of pastoral and wild. What a route for a trail, folks! Start at Burnett, follow the secret canyon upstream to headwaters on Carbon Ridge, and onward into Rainier Park.

Round trip 1 mile, allow 1 hour
High point 1650 feet, elevation gain minor
March-December

Three Sisters (Map — page 32)

You've seen it for years — everybody has — and never even knew it had a name. Actually, you may never have focused on it, busy as you were goggling at the great white bulk of Rainier. But if you ever did, the thought occurred that the view must be tremendous from this high ridge jutting to the edge of lowlands in the angle between White River and South Prairie Creek. It is. Indeed, there is no more stupendous panorama anywhere of Puget Sound country and the northern hinterland of The Mountain.

There are two distinctly different summits, Three Sisters 3 and 1 (2 is viewless). And two approaches — the easy way and the interesting way.

The Interesting Way

Drive from Wilkeson 5¼ miles to the 1950-foot Y (see South Prairie Ridge). Go left on road 1810, dropping to cross South Fork South Prairie Creek, to a Y in 2½ miles. Go left on 1810 (unsigned) a long 2 miles, rounding the ridge to the valley of the East Fork, to where the big wide road switchbacks uphill. Go straight ahead on a little old road 1¼ miles, to a turnaround marking the end of solid bottom. Park here, elevation 2750 feet.

Walk the road ¼ mile to where once it bridged the East Fork. Except in high water the wading is safe and easy, if interesting. On the far side the old (1930s?) logging-railroad grade is cleverly disguised as a creek bed and requires some salmonberry burrowing, adding interest. In 1 scant mile from the ford the grownover old road proceeds upvalley; turn left, where pathfinders have left plastic ribbons, and find genuine trail, No. 1178 in the Forest Service inventory and formerly a major thoroughfare (note telephone wire) but no longer signed or maintained.

First in 40-year-old second-growth, then in small firs of a burn, and then, astonishingly, in a scrap of virgin forest (1978), the rough but decent trail switchbacks a steep 1 mile to Modern Times, at 3800 feet entering awesome desolation of the 1970s clearcut in which lies the entire rest of the route, the views starting now and getting bigger by the minute. Friendly ribbons may guide the pilgrim up a twisty-turny, fireweedy cat track that traverses to the edge of a deep little valley and follows it up ⅓ mile to intersect a logging spur at 4000 feet. Now in sight is 4980-foot Three Sisters 1, with a topknot of snags. Henceforth, when in doubt, head for Old Snagtop. Obeying that rule, follow the road up the little valley, left around the head. Pass road 6070 switchbacking right, on a ridge shoulder at 4200 feet pass road 6069 switchbacking right, and descend a bit, now directly beneath Snagtop, to a sideroad at 1½ miles from the point at which cat track intersected logging spur. A decision.

Feeling pooped? Or, is the snow becoming a slog? Well, take the sideroad left, contouring ⅓ mile to an excellent promontory at 4200 feet, 4½ miles from the car. It's a most satisfying destination, the stunning view only excelled by that from the peak.

But bagging Snagtop is not unreasonable, though interesting. The all-road route (The Easy Way) is too roundabout from this approach. Simply point boots at the snags and follow game trails that connect logging spurs — the entire mountain is one vast elk barn, and smells like it, and everywhere has thoroughfares stomped by the heavy-hooved beasts. In about ¾ mile the boots attain the snags, 4980 feet.

The vista from Three Sisters 1 is a five-star goshamighty whambam zowie. Slashfire-blackened stumps spatter the brownish 1970s clearcuts, a vivid contrast to virgin green of Carbon Ridge, dazzling white of Rainier. Winthrop Glacier and Little Tahoma, Curtis and Liberty Ridges and Willis Wall, Ptarmigan Ridge and Echo and Observation, Mowich Face and Sunset Ridge. South over Carbon and Puyallup and Nisqually valleys, Spar Pole Hill and The Divide and Bald Hills and Black Hills. North over the White valley, Boise Ridge-Grass Mountain-Huckleberry Mountain-Dalles Ridge and high Cascades beyond, from Stuart to Chimney to Glacier to Baker. West, Tacoma and Seattle, Puget Sound and Olympics. The circuits overload. The brain explodes.

Round trip 10 miles, allow 9 hours
High point 4980 feet, elevation gain 2500 feet
June-November

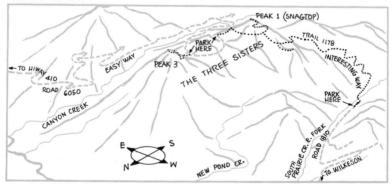

Crossing the East Fork of South Prairie Creek on Three Sisters trail

The Easy Way

Drive Highway 410 east from Enumclaw to 5¾ miles past the Mud Mountain Dam turnoff and turn right on a White River Tree Farm road signed "Bridge Camp Gate." (This gate, and the several others on the route, are always open except during closures for extreme fire danger, most common in late summer.) Descend to cross the White River. At the junction beyond, turn right, downvalley, on high-speed road 6000. In a long 4 miles turn right on the first major sideroad, rather obscurely signed 6050, to the Clearwater River. Ignoring lesser sideroads, drive another 9 miles to Canyon Creek crossing, 3400 feet. On the way are any number of great views over the White River to Grass Mountain and Enumclaw, and over Canyon Creek to Three Sisters. Also on the way are many old railroad trestles plus sideroads to Lyle and Cedar Lakes trails. From the crossing drive 3¼ miles, climbing to the ridgetop saddle at 3608 feet. Park here.

Note that all the country to here was logged by railroad, one of the last such operations in the Cascades, ending on the ridge in the mid-1950s. Then commenced the truck logging, which is just now completing the skinning of the high ridges. The bulk of the virgin timber remaining hereabouts is in Mt. Baker-Snoqualmie National Forest — and is proposed to be placed in a Clearwater-Carbon Ridge Wilderness.

From the saddle a meager road heads right, for Three Sisters 3, soon coming to a closed gate that frees the route of razzers. The way leaves the contouring railroad spur and turns up to the crest in shrubby silver firs and grassy meadows, delightfully pseudo-alpine. In 1½ miles is the summit, 3969 feet — and the obligatory radio tower. Views have been constant the whole way. For the denouement, though, push a couple hundred feet through a fringe of scrub to the bald brink of a cliff. Holy gee.

It's one long step down to Enumclaw. Buckley, too. And bug-infested Highway 410. The Weyerhaeuser Upper Mill. The reservoirized White River. All around is the immense second-growth wilderness of South Prairie and Canyon Creeks, only now being invaded from below by Second Wave clearcuts. And out there beyond the mountain front are the Osceola Mudflow, Lake Tapps, Big Valley, cities and towns and farms, Issaquah Alps, saltwaterways.

Round trip (3) 3 miles, allow 2 hours
High point 3969 feet, elevation gain 400 feet
May-November

Onward to Three Sisters 1. From the saddle drive 1 mile, rounding scrub-covered, viewless Three Sisters 2 to the saddle beyond and an obscurely-signed Y. Go left on road 6065. (The right, 6050, proceeds 1¼ miles to join the Interesting Way.) Ignoring lesser sideroads, drive ⅓ mile to a Y at 4100 feet. Park.

Walk the right fork, steep and rough, rarely molested by sports except in elk season. In ½ mile is a Y directly under the summit; go right, crossing the south face of the peak to the far ridge, recrossing, and again, and at 1½ miles attaining Snagtop.

Round trip (1) 3 miles, allow 2 hours
High point 4980 feet, elevation gain 900 feet
May-November

Microwave Hill (Map — page 36)

From the little hill that is the absolute far-out ultimate lower end of Ptarmigan Ridge, look up and up the miles and miles to the upper end on Rainier's white walls. And look down to the green valley where two of Rainier's rivers, the Puyallup and Carbon, hug opposite sides of the Big Valley, enclosing between them the seeming-toy village of Orting.

Drive Highway 162 to 1 scant mile southeast of Orting and at Crocker Grange Y turn south on Orville Road (to Electron and Kapowsin). In 3 miles, just before the bridge over the Puyallup, turn sharp left on Brooks Road 2 miles to the parking lot outside King Creek Gate, elevation 700 feet.

Walk through the complex of St. Regis offices and shops to a Y in ⅓ mile; turn left on Fox Creek Road. In ½ mile is another Y; go left on Microwave Road. Continue along, passing lesser spurs, emerging from forests where thinning is in progress to clearcuts of alder-conversion operations. On the open sidehill above a marshy valley the views begin.

At 1½ miles from Fox Creek Road is a four-way intersection; continue straight ahead but note the spur right, the route of the loop return. The microwave tower is now seen ahead, atop the hill around which the road curls; in 1 mile from the intersection, 3½ from King Creek Gate, are attained the 1448-foot summit and the Bell relay station.

The best view is short of the summit, at the top of a 1977 clearcut. Below are green pastures of the Puyallup-Carbon valley, houses of Orting. North are lowlands extending to Issaquah Alps and Seattle, Olympics as backdrop. West are vast barrens of the airstrips of McChord Field.

A looping return gives more views. From the clearcut edge walk Spur 5 out on the ridge leading from Microwave Hill to Spar Pole Hill. When the spur ends, proceed on a cat road. On the way are looks far south along the Puyallup to the Bald Hills, north from Rattlesnake to Boise to Grass to Pete, Enumclaw and Buckley and Three Sisters. And wow, hulking whitely huge over the green foreground, Rainier. At the foot of Spar Pole turn right on a powerline service road.

(A scant ½ mile down this road a spur goes left. For a sidetrip, walk it ¼ mile to the deadend, then pick the easiest way through logging slash a couple hundred yards to a 1500-foot saddle in the south ridge of Spar Pole. Climb right to a 1623-foot ridge with a fine view over Beane Creek to Fox Creek to Cowling Ridge to — gasp — Rainier. Or, climb left to the end of a spur that leads in 1 mile to the summit of Spar Pole Hill — the shortest route there.)

Forest fungi

A bit beyond the sidetrip spur the powerline bends left; instead, take the main logging road's right bend, down the hill to the four-way intersection, regained at 1¾ miles from the turnoff onto Spur 5.

Loop trip (excluding sidetrip) 8 miles, allow 5 hours
High point 1500 feet, elevation gain 900 feet
All year

Spar Pole Hill (Map — page 36)

From all over Puget Sound country the hill stands out prominently, the final high point of Ptarmigan Ridge before that long buttress of Rainier drops to the Big Valley. However, the once-famous view from the hill to all over Puget Sound country was swallowed up in greenery until 1977, when Second Wave alder-conversion clearcutting reopened the 360-degree panorama. But views are only part of the attraction — this is the champion classic hike of the Kapowsin Tree Farm, sampling all its many good things.

Whether from Puyallup or Buckley, drive Highway 162 to 3 miles east of Orting. Turn onto Patterson Road (signed "Crocker Heights") and follow its blacktopped twists and turns 4 miles to the end of public road at Voight Creek Gate. Park in the spacious lot provided by St. Regis. Elevation, 970 feet.

Walk by the gate the few yards to the restrooms and the first Y; go right, in tidy thinned forest. Cross a powerline, pass an unsigned spur right, over the powerline, and just beyond, at a Y ½ mile from the gate, go right on Fox Creek Road. Cross and then parallel the powerline, in a scant ½ mile coming to the handsome timber bridge over Voight Creek, a stream of "mountain tea" colored but not flavored by bark tannins. (Note: the gate here is closed in hunting season; Fox Creek Road, and thus Spar Pole, are always strictly for pedestrians. Unless you're a logger.) For a quick sidetrip, just before the bridge follow a path into the woods and downstream a few hundred feet to the falls, where the creek splits in several pieces to pour over a 10-foot rock ledge.

Proceed on Fox Creek Road, passing spurs right. (Including one confusingly signed "Sparpole Road" that could be used as a shortcut but as of 1978

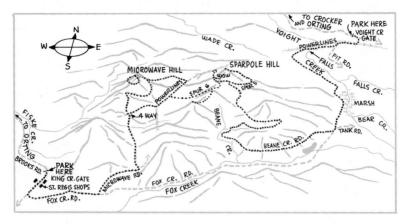

Voight Creek on road to Spar Pole Hill

would require some brushbeating.) The way is in a lush valley bottom, Voight Creek flowing in alder-cottonwood forest. But when Voight Creek is no longer there (entering from a valley to the left) the valley continues ahead, the wide bottom mostly a marsh. Then Bear Creek can be heard waterfalling in. The marsh ends, a low divide is crossed, and now the valley is occupied by Fox Creek, running the other direction. So things go in these eons since the glacier melted away and little creeks took over its big valleys. At 1137 feet, 2 miles from Voight Creek bridge, is a junction. Tank Creek Road reverse-turns left. Fox Creek Road (unsigned) goes straight ahead (to King Creek Gate, 3 miles distant, almost identically as far as Voight Creek Gate, so this approach is an alternate). Turn right on Bean Creek Road.

The way ascends moderately on old railroad grade to pleasing prospects of cozy, secluded Fox valley, clearcut in the early 1970s, retaining a meadowy look beneath steep forests. In 1 mile the road emerges from woods into 1977 logging and swings sharp right into the valley of Beane Creek, wide-open stark naked since the "alder-conversion" (deciduous forests logged, firs planted) of the early 1970s. Amid old stumps of First Wave clearcutting, little third-growth fir seedlings struggle to outgrow the brush.

Views expand as the road ascends the valley, passing spurs. Over the right end of Cowling Ridge appears the white heap of Adams. Then, over the left end, heap big Rainier. High on the side of Spar Pole, at 3 miles from Fox Creek Road, at 1720 feet, Bean Spur 5 switchbacks right. This is the way to the summit. Follow Spur 5 a short bit, turn off it left on a grassy old road leading to the summit plateau, viewless in 1977. At ¾ mile from the turnoff onto Spur 5 is the spar pole, left standing after First Wave railroad logging was completed about 1910 and plainly visible from downtown Orting.

But until alder-conversion reaches the summit, the views are below. Just a few steps from Spur 5 begins the long, slow curve around Wow Corner into a 1977 clearcut. Bean Spur 6 goes down left — this is the route from Microwave Hill (which see). The panorama is piecemeal. First, Rainier, the full length of Ptarmigan Ridge from glaciers, Mowich Face, Park Boundary Peaks, to Fox Creek. Beyond Cowling Ridge are the Puyallup valley, Adams, The Divide, and the odd Kapowsin Scarp, plus bits of Kapowsin Lake and Ohop Lake, and Nisqually valley and Bald Hills. Then, in a few steps, Rainier is lost but horizons open westward, over Microwave Hill to McChord Field and Tacoma, Black Hills and Olympics. More steps and the north widens, over Puyallup and Carbon valleys to Orting, Sumner, Seattle, Puget Sound, Prairie Ridge and Lake Tapps, Issaquah Alps, Buckley and Enumclaw beyond the White River on the Osceola Mudflow, and Boise, Grass, Pete, Three Sisters. And if you think all this is great, you ought to see the billion-twinkling light show at night.

Round trip to summit or Wow Corner 13½ miles, allow 8 hours
High point 1904 feet, elevation gain 1000 feet
All year

Cowling Ridge (Map — page 38)

Cowling is the highest point in the vicinity, 2435 feet, the dominant feature in distant views of the area, and from its Electron Lookout once provided distant views to lots of other areas. With lookout tower long gone and trees grown up thick as hairs on a dog's back, for years the views have been inward to mosses and liverworts and bugs. However, Second Wave clearcuts are again letting daylight in the swamp and year by year the horizons grow.

Drive to King Creek Gate (see Microwave Hill), elevation 700 feet.

Walk through the complex of buildings ⅓ mile to a Y; go right, signed "Road 6, Headworks" and etcetera. In the next 2½ miles the big main road winds

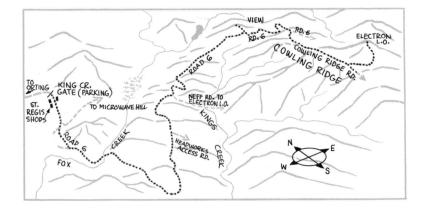

Trillium

around, passes pastures of a stumpranch converted to tree farm, crosses Fox Creek, passes spurs left and right, climbs a scarp to an alluvial terrace, and comes to a major Y at 1100 feet. The right is "Headworks, Access Road" — the way to the upper Puyallup and Rainier National Park, to whose boundaries St. Regis has logged. Go left (straight) ¾ mile over the flat to an intersection. The left is Fox Creek Spur. The right is "Neff Ranch, Neff Ranch Loop." (Not surveyed for this guide, the Neff Loop is the old route to Electron Lookout and still a favorite walk. Kings Creek is crossed. Fields are passed of the Neff Ranch, inhabited until about 1960, when the family traded with St. Regis for lands outside the tree farm.) Go straight on "Road 6, Divide Road."

Views begin in the next 2 miles as Road 6 steeply climbs a second scarp to a long, wide, nearly flat alluvial terrace mostly skinned in the early 1970s, giving fine looks over Fox Creek valley to Spar Pole Hill. At 1720 feet, 5¾ miles from King Creek Gate, views climax at a roadside hillock above the old glacier valley in which Fox Creek now drains one way, Voight Creek the other. Out the former slot see the Puyallup valley and lowlands, out the latter see the Carbon valley and lowlands and Issaquah Alps. Between the two slots stands Spar Pole Hill.

Round trip to View Hillock 11½ miles, allow 8 hours
High point 1720 feet, elevation gain 1000 feet
All year

The future lies above. Continue on Road 6 as it swings around a lush-forested, steep slope of Cowling Ridge, ascends to the crest, and at ¾ mile from the hillock comes to a new-in-1977 sideroad right, at about 1900 feet. This is Cowling Ridge Road; take it. (Road 6 proceeds straight, to lots of lonesome walking in quiet woods, including a roundabout route to Electron Lookout.) In ¼ mile a sideroad goes right ¼ mile to a clearcut that was in progress during the survey in late 1977, promising to open a view to golly knows what; from the edge of the ridge here at 2000 feet there ought to be a famous vista west over the Puyallup valley to the lowlands.

Watch this space — Cowling Ridge — for future views.

Collectors of old lookouts can proceed on Cowling Ridge Road ¾ mile to the summit plateau and there, at a Y with the old road, turn left ½ mile to the clearing where stood the Electron tower.

Round trip to New View 14 miles, allow 10 hours
High point 2000 feet, elevation gain 1300 feet
February-December

Brooks Hill Loop (Map — page 40)

Views and waterfalls and all that sort of thrilling scenery ain't everything. Peace is something. Miles of quiet walking in lonesome forest. And here is a rather special forest. While much of the Kapowsin Tree Farm is a typical wild tangle of rank second-growth of mixed species, a lot of it has a kempt, European, park-like look — all trees of the same species (Douglas fir), all about the same size, neatly spaced. That's what thinning does. If you must have drama with your peace, come in winter, when a few inches of snow vividly record the traipsings of an unsuspected population of critters. Or in the

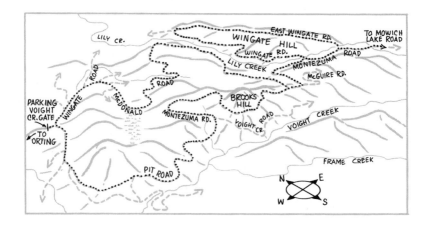

fall rains, when the forest floor is a Lilliputian Oz of mushrooms; in October the woods are thronged with non-violent hunters but there's no shortage of sport — the farm could swallow up all the fungus nuts in the state and fill everybody's bucket with chanterelles.

Drive to Voight Creek Gate (see Spar Pole Hill), elevation 970 feet. Walk by the gate the few yards to the restrooms and the first Y. The loop is fine either way but will here be described in the anticyclonic direction, most mentally comfortable for righthanded (left-brained) people. So, go left on Wingate Road ¼ mile to the next Y; go right on Wingate. In a few yards is the next Y, unsigned, at the edge of the large field of a grass-and-cow farm being converted to tree farm; go right. At the next Y, still by the field, where fruit trees remain, Wingate goes left; go right on (possibly unsigned) McDonald Road. Here, 1 mile from the gate, the major junctions have been passed and the simple rule is to dodge lesser spurs and stick with the "main-looking" road.

The way goes up and down, winding around plateaus and sidehills, crossing the small vale of Waterhole Creek and swinging into the valley of Lily Creek. At about 6½ miles, roughly the midpoint of the loop, is big excitement — a three-road junction. McDonald Road, the route thus far, ends at Montezuma Road, off which a few feet left branches McGuire Road; for possibilities there, see below. To finish the job in hand, turn right on Montezuma, contouring above Voight Creek valley on the slope of Brooks Hill, whose 1969-foot summit is close above but viewless.

The route starts down and after a switchback comes to a Y at 3 miles from McDonald Road's end. Voight Creek Road goes straight; turn right on (unsigned?) Pit Road, signed "Voight Creek Gate." In 1½ miles is a Y; the main road goes left and will get you there but for a shortcut go straight on a grassy road that climbs a little hill and plummets to the Voight valley, in ¾ mile joining Road 6. Turn right and in a few feet right again on the road signed "Voight Creek Gate," which is attained in the final ¾ mile, 6 miles from McDonald Road.

Loop trip 12½ miles, allow 8 hours
High point 1900 feet, elevation gain 1300 feet
All year

A walker can circle around on these pleasant footroads until thoroughly looped. For example, should a person seek more exercise or chanterelles than provided by the Brooks Hill Loop, the Wingate Hill Loop can be tacked on as a loop off the loop. Where McDonald Road ends (see above), go left on Montezuma Road 1 long mile to where Wingate Road turns off left over little beaver-dammed Lily Creek. To do this loop in the cyclonic direction, to correct any possible tilting of the brain, continue straight on Montezuma another 1 mile and turn left on East Wingate Road, signed "Impassable." Cross Lily Creek, contour the side of 1935-foot Wingate Hill to Wingate Road, which leads back to Montezuma to complete a 5½-mile loop.

Other loops can be made by throwing in Wingate Road and McGuire Road and stirring well.

Worthy of mention as a link in the hiking route from Orting in Puget Sound lowlands to Spray Park on Mount Rainier are the 2½ miles of Montezuma Road leading from the East Wingate Road to Highway 165, the Mowich Lake Road.

Mt. St. Helens from side of Evans Peak

Evans Peak (Map — page 43)

No view of The Mountain but one of the greatest views there is from The Mountain. Straddling the park boundary, partly in and green-wild and partly out and brown-scalped, the "Park Boundary Peaks" are the farthest out mile-high points on Ptarmigan Ridge, prominent landmarks from all around the lowlands. Westernmost is Evans Peak, from whose 5000-foot summit the slopes plunge abruptly to 3000 feet, nothing to block ringadingding views to cities of the plain.

Drive Highway 165 from Wilkeson to the Fairfax Bridge and ¾ mile more to a Y; go right on 165, the Mowich Lake Road, and ascend to the crest of Ptarmigan Ridge. About 7¾ miles from the Y, at the second saddle hit by the road, at 3300 feet, note a road going left, the faded sign saying "178." Drive this road (or, if gated due to logging operations, walk) as it swings into the skinned valley of Evans Creek. On the far side see Evans Peak — the clearcut

42

near the summit is the goal. Obviously the peak and all the upper creek valley belong in the national park. Road 178 crosses Evans Creek at a point where a large campground could be located, satisfying a much-felt need on this flank of Rainier. At 1¾ miles from the Mowich Road, at 3550 feet, is a Y, and a second good starting point for a walk. However, it is permissible to drive on; turn right on road 1754 and proceed up the valley 2¼ miles to a subalpine meadow at the head of the main branch of the creek. Note virgin forest on 4900-foot August Peak above — that's the park boundary. Park here, elevation 4100 feet.

Walk the main road (ignoring wheelers who see little and enjoy less) as it swings around the side of 5100-foot Poch Peak (pronounced "Poh") in patches of virgin timber left to seed the clearcuts. The road enters a branch valley of Evans Creek and at 1½ miles hits a 4432-foot saddle between Poch and Evans Peaks, with views of St. Helens. A new (1977) logging road swings out from the saddle around Poch Creek to Peak 4898, an interesting walk too; for this trip, though, go left on road 1754A onto Evans. At 1 long mile from the Poch-Evans saddle the road ends at 4680 feet on a promontory landing. A cat road continues higher, and the clearcut can be scrambled and battled to the 5000-foot summit, but to no good purpose. The landing panorama suffices.

And how. The subridges and small valleys of Ptarmigan Ridge extend westward through Voight Creek drainage to Cowling Ridge, Brooks and Wingate and Spar Pole and Microwave Hills. Down left is the confluence of the Mowich and Puyallup Rivers and across the gulf is The Divide and beyond are Bald Hills and Adams. Down Evans Creek and Poch Creek is the Carbon River. Visualize the Fairfax (Bailey Willis) Trail climbing from there to here, up Evans Creek, and look beyond to Burnt Mountain and the White River plain — the Osceola Mudflow. But hey, that was only one — also visualize the Electron Mudflow down the Puyallup. See where they both went — Orting, Sumner, and nearly to Tacoma, marked by the stack of the ASARCO smelter and the plume of the St. Regis pulpmill. See the saltwater shore from Commencement Bay to Des Moines. And if your brain isn't too addled by ecstasy, stay for the sunset over the Olympics, the night light show. Ask: why isn't Evans Peak in Rainier National Park?

Round trip 5 miles, allow 4 hours
High point 4680 feet, elevation gain 600 feet
June-November

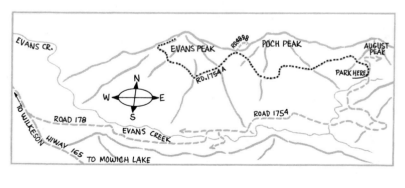

Swan Creek Canyon

PUYALLUP RIVER

The White River issuing from Emmons and Winthrop Glaciers, the Carbon River from Carbon Glacier, the Mowich River from Mowich Glacier, and the Puyallup from Tahoma and Puyallup Glaciers, all flow as one into Commencement Bay, the sum of the rock-milky melt, snowfed trickles and rainfed springs, from the entire northeast and north and most of the west slopes of The Mountain. Some stream. Rainier's biggest.

Why, then, is its chapter comparatively skimpy? Well, Tacoma is mostly assigned for bookmaking convenience to the Puget Sound Trail. And due to tricks of geologic history and caprices of the surveyor, much "properly Puyallup" country is assigned to adjoining drainages. Finally, the river upstream from the mountain front belongs to Puget Power and St. Regis Paper and is totally unavailable to public vehicles and to just a limited extent easily exploitable by public boots. Someday this will not be so — Rainier National Park will be enlarged to rational boundaries and a highway will bring tourists to campgrounds, hikers to trailheads, where now only loggers throng.

What walking the chapter does contain is all top-drawer — open the whole year except for one trip, mostly within minutes of major neighborhoods of Puget Sound City. The proposed Tacoma-to-Tahoma Trail is of not merely local but national significance.

One wants to be respectfully humble when discussing this mighty river. Down it from the White 6000 years ago rumbled the Osceola Mudflow. And down the Puyallup proper a mere 600 years ago rumbled the Electron Mudflow, which buried Orting under 15 feet of boulders and muck; floods devastated the rest of the valley, dumping 5 feet of mud at Sumner. Another bad day for the Indians.

USGS maps: Tacoma North, Tacoma South, Puyallup, Sumner, Orting, Kapowsin, Golden Lakes

Swan Creek Canyon (Map — page 46)

A wildland's value varies inversely with the square of the distance from home. What would be merely nice in the heart of a national park is beyond price in your backyard. Thus is magnified the preciousness of Swan Creek Canyon, a refuge of green wild peace on the exact city limits of Tacoma.

Drive I-5 to Exit 135 and go off to Highway 410, following "Puyallup" signs. Well out of the interchange, 410 bends left; diverge right, past Puyallup Tribal Smoke Shop, on Pioneer Way. In ¾ mile, just before Waller Road, note an old farm on the right and a chain-closed lane. This is the unsigned entry to an unsigned Tacoma-Pierce County park of 200-plus acres. Park on the wide shoulder across Pioneer Way, elevation 20 feet.

Follow the lane through pastures and orchard into woods. As the canyon is entered the roars and growls and belches and sneezes of civilization are muted, freeing the auditory scene for creek chatter and bird babble. In a scant ¼ mile the way touches the creek, here flowing over a fish-ladder weir. Though the road-trail continues, cross the weir to a new trail, nicely graded but defensively built to exclude the razzers who snarl and spin around the uplands but are no problem down here.

Giant cedar stump with springboard notch in Swan Creek Canyon

And so, enjoy. Now beside the gravel-rattling creek, now contouring high on the sidehill, the upsy-downsy path ascends the valley in the snug isolation of a spacious wild living room, a green grotto under arching maples and alders. The way burrows through vine maple, passes giant cedar stumps, trickling tributaries. The forest floor and understory are an arboretum — skunk cabbage and maidenhair fern, youth-on-age and ginger, devils club and elderberry — and escaped exotics to knit the brows of wildflower watchers. Historical interest is added by relics of an ancient waterworks — wire-wrapped wooden pipes, mossy concrete cisterns and a springhouse. Above the latter, Swan Creek diminishes sharply.

The creek dwindles, the canyon narrows. The forest changes from fern-

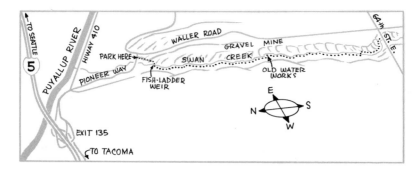

11th Street Bridge over the Puyallup River

hung maples to Douglas fir and hemlock and salal. At a long 2 miles the new-built (1978, by park personnel and volunteers) trail ends, where an old road (for pioneers' wagons?) once dipped into the canyon to cross. Hippety-hop over the creek and proceed on lesser trail a final scant ½ mile to trail's practical end where the creek flows in a culvert under 64th Street.

Despite sidetrails constantly branching off to residential neighborhoods and schools and grownover gravel mines, in all this distance not a house is to be seen and the rantings and ravings of civilization are far away.

Round trip 5 miles, allow 3 hours
High point 320 feet, elevation gain 600 feet
All year

Tacoma-to-Tahoma Trail (Map — page 48)

This was the way taken by Tolmie on his botanizing trip in 1833, the first white man to walk the slopes of Rainier — or Tahoma as some think it is better called. It's a way that walkers of today can take as well, following banks of the

PUYALLUP RIVER

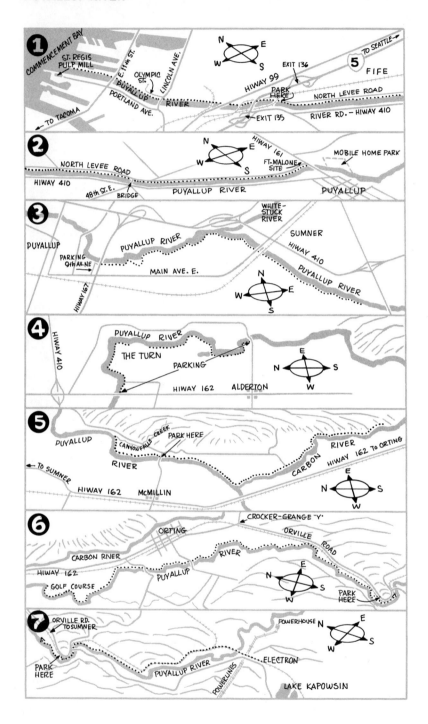

Puyallup River from Commencement Bay by industrial plants to pastoral floodplain to forests of the mountain front, and thence via several alternatives to wilderness of the national park. Close to where people live, open the whole year, the Tacoma-to-Tahoma Trail is an idea whose time should come. But a pedestrian needn't wait — the trips described here sample the river's moods and suggest the potential. They also provide, right now, a lot of nice days.

Commencement Bay to Fife

The best grimy-industrial tour in the book, this walk over the Puyallup delta — the Port of Tacoma — is most exciting on a work day when all the satanic contraptions are bumping and grinding and honking and bellowing, infernally fascinating. Yet serenely sliding through the bustle is the quiet river, green-brown from pollution by glaciers and farms, afloat with ducks and gulls and fishermen, but not with ships because the river — or Puyallup Waterway as the final stretch is called — is rarely used for docking; this activity is confined to the half-dozen other waterways dredged in delta silt.

Drive Highway 410 to about halfway between I-5 and Puyallup. Between the Mile 3 and 4 posts, at 48th Street, turn north over the river on a narrow old bridge. Turn west on North Levee Road 3 miles to its end at a railroad bridge. Park here, elevation 20 feet.

Cross the railroad tracks, drop to the dike, and away you go downstream. The levee is unobstructed, the gravel road little used. In all of **Footsore** this is the premier walk for bridges, some old, some new, some supported by piers of wood or concrete, others on concrete pillars. In sequence there are: a railroad bridge, I-5 monster bridge, another railroad bridge, old Highway 99 bridge, a third rail bridge (there's a lot of good train-watching), Lincoln Avenue Bridge, a fourth rail bridge, this a swing-opener to let ships through, and finally the beautiful 11th Street Bridge with a tower-lift center section.

Along the way are views to downtown Tacoma on the hill above the delta. At the end are views over the bay to ships coming and going and sitting at anchor, and to the ASARCO Smelter stack, Point Defiance, Vashon and Maury Islands, and the Olympics. Also at the end is the special treat, the chief entertainment — the Katzenjammer Castle of the St. Regis pulpmill, hissing, squealing, humming, and roaring, pouring clouds of steam from a dozen stacks and a hundred cracks in the walls — the greatest plume in all Puget Sound country north of the Chehalis Steam Plant.

Round trip 5 miles, allow 3 hours
Practically no elevation gain, this and all following trips
All year, this and all following trips

Fife to Puyallup

Waterway narrows to River, sedately but powerfully flowing between dikes. Industry ends and farms begin. Birds flit in riverbank brush, fowl fly and dive, fish swim. The view of Tahoma is famous.

To do the complete route, drive as before to the west end of North Levee Road. Walk back east on it, passing the first farm, and in a short bit drop to the waterside footroad, where just about any day of the year fishermen are parked, quiet and friendly. The beer cans mainly are dropped by squirrelers at night; razzers are rare in daytime.

Puyallup River and Mt. Rainier

An old tradition among Puyallup High School students is to decorate the concrete walls of the levee. The gaudy artwork is diverting; due to weathering and moss, none lasts long.

There's time for pondering, looking across the foreground of murky stream to the far glaciers. This is one of only three outlets of The Mountain's waters, the others being the Nisqually and Cowlitz Rivers. Here in the Puyallup are also the White, the Carbon, the Mowich, and all their tributaries.

At 5½ miles is the Highway 161 bridge, the proper turnaround. But first visit the historical marker noting the construction here by U.S. soldiers in February 1856 of Fort Maloney to protect the John Carson ferry, thought necessary after Indian attacks of the previous October. Here the Military Road from Steilacoom to Bellingham crossed the river. For more history, enter Puyallup and in ½ mile from the bridge turn left to Pioneer Park and the restored 17-room mansion of Ezra Meeker, who arrived in Puget Sound by wagon train in 1852 and platted the town in 1877.

Round trip 11 miles, allow 7 hours

Puyallup to Sumner and the White-Stuck River
Yes, this is the junkiest section of the route, strictly for local folks and fanatics. Yet, surprisingly, there are lonesome wildwoods, a fringe of riverside

50

cottonwoods and alders that screen most of the industry and commerce and traffic. The main interruptions (of route and mood) are the proliferating trailer parks; society has decided these establishments and their residents are expendable and thus may be permitted to crowd by the river, awaiting the next Electron or Osceola Mudflow. But if this segment is sort of depressing, it has one truly Momentous Event — a Major Confluence.

In Puyallup follow East Main to 9th Street NE and turn off to a parking area under the Highway 167 bridge.

A woodsy riverbank path passes a lovely black-sand beach. A deep tributary ravine forces a detour up through a shopping center parking lot; return on a trail bridging the creek to a dike road. Vast wasteland fields are passed; the other side of the river is woodsy-wild, then freewayized. An enormous sandbar invites waterside walking.

At 1¼ miles is the Momentous Event — the confluence of the Puyallup and the White-Stuck, the two uniting downstream of a long peninsula whereon Sumner is located. Pause to ponder. And listen for loud noises upstream.

The dike road continues by a large garbage dump closed in 1975 and perhaps planned for public green space of some sort. At ½ mile from the confluence are bridges of highway and railroad. In ¾ more mile of woods, with a trailer park and then fancy apartments on the other bank, the road dwindling to trail, the swath of a high-pressure (natural gas?) pipeline makes a good turnaround; in ¼ mile more private homes block the riverbank.

Round trip 5 miles, allow 3 hours

The Turn
Though a walker with only as much gall as the surveyor can do every step from Sumner to Orting, touring trailer parks isn't the happiest sport. This section therefore is best sampled by short strolls from several convenient access points.

The transition is completed to a farming valley, the fields of crops and cows picturesquely framing old homes and barns. At crossroads are little old country store/postoffices. It's hard to believe Tacoma is so close. The near views are over the flat floodplain to forested walls of the Big Valley, 2 miles wide at first, narrowing to 1 mile. The far views are to Ptarmigan Ridge, the Park Boundary Peaks, and Tahoma.

From Highway 410 drive Highway 162 to the bridge over the Puyallup and park on the south side in a fishermen's lot.

A footpath drops to the riverbank slope and follows the river bend (first of three in less than 1 mile) north to a sand point jutting splendidly into the angle. The path is forced from the water by brush and enters a magical place, huge old maples arching over the greensward, a fit picnic spot for Robin Hood and his merry men. Next to the maple grove, and part of the large farm to which all this belongs, operated by Washington State University as the Puyallup Research and Extension Center, is an experimental plantation of cottonwoods in neat rows. Just short of a barbed-wire fence a path turns left to the river, the stock fence easily crossed. Soon comes The Turn — an abrupt 90 degrees — and another dandy jutting sandbar. Bar-walking can be continued a bit farther, the river flowing through wildwoods on both banks, before a farmhouse halts toleration.

Another Momentous Event has occurred. From Sumner to Commencement

Morning glories blooming on bank of Puyallup River

Bay the Puyallup flows in a west-east valley. But here it issues from the north-south Big Valley of Pleistocene time, glacier-melt time, the valley that is continuous from Elliott Bay (and Lake Washington) to the Nisqually River, and in this part and that utilized nowadays by a flock of rivers.

Round trip 2½ miles, allow 1½ hours

Alderton

Strictly river and wildwoods, only glimpses of farms.

Drive Highway 162 to Alderton and at a "Public Fishing" sign by the post office-grocery turn east ½ mile. Just before the bridge is a large Game Department parking area.

The dike north has a public walking easement donated by Sumner Sportsmen Association. The way is green, passing a large marsh-lake abounding in birds. Subdivision and trailer park halt progress just a shout short of the previous segment.

Round trip 1½ miles, allow 1 hour

McMillin
Trailer parks and such are left behind, the river becomes purely wild-pastoral. But between the previous segment and this is a long gap — surveyed but not recommended because of brush, awkward farm fields, and dike-side houses.

Drive Highway 162 to McMillin and turn east ½ mile to the bridge. Cross and park on a shoulder. Note the pipeline crossing the river — in it flows the Green River to slake Tacoma's thirst. Walk upstream and downstream, but not simultaneously.

Downstream. A gated road bars razzers but permits quiet walkers to amble the lonesome dike. To the right is a slough-marshy forest that has excluded agriculture, established solitude. A wide gravel bar is being mined here; when the truck road ends a sandy trail continues to sheer poetry. Out from under arching alders Canyonfalls Creek stealthily sneaks in. Birds chirp and flit in secret shadows. The sand peninsula at the mouth is a grand spot to sit and eat lunch and watch the river and the ducks.

Upstream. The dike road, boulder-blocked to halt wheels, begins with a pasture left, a great bar right. Both sides of the river are now wildwoods. At a scant 1 mile is another Momentous Event, the confluence of the Puyallup and Carbon Rivers. The walk can continue up the Carbon 1 mile to dike's end at the rearing up of the gravel-and-forest cliff (see Carbon River Parkway Trail).

Round trip downstream 1½ miles, allow 1 hour
Round trip upstream 4 miles, allow 3 hours

Carbon River to Canyon Bridge
If cow-watching is your game, here's the Puyallup walk for you. But there are also gulls, ducks, hawks, herons, fish, golfers, and The Mountain.

Due to private roads and fences, this segment has no practical access at the downstream end, or indeed any decent put-in anywhere except at the upstream end. But that's good — difficulties forbid razzers. Drive Highway 162 southeast of Orting 1 mile and at the Crocker Grange Y turn south on Orville Road, signed "Electron." In 3 miles, as road and river are partway through a horseshoe bend left into the short canyon where Orville Road bridges the river, park on a large shoulder to the left, elevation 350 feet.

Walk the short gravel lane to the railroad tracks and follow them downstream a bit to the start of the dike, gained by a slither-scramble down columnar-basalt riprap. That's the last difficulty — the dike just goes on and on, crossed by frequent stock fences easily circumvented, the lack of signs demonstrating a high level of toleration of pedestrian trespassers. Except for the occasional farm vehicle, wheels rarely roll the road.

At the start the Puyallup valley is canyon-narrow, soon widening to a modest floodplain, then abruptly to a mile from green wall to green wall, the

Cows watching people

veritable Big Valley. Cows moo, dogs bark, guns of Fort Lewis boom. From cottonwood forest the river emerges to farms and sorties out in the middle of the broad valley. Off east can be seen the Carbon valley and the tip of Ptarmigan Ridge, Microwave Hill and Spar Pole Hill, and — gasp — Tahoma.

Gravel bars and beaches of black volcanic sand offer alternates to the dike. Marshes and sloughs are passed, barns and more cows, and at a scant 4 miles, the bridge of the Orting-Kapowsin Road, which due to fences is not an access.

Now, the best part. The river turns westward to the foot of the high, steep, wild-forested valley wall and at a scant 2 miles from the bridge reaches Hi Cedars Golf Club, where golfers quaintly wheel around the kempt greensward in cute buggies. For 1 long mile neat greens and fairways are on one side of the dike, the river and green-tangled wall on the other. Where Orting High students of the Class of 1941 put their numbers on a boulder (as have other classes on other boulders the entire route) is the proper turnaround. Lunch by the river, gazing over the green plain to The Mountain.

It is 1 more mile to the confluence with the Carbon, all but the last bit walkable, but not pleasantly due to mean-it fences and hellberries. The main

54

attraction is the boulder of the Class of 1937.

Round trip 14 miles, allow 9 hours

Canyon Bridge to Electron

Scattered stumpranches display the last cows and barking dogs, the crops become those of the Kapowsin Tree Farm, a lonesome wildwood. Razzers continue to be foiled by lack of access, the walking is free of wheels.

The segment can be done from either end but not easily from any midpoint. The logical start is the downstream end. So, park at the same spot as for the previous segment.

Walk the railroad tracks upstream through the rock-walled canyon, a notable little spectacularity. Just past the bridge drop off the tracks to river sand, leap or wade Fiske Creek, and scramble onto the start of the dike. For a scant 2 miles the elevated causeway proceeds by marshy woods and stumpranch pastures, the last habitations. Sands and gravels offer alternate walking. Across the river the torrent of Kapowsin Creek gushes in.

When dike ends, clamber boulders to the railroad track, which here returns to the river after an absence and provides the rest of the route. The way now is true wildland, river gravel and fine forest hillside edging the tracks, which in 1 long mile cross Fox Creek, cutting the base of a rock wall; beavers have dammed the small stream. The tracks leave the river — but the splendid fir forest invites exploration of a riverside route. In a final long ½ mile the tracks return to the river and cross it — precisely where it exits from the mountain front, here consisting of the Kapowsin Scarp.

Startling the lonesome walker, at the bridge are houses. Indeed, this is Electron. And in ¼ mile more is Electron Road, an alternate put-in, elevation 580 feet. To get here drive Orville Road south from the Canyon Bridge 4 miles.

If more walking is desired, continue to Lake Kapowsin (which see).

Round trip 7 miles, allow 5 hours

Electron to the Glaciers

Not wishing to hog all the glory, the surveyor left the remainder of the Tacoma-to-Tahoma Trail for others to pioneer. The route is obvious enough.

From the bridge it's 1 mile upstream on river gravels to Puget Power's Electron Powerhouse at the foot of Kapowsin Scarp, up which a cog railway once carried tourists to an excellent vista point beside the reservoir. This was a pretty impressive hydroelectric operation in 1904, but interest waned after Grand Coulee and the rest.

The fascinating Electron Flume enters the reservoir, often carrying most of the Puyallup River from the Headworks weir some 9 miles upstream. An expedition up the flume was aborted by the umbrella weather that made the narrow plank walkway treacherous; Puget Power probably wouldn't have been too crazy about the scheme anyway. Yet note that these 9 miles in the Kapowsin Tree Farm are pretty much a roaring wilderness, the river absolutely wild.

The St. Regis closed-to-public-vehicles Access Road leads from King Creek Gate to the Headworks. And from the Headworks (see Confluence of Mowich and Puyallup Rivers) St. Regis roads go some 6 miles or so to the national park boundary, nearly meeting the in-park West Side Road, which leads to trails.

St. Regis log dump on Lake Kapowsin

Lake Kapowsin (Map — page 56)

At the foot of the 1000-foot-tall Kapowsin Scarp, the abrupt front of the Cascades, lies Lake Kapowsin, dammed by the Electron Mudflow, highway-civilized on the west side but on the east side partly wildlike-peaceful, partly occupied by one of the largest log dumps in the Western World.

Drive Highway 162 from Orting 1 mile southeast to Crocker Grange Y and turn south on Orville Road, signed "Electron." In 7 miles is the barely-noticeable hamlet of Electron, elevation 580 feet. The best parking is a bit north of Electron Road where a powerline crosses the railroad tracks.

Walk south on the tracks, used only by trains hauling logs to Commencement Bay, some to be used for making pulpmill steam, most to be loaded on ships. The rails instantly leave highway and homes for wildwoods, proceeding

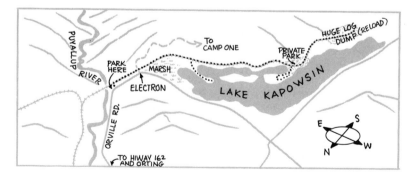

south in the narrow extension of the glacier-era Big Valley that continues through the Ohop Valley to the Nisqually River. The way soon skirts a grand broad bird-crowded marsh which at 1 mile from Electron yields to open water of the forest-shored lake. The tracks cut across the neck of a peninsula; as they return to the shore, spot a path to the peninsula tip, a mossy-grassy rock bald, a glorious place to picnic with the ducks.

The next 1¼ miles offer a succession of entertainments: a long near-shore island secluding a serene waterway; a charming bay sprouting hundreds of old pilings from the old log dump; the peninsula enclosing the bay, the old truck road providing a pleasant sidetrip out in the wild tangle; a delightful little St. Regis park (private — no public road access), Mary Lea Griggs Recreation Area, with picnic shelter, green lawns, big firs, and lake views.

Now for something completely different. Beyond the park the tracks enter the St. Regis log dump, the "reload" from trucks to rail cars. Nearly 1 mile long and about ⅓ mile wide, the dump has hundreds of decks of logs ranging from second-growth thinnings of the Kapowsin Tree Farm to ancient giants, 4 and 5 feet in diameter, some up to 10 and 12 feet, currently being mined from high ridges bounding Rainier National Park. Stay out of the way of trucks and loaders and working folk and walk on, goggling and gasping, to the track end. There's enough timber here to keep Japan in wood for maybe an hour and a half.

Round trip 6½ miles, allow 4 hours
High point 650 feet, minor elevation gain
All year

Confluence of Mowich and Puyallup Rivers (Map — page 59)

Few folk except loggers ever gaze up the Mowich River to the 13,000 feet of The Mountain standing hugely above the lonesome valley unknown to tourists. Come see. And join the campaign to extend Mount Rainier National Park outward here to its natural and logical boundaries.

Drive Highway 165 (see Evans Peak) about 11 miles from the Fairfax Bridge toward Mowich Lake. Some ¼ mile past the Mile 2 (from the park boundary) post, at 3238 feet, spot a narrow sideroad diving down to the right. Drive (or if nervous about it, walk) ¾ mile to Camp 2 Gate. Park here, elevation 2950 feet.

The waters babbling in the bushes are of Voight Creek, a geological curiosity that rises nearby and "hangs" on the side of the ridge above the Puyallup valley, paralleling the latter in an "oversize" valley all the way to lowlands. Beyond the gate is a cabin that is all that remains of Camp 2, a big, famous establishment of St. Paul and Tacoma (later bought by St. Regis) in the railroad-logging 1930s. Long before that the vicinity probably was the location of Grindstone Camp, where the Grindstone Trail branched off from the Bailey Willis Trail and led to Mowich Lake and Spray Park. Everybody frets about the paucity of camping on this side of Rainier — why not extend the national park out to here, build a big new Grindstone Camp, and from it rebuild the Grindstone Trail to Mowich Lake, as well as adding trails to vista points?

Pass the gate, which except for a part of hunting season excludes all public

A telephoto of Mt. Rainier from "Big Bang View"

wheels, keeping the peace on the quiet footroads, which mainly are old railroad grades going long distances on the level or nearly, linked by steeper modern truck roads. A person could get bewildered; remember that the route most traveled by company trucks is from Camp 2 to the valley bottom, exactly where you want to go; when faced by a choice, take the road that seems to have the most traffic.

Walk in tall second-growth down the Voight valley 1 mile to a Y, the right signed "Voight Creek Road"; go left, signed "Camp 7," uphill. Making a great big U turn, the road swings out of the Voight valley, around the end of the ridge at 3050 feet, and heads toward Rainier. At an unsigned Y the road to the valley goes right.

But first (or maybe only, for a round trip of 6 miles) go left on the lesser road a scant 1 mile to Big Bang View, incomparably more fantastic than anything obtained from the Mowich Lake Road and worthy of world fame. Look up the broad, flat-floored valley of the Mowich to the magnificent ice sweep of the Mowich Face. On the left, Tolmie and Hessong lead to Tillicum Point, Echo and Observation, the upper ramparts of Ptarmigan Ridge. On the right, Sunset Ridge (logged to within less than a mile of Golden Lakes!) is part of the panorama continuing over the Tahoma and Puyallup Glaciers to Success Cleaver. And across the Puyallup valley are logging roads and stumps of impressively-naked The Divide.

To continue to the valley, take the right, and at the next Y, about 1½ miles from the Voight Creek Road junction, where the right is signed "Marsh Road," take the left, 2970 feet. In ½ mile, at 2688 feet, Divide Road goes right; go left, straight down, soon bending onto railroad-flat grade. When the flat proceeds straight, at 2500 feet, turn left and down, soon coming to another Smashing View of The Mountain. At 2100 feet, 1¼ miles from Divide Road, is a T with Incline Road; go left. In a short distance is a Y; go right. Where Spur 10 goes right, go left, signed "Camp 7." Where Spur 11 goes right, ditto. At 1¼ miles from Incline Road the way flattens at 1850 feet, with another Smashing View up the Mowich to Rainier, and also now up the Puyallup to its forks. In 1 scant mile more the valley bottom is reached at roughly 6 miles from Camp 2. Here is a T with the valley-bottom road. Walk both ways.

Downvalley on Access Road ½ mile, past the bridge over the Puyallup, leave the road and cross gravels to a view of Puget Power's Electron Headworks (see Tacoma-to-Tahoma Trail), 1620 feet. The ancient (1904) hydroelectricity device seems an oddity so deep in second-growth wilderness. At times the entire Puyallup is diverted by the weir into the Electron Flume (sorry about that, fish) and the river bed can then be crossed to inspect the operation.

Now, the Confluence. Walk a few yards upvalley to the bridge (and Rainier view) over the Mowich. Walk gravel the short bit to the bouldery point, 1650 feet. Sit with one hot foot cooling in the Puyallup, the other in the Mowich. Imagine how grand and fitting it would be if the national park extended to here. Think how embarrassing it would be for a foot-soaker if another Electron Mudflow roared down.

Round trip (including sidetrip to Big Bang) 15 miles, allow 10 hours
High point 2950 feet, elevation gain 1500 feet
May-November

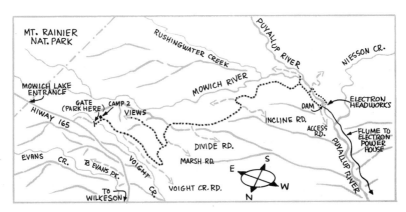

Nisqually River from bluff at end of Church Kalama Road

NISQUALLY RIVER

Southernmost of Rainier's great ice-fed, rock-milky rivers to enter Puget Sound, the Nisqually long has been for all the world the classic approach to The Mountain. Not merely regional in significance but international would be the proposed saltwater-to-glaciers parkway from national wildlife refuge to national park. For local folk, though the Nisqually province is quick of access only from southern neighborhoods of Puget Sound City, it has so much superb walking, so many flabbergasting vistas, as to be well worth now and then busting the Two-Hour Rule.

The enormous glaciated tableland of the "South Puget Plain" is represented here solely by the Parkway. Private ownership complicates most of the subprovince, as does the public ownership of Fort Lewis. The eastern portion, however, is largely in the Vail Tree Farm, with hundreds of miles of lonesome roads, quiet roaming through sky-open young plantations and green-tunnel second-growth (and more and more third-growth), by lakes and bogs and marshy-slow creeks. If the shrift given by this book is too short for you, get a copy of the Weyerhaeuser map and go independent.

The northernmost subprovince is that of Ohop Creek, evidencing the derangements of the ancient landscape by glaciers from Rainier and Canada, as well as Electron and other Mudflows. Just an itty-bitty thing, the creek holds title to two oversized valleys, in its upper length occupying an apparent former valley of the Puyallup River (and Glacier), and in its lower the mountain-edge valley of the Really Big River. Ohop walks, mostly all-year, range from moody-in-winter woods to the best animal show in the Northwest to a fantastic Rainier vista.

The central subprovince is that of the Mashel River, a stream known to hardly anybody but loggers; with its major tributaries, the Little Mashel and Busy Wild Creek (wonderful name!), it drains a broad area between the Puyallup-Ohop valley and the Nisqually proper, but is cut off by transverse ridges from Rainier and thus rendered obscure. Few areas of the Northwest are so totally privately owned and so absolutely skinned. But oh the views in the big-sky, moor-like land of 50 billion stumps! Among them are supreme vantages for planning the ultimate westward expansion of Rainier National Park — out on Ptarmigan Ridge to take in the Park Boundary Peaks, out along Sunset Ridge and Rushingwater Creek to the confluence of Mowich and Puyallup Rivers, out across the South Fork Puyallup to take in Puyallup Ridge and Beljica — though it wouldn't be inappropriate to go one more ridge west, over Deer and Niesson Creeks, to take in Busy Wild and Thing and The Divide. Mashel country is split between Weyerhaeuser and St. Regis; the former's roads are just about always open to the public, those of the latter never are, this segment of the Kapowsin Tree Farm closed even in hunting season, and every interface with roads of other ownerships stoutly defended. All roads are now deteriorating or soon will, because in several years virgin forests of the vicinity will be liquidated and centuries will pass before second-growth on the high ridges again summons chainsaws. Avoid hunting season, when the bands of elk attract armies of cow-shooters, and you may walk the naked hills dawn to dusk and never see a soul or a razzer, and scarcely a beer can. Extending from mountain front to subalpinity, ranging from all-year to late-spring-to-fall, Mashel walks are some of the most scenic and lonesomest around.

The next subprovince south is essentially another aspect of the Mashel. On the divide between it and the Nisqually, reaching from the mountain front at Pack Forest to near the park boundary on Puyallup Ridge, are great trees and masses of stumps, and saltwater-to-glaciers views that will become famous when the infection in these pages is caught.

South of the Nisqually is an astonishing intermingling of First Wave and Second Wave. How did such magnificent old trees survive so long at such low elevations, so near the mills? Well, not to worry, their time has come. Miles and miles of private and Gifford Pinchot National Forest logging roads are replacing miles and miles of trails. The walking has been scarcely even high-graded, fine though it is, because most people with so much time and gas invested driving to here will proceed a bit farther to the security of Rainier National Park. A second reason the survey skimped this final subprovince is that here begin the South Cascades, beyond the ken and scope of **Footsore**.

USGS maps: Nisqually, Weir Prairie, McKenna, Harts Lake, Bald Hill, Tanwax Creek, Eatonville, Ohop Valley, Mineral, Morton, Kapowsin, Mount Wow

For a free map of the road system on Vail Tree Farm, write Weyerhaeuser Company, P.O. Box 540, Chehalis WA 98532

Nisqually River Parkway (Map — page 63)

When Dan Evans, remembered as the Governor of Washington who worked for a North Cascades National Park and an Alpine Lakes Wilderness, proposed a parkway extending up the Nisqually River from the national wildlife refuge to the national park, you'd have thought from the screaming and howling he'd advocated the overthrow of apple pie. Yet a dispassionate survey finds little ground for rational objection. The river's rampaging over the ages has resulted in gravel soils unfit for agriculture, uninhabitable jungles and sloughs between unstable scarps of glacial drift, a corridor of wildness from glaciers to saltwater, the only major interruption being the Tacoma dams and reservoirs. What's to be done down there in the Big Ditch but farm trees and re-create people? Not much.

At present the potential is fully realizable only by heroes. (Being punchdrunk from too many smacks in the face by alder whips helps.) The surly surge of gray-green rock milk meanders restlessly from one ditch wall to the other. A walker sets out to happily amble a gravel bar — and the river swings over and cuts the foot of the scarp. A path promises to lead miles through wildwoods — and comes to naught in evil swamps of a slough. The very factors that have kept trammeling man at a distance restrict the motions of re-creating man.

No silly attempt has been made by the surveyor to punch a path from saltwater to glacier — that task must await the trail crews of the Parkway future. However, a number of representative spots have been noted with paths to walk, gravel bars for kids to fool around on, places where one can meet the Nisqually and ponder its fate.

Near the Delta

The delta and mouth are in the Nisqually National Wildlife Refuge (see Puget Sound Trail). Hospitality of Nisqually Indians and U.S. Army permit sampling of the final flow of the river before the delta. A floodplain averaging ½ mile wide, covered with Carter Woods, Blake Woods, Collard Woods, and just plain woods, lies between 160-foot tanglewood walls of 7th Infantry Bluff north and 38th Infantry Bluff south.

From Exit 116 on I-5 drive through Old Nisqually on the Old Pacific Highway to Highway 510 and turn left for Yelm, pursuing that destination at all subsequent junctions. But before getting there, a short way east of the Nisqually

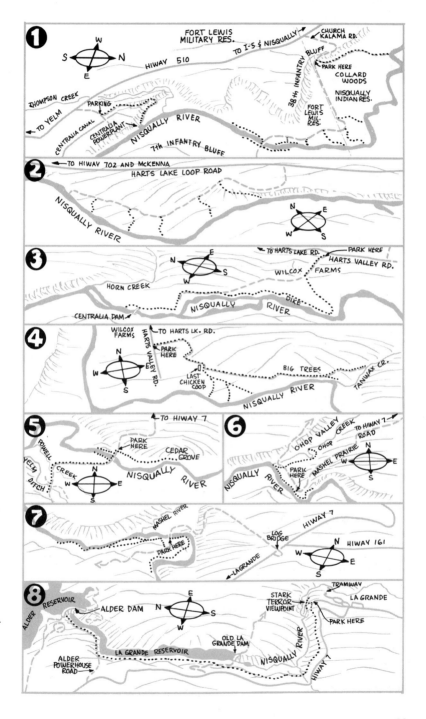

Indian Smokeshop turn north on Church Kalama Road. In ¼ mile the road turns sharp right at the bluff rim; pause here for a splendid view down to meanders of the river through alder bottom and out to delta pastures glimpsed 3 miles downstream. Continue on the road as it narrows, becomes gravel, and steeply descends the bluff.

For the first walk, park just after reaching the valley bottom, elevation 90 feet. Walk the road downvalley at the bluff foot, passing fish-farming ponds, and at a long ½ mile reaching the river just at the big meander seen from the bluff.

For other walks, continue driving ¾ mile over the bottom, passing scattered homes of Nisqually people. The road leaves homes, turns upvalley, enters Fort Lewis, here ungated and open, and proceeds upstream ¾ mile to a gated plank bridge over the river into the fort, whence come alarming "blams" and "crumps" that discourage trespassing. All along are sideroad-paths through nice groves of cottonwoods to nice gravel bars of a truly wild river.

Round trips up to 5 miles, allow up to 4 hours
Minor elevation gain, this and all other walks
All year, this and all other walks

Centralia Powerhouse

A sort of cute little old hydro plant. The lower terminus of the Centralia Canal that feeds it. And a narrows of the Nisqually, a canyon where bluff walls closely crowd the floodplain-less river.

Drive Highway 510 to 2 miles northwest of Yelm city limits and turn off on the gravel road signed "Centralia City Light Hydro Plant." In ¼ mile park atop the bluff, inspect the Canal, then walk the winding road down the canyon of Thompson Creek ¾ mile to the powerhouse. No walking to be done there. Just looking. Those jungles on the other side of the river, that's Fort Lewis.

Round trip 1½ miles, allow 1 hour

Near McKenna

Again there is a wide floodplain, utilized a little for cow farms, mostly for tree farms.

From McKenna (where the river can be seen from the bridge, but with no walking) drive Highway 702 east a long ½ mile and turn southeast on Harts Lake Loop Road. In 2¼ miles turn south on a rough logging road that proceeds in plantation 1½ miles, over the plateau and down the drift bluff, to floodplain and river, elevation 340 feet. Across are pastures. Here, bordering young firs of the plantation, is riverbank tanglewood, penetrated by paths.

Round trips up to 2 miles, allow up to 1½ hours

Harts Valley to Centralia Dam

Ah, serenity. A happy bowl, opening on an emerald plain, a vale of green peace tucked away between river and forest, one of the grandest farm walks in all the **Footsore** world.

Yelm Ditch

From Highway 7 south of Spanaway turn off on Highway 507, signed "Roy, Centralia." In about 1 mile turn left on Harts Lake Road and proceed due south for miles and miles, through Fort Lewis, over the vast South Puget Plain. The road bends west around the rim of the amazingly cirque-like (but that's ridiculous) basin of Harts Lake. At a Y where Harts Lake Loop Road (an alternate approach, from McKenna) proceeds west, turn south, downhill, on Harts Valley Road, signed "Wilcox Farms."

Behold! And wonder — what's the explanation of this horseshoe bowl cupped in 150-foot drift bluffs, this inlet-lacking lake, this wide, river-lacking plain extending from the lake to merge with the Nisqually floodplain? The plunge basin and outwash plain of a great falls of a great river issuing from the ice front? Well, whatever . . . The result has been a large expanse of un-Nisqually-like rich black soil. In 1909, to quote the milk carton, "Grandfather Judson Wilcox established the Wilcox Farm on the fertile land around Harts Lake." The third generation now operates a family factory-farm of 1000 acres with 750,000 chickens in dozens of enormous metal coops plus cows crops all over the emerald plain. It's a scene from another world. Someplace in

Cedar Grove

Europe, maybe. Farm policy bans public vehicles on lanes but permits public feet. So, peace be with you in your walking.

From the Y drive 1½ miles down by the Wilcox Farm Store (eggs, milk) and farm headquarters (see Rainier!) to the plain. Just after passing the foot of the last hillock and crossing the ditch of Harts Lake Creek, where a lane goes off right, park out of the way, by the ditch, elevation 354 feet.

Walk the lane right, through fields by the creek, ¼ mile to a Y. Take the left a long ¼ mile to field's edge, woods, and the upstream end of one of the Nisqually's very few dikes. If little children are in the party the trip likely will end right here, on the enormous wonderful lava-boulder, black-sand bar, with an infinity of material for building castles and tossing in water.

Adults though, will want sooner or later to walk the dike ½ mile to the downstream end, wild forest on the across-river wall, and then take a farm lane 1 scant mile, beside a slough, to the Centralia Dam, the weir that diverts water into the Centralia Canal. A gravel bar below gives a view of the structure and is a nice spot for a picnic.

Round trip 4 miles, allow 3 hours

Harts Valley to Tanwax Creek

After the picnic lunch, take an afternoon walk from the emerald plain to wildwoods, through a startling grove of big trees, to a lonesome river and a pretty creek.

Drive from the previous parking place ½ mile more to the end of public road at a four-way intersection. Park well out of the way. Elevation, 358 feet.

Walk the lane due east by the first of the huge coops from within which comes the muted, bee-like, vaguely ominous hum of thousands of chickens gabbling. Beware of exhaust fans! Those chicken winds could fell an ox. (Note the staggering cows.) Stick to the obvious main lane headed south past more coops and little forested monadnocks, in views to the Bald Hills. In ¾ mile is the last coop. Go past the end, turn right, and along the far side to the fourth ventilator window. Here an old woods road on the left has been bulldozed shut but an obscure path climbs the dirt barrier and quickly finds the road, now a trail. (Note: down the building a bit farther is an obvious lane left. This ain't the way, though it does branch into countless rude paths to the river.)

The trail climbs onto an ancient river terrace and winds between a lower bank and an upper bluff. Second-growth yields to a grove of amazing, tall, 4-foot Douglas firs and cedars, a surprising survival. Then come mossy-ferny big-maple and vine-maple woods. The path touches the bluff edge, with views (and game trails) down 50 feet to the river, here meandering in two big bends through lonesome gravel bars and alder-cottonwood forest. The path turns inland a final bit to maple-arched Tanwax Creek and trip's end, 1¼ miles from the last chicken coop. Beyond the pretty stream are stumpranches, a Christmas tree farm, and a peckerwood sawmill.

Round trip 4 miles, allow 3 hours

Cedar Grove and Yelm Ditch

Gravel bars, a grove of great cedars, and a curious artifact of ancient engineers.

Drive Highway 7 to Ohop Grange Hall and turn west on Tanwax Extension Road (not so signed at the turnoff). In 1¾ miles, at the intersection with Kreger Road, jog right onto a rough log-haul road. Proceed westerly on the main road, dodging lesser spurs, 1¾ miles to a Y where both forks are equally major. Go left and again dodge spurs another 1¾ miles to another such Y. Again go left, dropping off the scarp and in ¾ mile coming to a log bridge over the river. Park here, elevation 390 feet.

Walk back from the bridge to a mucky lane which leads into a grove of cedars up to 4 feet in diameter, 5-foot spruces, and assorted big maples and whatnot. Trail ends by the river in ½ mile.

The second star attraction is across the river. Walk the main road over the bridge ¾ mile to an intersection. Here study a weird waterway, obviously dug by man, now much-dammed by beaver and overgrown with aquatic plants, though the water pushes briskly through. This is the Yelm Ditch, shown on the map as starting upvalley a couple miles, proceeding all the way to Yelm. Was it for irrigation, or electricity? When? No trace of the ditch was found near Yelm itself. Investigating the course might be interesting.

Gravel bars can be walked up and down the river on both sides of the bridge. Upstream on the south side is a scraggly farm, doubtless producing more solitude than sustenance.

Round trips up to 3 miles, allow up to 2 hours

Ohop Creek Confluence
Leaving behind picturesque pastures, Ohop Creek finishes its run to the Nisqually in a swampy-forest valley nearly ½ mile wide. This is the southern end of the Big Valley that terminates on the north in Elliott Bay and Lake Washington. A truly Momentous Spot.

Drive Highway 7 south and east over Ohop Valley toward Eatonville. At 1 mile from the turnoff to Ohop Valley Road turn right on Mashel Prairie Road. Drive this log-haul road past lesser sideroads 1 long mile to an intersection; turn right 1½ miles, dropping to the Ohop Creek valley and the river, elevation 450 feet.

Path and gravel bar lead ¼ mile upstream to a rock nose jutting into the water. Wildwoods line the wild river. A 40-foot hard-rock wall continues upward into a 250-foot freshly-logged (Second Wave) drift scarp.

Walk fishermen's paths and flood channels downstream beside the river ½ mile to the far side of the Ohop valley, where slow, dark Ohop Creek is swallowed up by the fierce rock-milk torrent. A woods road leads up the marshy, bird-busy creek.

Round trip 2 miles, allow 1 hour

Mashel River Confluence
A wild river — no, **two** wild rivers. Cool shadows of big trees. Quiet. Solitude.

Drive Highway 7 to a few yards south of the Highway 161 turnoff to Eatonville, and to a few feet past a log bridge over the highway. Turn left on a gravel log-haul road that circles around to cross the log bridge. Proceed 1¼ miles, winding down into the canyon of the Nisqually River, which in this stretch isn't messing around on any floodplain. Cross the river and park on the shoulder, elevation 520 feet. Walk upstream and down.

Upstream. Walk through a campground in firs and other conifers so big one wonders why they've been spared, to whom they belong. Above the river leaps a 200-foot cliff of iron-stained gravel pocked with bird caves — swallows' apartment houses. The forest floor is carpeted in season with blossoms of starflower and candyflower, lily of the valley and trillium, solomon's seal and Oregon shamrock. Myriad paths branch off, and gravel bars can be walked, as well as a cutoff river channel. In ¾ mile the last path peters out on a "beach" of rock shelving into the water. Above are green shadows of La Grande Canyon and only ½ mile away is the powerhouse, but until Parkway trails are built you can't get there from here. Not unless you're a fisherman, and insane.

Downstream. Walk the road away from the river around a bend until a way can be found into and out of the moat backhoed to keep wheels out of the woods. Follow an old road by old camps ½ mile to the end. Trail burrows another ¼ mile, ending on mossy slabs shelving off in rapids. Lovely! Lonesome! The route can be continued via scrambles in steep brush to a gravel bar, but the surveyor quit and thus doesn't know how far a doughty adventurer

Nisqually River below LaGrande Powerhouse

could proceed into wildness beneath the 200-foot canyon-wall jungles that guard the solitude.

On the other side of the bridge paths lead the short bit to the other wild river, the Mashel, and the confluence.

Round trip 3 miles, allow 2 hours

La Grande Canyon

The most spectacular section of the Nisqually between glacier and delta. But Tacoma City Light got there before us and drowned it. And since then has done little to ameliorate the crime by exploiting what remains of the scenery. Nevertheless, there is a walk that provides an impressive display of concrete plus a moment of sheer terror.

Drive Highway 7 to the headquarters of Tacoma City Light at La Grande. At the big sign, "La Grande Hydroelectric Plant," turn off right on the gravel road ¼ mile to a small parking area just short of a gate. (Alternatively, park by the highway at the picnic area. While walking to the gate take a sidetrip to the top of the tramway and watch the little passenger platform rise or fall from or to the powerhouse 350 precipitous feet below, in the canyon depths, inaccessible to visitors and also invisible, since no vista point has been provided.) Elevation, 940 feet.

Walk by the gate; feet are permitted but not public wheels, so the way is quiet, a very nice footroad for winter exercise in umbrella time. A bit past the gate is a trail signed "Do Not Proceed." A person so foolish as to ignore this advice may descend an old road to concrete supports of an aqueduct, now removed, that once carried water over the canyon. A path leads to the base of the supports — and shrieks, and vertigo, and peril. The canyon here is deeper than wide, and the rock-slab lip overhangs, as one discovers in horror upon peering over to see down the mossy-ferny precipice 300 feet to the river bed (usually dry, the water diverted through the powerhouse). For a small expenditure Tacoma could erect safety fences and a view platform that would become famous for fainting tourists.

So don't do that, folks. Instead walk the lonesome road up the canyon. Logging trucks can be heard on the highway above but all is peace down here. The best view of the river bed is in 1½ miles; below rock walls is a green pool at the base of old La Grande Dam, built in 1912, rebuilt in 1944, half-hidden in trees, almost seeming to belong there. A sideroad drops to the dam for a close look at finger-narrow La Grande Reservoir, green with glacier-milled rock flour. In another 1 mile, past a second gate, is a junction with Alder Powerhouse Road, open to public wheels. But walk on anyhow the final ¾ mile to the powerhouse in deep, clammy, perpetual shadows of 840,000 tons of concrete, 330 feet high, 1500 feet long, built in 1944. A stupendous lump. Amuse yourself imagining an Osceola-like mudflow spilling over the dam. Look out below.

Round trip 6½ miles, allow 4 hours

Alder Dam to Nisqually Glacier
Another thing Tacoma hasn't done is build a trail along the 7½ miles of Alder Reservoir, which presently offers picnicking, fishing, boating, but no walking worth mentioning.

Though given only a cursory eyeball survey, the 20 or so miles (as the water runs) upstream from the reservoir head at Elbe seem to have a sufficiency of floodplain woods and gravel bars to easily permit a Parkway trail. And that takes you to the national park boundary and away you go to the ice.

Fort Lewis

Established in 1917 to train doughboys to fight Kaiser Bill and his Huns, this 140-square-mile military preserve now prepares troops for NATO forces on the North German Plain, whose terrain resembles that of the South Puget Plain. The artillery sounds sometimes for days without cease, 105mm and 155mm howitzers and 8-inch guns firing maybe 50,000 rounds a year, cracking chimneys and nerves in Yelm and often, on dismal winter days, leading lonesome walkers in Cascade foothills to run for the car, supposing a thunderstorm is coming.

Driving the public highways traversing the landscape that reminded Tolmie, in the 1830s, of the parks of 18th-century Whig grandees, one is tantalized by how much walking there is to do in this mostly-wild magnificence that extends from Tacoma to the Nisqually River, Puget Sound to the Cascade front. But those guns . . . And those moments when a trespasser suddenly finds himself surrounded by soldiers armed to the teeth and tries to remember how to say "I surrender!" in Russian . . .

As it happens, there is a legal, safe, if complicated way to explore the prairies and woods, notably spectacular in the spring flowering. Obtain the USGS maps covering the fort. Study out a nice-looking trip. Better, several trips. Write an application for an "organized group." Send it, a month or more in advance, to Headquarters, 9th Infantry Division and Fort Lewis, Fort Lewis, WA 98433, Attention: Public Affairs Officer. Not all requests can be honored but if you apply early enough, with enough alternatives, chances are good of a wonderful and legal walk.

St. Paul Lookout (Map — page 71)

The best places to **feel** The Mountain are near but not too near, high but not too high, close enough so it doesn't seem a Hollywood backdrop, far enough so the immensity doesn't overpower a sense of scale. St. Paul Lookout is just right. In fact, St. Paul Lookout is one of the champion viewpoints of 13,000 feet of icefalls and lava ramparts.

Drive Highway 162 from Orting 1 mile southeast to Crocker Grange Y and turn right on Orville Road, signed "Electron." In 7 miles pass Electron Road and turn left on a blacktop road signed "Electron Flume" and "St. Regis Paper Co. Logging Offices." At a Y in 2 miles, where the right goes to St. Regis headquarters, angle left on gravel Camp 1 Road. Switchback up the Kapowsin Scarp to the plateau and a T in 3½ more miles. The left is to Electron Flume; go right and in 3 miles be surprised to enter the boondocks settlement called "Ohop" by maps and by everyone else, Camp 1, dating from railroad logging by St. Paul and Tacoma Lumber Company and now inhabited by employees of the successor St. Regis. At a Y in town go left to the end of houses and a small parking area at a gate, elevation 1450 feet.

The gate, never open to the public, making all this Kapowsin Tree Farm country razzer-free, is on the North Ohop Road. Walk it a few yards and turn

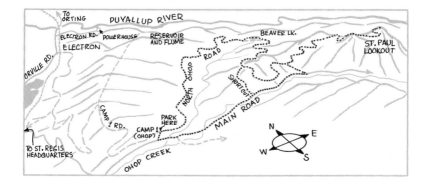

right on a road that goes a scant ¼ mile to Main Road, which follows Ohop Creek.

(For lonesome woods walks the year around, keep North Ohop Road in mind. Few will wish to follow in the surveyor's sore-footsteps as a route to the lookout, winding all over hell and gone as it does along North Fork Ohop Creek. But it's just quiet as nowhere out there, the second-growth too skimpy to be worth management by man so the job is left to nature. At 4 miles is a good turnaround, on the shore of "Beaver Lake," where the engineers have dammed the creek beautifully and flooded a stretch of road ¼ mile long, a chilly wade in winter. Solitude? This is where they invented it.)

Turn left on Main Road, along which trucks highball 50mph to the reload on Lake Kapowsin (which see) from timber mines on the boundary of the national park. But never, not even in hunting season, do public wheels molest Main Road.

At 2 miles is a connection off left to North Ohop Road, a nicer way to the lookout than Main Road, but longer and confusing, though easy to follow on the return and thus recommended for that direction only. For the quickest and surest way, stick with Main Road another 1½ miles to the foot of the St. Paul ridge. Spot an undriven, grassy road switchbacking up left, leading in ⅓ mile to North Ohop Road.

Turn right and start climbing in big-fir, then small-fir forest on the lovely, rarely-driven (never by public) footroad. Windows open as the road contours a subpeak to a 2600-foot saddle and a grand view south. But tarry not, the big show is close. The road starts steeply up the final peak, passes intriguing towers of shattered lava, switchbacks twice, passes a moldering log cabin, a decrepit privy, and at 2970 feet, 3½ miles from Main Road, gloryosky!

No matter the lookout tower is gone. The ridge prow is naked, nothing to block the view. A steep 1500 feet below is the great broad flat valley where Mowich and Puyallup Rivers and Niesson Creek join, the valley an awesome 2 miles from wall to wall. Some geological foolery has occurred; one speculates that once the Mowich flowed to lowlands alone in what is now the Puyallup valley, and the Puyallup occupied what is now used by little Ohop Creek. Did the Electron Mudflow down these valleys have a hand in it?

The view north is to Ptarmigan Ridge, Carbon Ridge, and South Prairie Ridge, and the view south is to scalped heights of The Divide and out to Ohop Lookout and lowlands. But that's not what you came for. Sit on the prow and munch your cookies and stare, and stare, at the Mowich Face enclosed by Ptarmigan and Sunset Ridges, and at Puyallup and Tahoma Glaciers and Success Cleaver. On Klapatche Ridge between the forks of the Puyallup, see the West Side Road on the park boundary. See the logging roads that go to the very boundary, literally into alpine meadows.

Round trip 14 miles, allow 8 hours
High point 2970 feet, elevation gain 1500 feet
April-November

Ohop Valley (Map — page 74)

Two lakes, creeks and pastoral vistas, and lonesome wildwoods in the valley where once the Really Big River rolled along the mountain front but now

Ohop Valley

just meager Ohop Creek oozes through the weeds. No wheels intrude; peace is guaranteed. A good walk for moody winter — and flowery spring.

From Highway 161 drive Kapowsin Road east to Kapowsin crossroads and turn right to Kapowsin Lake. Having crossed the railroad tracks, so they now are by the shore, park on any commodious shoulder with access to the tracks. Elevation, 550 feet.

Paths from tracks to shore give fine views over forest-ringed Kapowsin Lake to pilings once used to organize logs dumped in the water by railroads, to the present dry-land St. Regis reload, and to the abrupt lift of Kapowsin Scarp. The end of the lake is passed, swampy woods entered, and then a large, ancient orchard where unkempt apple trees feed herds of loud birds. The way crosses a wide alder bottom to the far valley wall and proceeds along the slope in mixed forest with pleasing views out over marshy floodplain pastures, handsome barns, comfortable farmyards, cows and horses and crowing roosters.

At 2½ miles is the only and brief intrusion of wheels, at the crossing of Clay City Road (just uphill are an interesting Mutual Materials clay pit and brick-and-tile manufactory). Just beyond is 25 Mile (Little Ohop) Creek, nice. That's the last thing that could be called big excitement, but there are two more pretty tanglewood creek valleys, and plenty of solitude on a trail only used by log trains. Disappointingly, there are merely screened glimpses of far-below Ohop Lake. At 2¼ miles from Clay City Road the tracks bend left, out of the valley, to Eatonville. Time to turn around.

Round trip 9½ miles, allow 6 hours
High point 720 feet, elevation gain 150 feet
All year

This is the long and quiet walk in Ohop Valley. But the charm of that picturesque vale is best felt on a deadend farm lane that permits peaceful absorption of the Ohop quintessence.

Where Highway 7 coming from the north drops off the bluff into Ohop Valley, turn right on Kelstad Larson Road and immediately park. Scarcely a wagon wide and used by only three families, whose barns and fields and cows are what it's all about, the lane ends in 1¼ miles in a farmyard. These are the most joyous couple of loitering hours you'll ever spend in the Ohop, which cows can walk from end to end, the lucky beasts. Ohop grass is said to be especially delicious; it sure looks it.

Northwest Trek Wildlife Park (Map — page 75)

No zoo, this, but rather a unique 600-acre wildlife park of Tacoma Metropolitan Park District, maintained in cooperation with Tacoma Zoological Society. Northwest Trek began with the loving care by Dr. David and Constance Hellyer, who acquired the property in 1937 and in 1972 gave it to the public. Now hundreds of thousands of visitors a year take the 5½-mile, 1-hour Trek

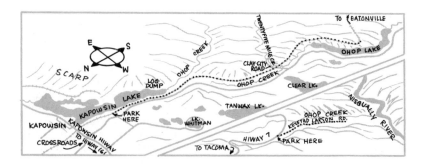

Tour, riding quiet trams through areas where animals roam free, only people are fenced in. The park is open daily April through October, Wednesday-Sunday the rest of the year.

Drive Highway 161 south from Puyallup toward Eatonville. (Or, drive Highway 7 south from Tacoma and at a Trek sign opposite Highway 702 jog to 161.) Just south of Clear Lake turn in on the park entrance and drive ¾ mile to parking areas from which paths lead to Trek Center, elevation 760 feet.

By all means take the Trek Tour and see deer, elk, moose, woodland caribou, bison, wolverine, bighorn sheep, mountain goat, and more, roaming gone-to-nature farm fields and second-growth wildland woods half-a-century old.

But do some walking, too, on the 5 miles of nature trails; these are in a different area than that of the Tour, which cannot be visited on foot.

For openers, left from the Center is a loop of blacktop paths totalling ½ mile, passing animals in natural habitats (beaver, porcupine, otter, fisher, mink, skunk, weasel, marten, raccoon), a children's Baby Animal Exhibit, and — supreme thrill — an overlook from which one looks down on nonchalant bear — and wolves loping through woodlands.

For the long walk, go right from the Center toward the Tour Station above Horseshoe Lake, beyond which rise summit snows of Rainier. On the way, opposite a pair of uncaged, unchained bald eagles perching there watching the parade, is the trailhead. From it are a number of loops of various lengths, sampling the various forest systems — marsh, young fir, alder-maple.

For an introductory tour, do the perimeter loop, taking all right turns, and thus in about 1 mile reaching the brink of the plateau, the Ohop Valley scarp, and screened glimpses of Ohop Lake. In about ⅓ mile more, at Station 6, starts a sidetrip, the best part. Turn right and proceed along the bluff in cool green lush forest, past the end of Ohop Lake, out along the slope of Goat Ridge, to Sweetwater Spring, 1 mile from the loop. Sit a while, dip a delicious sip or so from the boxed-in pool, and return to Station 6. Again on the perimeter, return to the eagles in a final ⅔ mile.

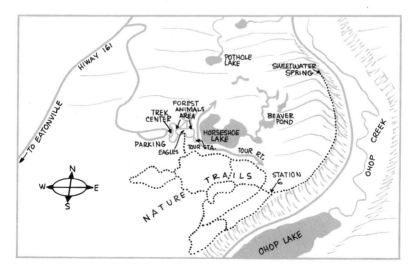

A pine marten at Northwest Trek

Dress and behave appropriately and you may be taken for one of the exhibits, as was the surveyor, who was eagerly asked by a party of foreigners, "Sir, are you a logger?" The honor modestly accepted, there is now some corner of England where his photo is displayed as representative of the species.

**Introductory tour 4½ miles, allow 3 hours
High point 760 feet, elevation gain 200 feet
All year**

Ohop Lookout (Map — page 77)

Though on the abrupt mountain-front scarp above Ohop Valley and Eaton-ville, Ohop Lookout will not give the broad lowland vistas it did from the now-gone tower until some judicious pruning is done. However, the peak offers two fine and very different hikes from opposite directions: one, short, has splendid views from a Second Wave clearcut; the other is virtually view-less but is a classic green-tunnel far-out wildland chanterelle sort of hike.

Short Hike With Views

From the stoplight intersection in Eatonville, turn east from Highway 161 on the Alder-Eatonville Cutoff, confusingly signed "Elbe." In ½ mile, at the city limits by Paul Kreger Memorial Field, turn north on a road signed "Weyerhaeuser High Yield Forest." At a Y in a scant ½ mile go left over the railroad tracks and climb into an area first of gravel-mining, then tree-farming. In 2 miles from the Alder Cutoff is a Y of roads 6000 and 1000; go left on 1000. In ½ mile more, at a possibly signless Y, diverge left on lesser road 1550.Con-tinue ¾ mile, crossing Lynch Creek and Berg Creek. Park by the latter's bridge, elevation 1250 feet.

Walk a few yards to a Y; go left, contouring to a ravine, then climbing through big-fir forest to a spur crest. Here's the first view — go left a bit to the dropoff and look over the Ohop Valley to lowlands, and to the spectacular 400-foot precipice of bare rock on the end of Ohop Mountain. At a scant 2 miles is a Y; go right, uphill, in a 1950s plantation, open and airy. Around 1 mile from the Y is the trip climax. The nice little footroad swings to the tip of a spur, a pasture-like, vetch-infested, wide-open promontory. The top, 1850 feet, is the lunch spot-turnaround.

Looking like a Christmas card, cozy little Eatonville is tucked below in the hollow of the Mashel valley. Beyond is Hugo on the "mountain island" of Pack Forest, and then the Nisqually valley and the Bald Hills. West is the sprawl of the South Puget Plain, woodlands dotted with lakes and farms and towns. Beyond are saltwaterways and Black Hills. East is the Mashel valley, with Dobbs and Mashel and Busy Wild and Thing and — The Mountain. (Those rumbles out west — that's not thunder, that's World War III being rehearsed in the vastness of Fort Lewis.)

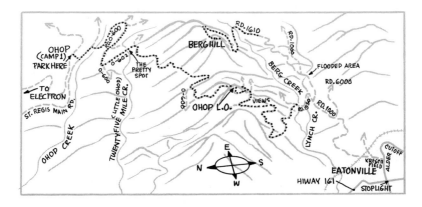

Ohop Valley from viewpoint on way to Ohop Lookout

Walking beyond here yields only glory and nostalgia. In 1 long mile (at all forks take the left) is the summit, 2335 feet, and the site of the old lookout tower, ringed by tall firs. There is a slot view north, enough to tantalize — over green fields of Surprise Valley can be seen waters of Kapowsin and other lakes, valleys of Puyallup and Carbon Rivers, and the Issaquah Alps and Seattle.

Round trip to summit 8 miles, allow 5 hours
High point 2335 feet, elevation gain 1100 feet
All year

Long Hike With Solitude and Wildness
Drive to Camp 1 (see St. Paul Lookout), elevation 1450 feet.

Walk by the gate up North Ohop Road the short bit to a sideroad leading right ¼ mile to Main Road. Turn left on the truck boulevard ⅓ mile. Turn right on lesser-but-still-major road 0-600. This portion of Kapowsin Tree Farm is never open to public wheels, not even in hunting season; you'll never meet a razzer; the only traffic here is St. Regis crews thinning second-growth and gypos mining (legally) cedar. The road crosses marshy ponds and Ohop Creek and climbs the valley wall to a rolling plateau extending for miles. At 1½ miles from Main Road are a pair of Ys; at the first go right; at the second go right on 0-600 in thinned forest, dodging spurs. At 1550 feet, 1¾ miles from Double Y, where the old railroad grade of the route proceeds straight ahead, overgrown, two roads go left; both will get you to Ohop Lookout but the right, 0-600, is a mile longer. So go leftmost, making a U turn to do so, on 0-602. In ¼ mile is a triple fork; go straight through on the center lane. In ¼ mile more is the highlight of the trip, the way emerging from green tunnel to big-sky beaver marshes and then crossing Twenty Five Mile (Little Ohop) Creek. A lovely spot, 1600 feet, 4½ miles from Camp 1. The birds, the beaver dams, the flow of "mountain tea" under big old logs of the bridge, the solitude, the picnic lunch — who needs more?

Why go on? Ah, to walk far far from anywhere to absolute nowhere, completely out of the world. That rumbling westward — it's some tumult of the gods. The footroad grows grassier and grassier. At a long ¼ mile from the creek is a Y; go right on 0-6021. Now climb from the plateau-valley, cross the ridge to Berg Creek drainage, and at 2¼ miles from the last previous Y come to an 1800-foot T with a better road (0-600 — see above). Turn left and in 2 miles, after joining the better road from the south, attain the summit, 9 miles from Camp 1.

And slogging homeward in spooky gloom of winter twilight, maybe meet a band of elk munching in the marshes, or suddenly hear from every side the call of the wild — a dozen coyotes in simultaneous serenade. You may even, as did the solitary and lonesome surveyor, find the enthusiasm to break into a jog, which becomes a run as little footsteps are heard following in the night.

Round trip to Little Ohop Creek 9 miles, allow 6 hours
High point 1600 feet, elevation gain 150 feet
All year

Round trip to Ohop Lookout 18 miles, allow 12 hours
High point 2335 feet, elevation gain 1000 feet

View south from Berg Hill over Mashel Valley

Berg Hill (Map — page 77)

A step farther inland than Ohop Lookout, yet low enough and close enough to the mountain front for winter hiking, a scalped peak gives views from Olympia to Tacoma, saltwater to glaciers, a million stumps and a million shrubs doing nothing to block the panoramas.

Drive from Eatonville to the 6000-1000 Y (see Ohop Lookout) and keep left on road 1000. In ½ mile is the Possibly Signless Y where road 1550 goes left to Ohop Lookout; stay right on 1000. Soon begins an interesting flatland where the road and Lynch Creek discuss which belongs where; in the rainy season hikers may not wish to get their wheels involved in the argument; the car may be parked (elevation 1300 feet) and a bit of stimulating wading done, adding 4 miles to the round trip. Otherwise, drive on. At a Y go left on 1000 or right on 1580 — the two soon rejoin. A bit past the reunion, at about 2 miles from Lynch Creek ford and 3 miles from Signless Y, is a Y at 1655 feet. Park here.

Walk left a few steps to a Y and go left on road 1610. At a T in ¼ mile go right on 1610, swinging into the cute little gulch of Berg Creek to the crossing at 1625 feet, ¾ mile. Now begins a steady ascent on a rough footroad in naked country dotted with shrubs of a late 1960s plantation. Views are constant. Many are the sideroads but it's hard to go wrong. Up, up, up goes 1610, to a quarry that has bitten a chunk from the peak's rotten volcanic rubble, and at 1¾ miles from Berg Creek, to the summit, 2400 feet.

East over headwaters of Lynch Creek are The Divide, Mashel, and the

80

glaciered glory of Rainier. North over the head of Berg Creek is the intriguing wildwoods plateau that is traversed by Little Ohop Creek and that drops off abruptly in the Kapowsin Scarp; smoke from chimneys of far-out Camp 1 can be seen, and Ptarmigan Ridge to its end in Spar Pole Hill. West are Ohop Lake, downtown Tacoma, Nisqually Reach, Black Hills, and Olympics.

Round trip 5 miles, allow 4 hours
High point 2400 feet, elevation gain 900 feet
February-December

Mashel Mountain (Map — page 81)

Enwrapped in headwaters of Mashel River, the first really high peak east of Eatonville commands a stunning panorama of 50 billion stumps. Ah, but that's only a fraction of the show — Rainier is so hugely near its white brilliance is blinding, and when the smog thins there are cities and saltwaterways to be seen as well.

Drive from Eatonville to the 1000-6000 Y (see Ohop Lookout) and go right on 6000, which leads by many junctions nearly to the summit, pocked on the way by 50 billion chuckholes. Drive (slowly) to a Y in 2 miles; stay left and twist up from the plateau onto the west ridge of Mashel. At 5 miles from the 1000-6000 Y is a junction at the foot of the final climb. Elevation, 2050 feet. Probably park here; views don't begin for a bit but the road becomes steep and narrow and often rude.

Walk straight, right, uphill, on 6000. At a spurtop Y at 2300 feet, go left on 6000. At a ridgecrest Y at 2500 feet, go right on 6000. Aside from that, just ignore obviously lesser sideroads. In 1¼ miles, at 2650 feet, is a promontory of volcanic rubble that has been quarried to a faretheewell. If you're still driving, park here; the views become stupendous and now will leave you no time for a steering wheel.

In a scant 1½ miles (a gasp at every step), 6000 swings above the saddle between the south and north peaks of Mashel. Here, at 3200 feet, turn left on a brushy, unmaintained, undrivable spur perhaps signed "65___" (part of sign missing). Second-growth now closes off the view. At a Y in ⅓ mile, go right. A bit beyond is another Y; walk both forks.

First, left. In ¼ mile the way flattens. Just before reaching the highest point

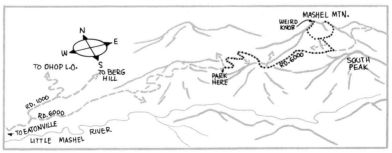

Weird Knob

of the road, find a faint trail right, leading 50 feet through young trees to a Weird Knob of funnily-eroded volcanic rock. This is the summit, 3560 feet. By the early 1980s the pushy trees will have closed off all the view, but the knob is worth it. It's weird.

Now, right. The way bends left around a corner in ⅓ mile to wide-open stump slopes. Scamper up a bald summit only a couple feet lower than Weird Knob. Good gracious. Over a long lunch, inventory the horizons. Sakes alive.

The view east is unique, over the headwaters maze of the Mashel to scalped ridges decorated with gaudy gashes of logging roads in ocher volcanic soils. Atop a 4930-foot nakedness is a monster boxy Thing one speculates is the Bell System's Outer Space Connection, designed to pick up TV programs on the UFO Network. Beyond is Puyallup Ridge, partly stumps (Kapowsin Tree Farm) and partly green (national forest). And then just ice, just Rainier, and beware that bulging eyes don't pop out of your skull.

That's east. What's otherwhere? From the summit and on the ascent, The Divide, Ohop Lookout, Eatonville, Park Boundary Peaks, Ptarmigan Ridge, Spar Pole Hill, Carbon Ridge, Boise Ridge, Pete, Lake Tapps, Big Valley, Issaquah Alps, South Puget Plain, Olympics, Fort Lewis, Commencement Bay and Tacoma, Nisqually Reach and Olympia, Black Hills, Bald Hills, Alder Lake, High Rock, Adams, St. Helens.

Round trip from 2050-foot junction 8 miles, allow 6 hours
High point 3560 feet, elevation gain 1500 feet
March-November

The Divide (Map — page 83)

Build a highway and put a visitor center on top and The Divide, the high ridge between the Puyallup and the Mashel, way out in the middle of a lonesomeness unknown to the civilized world, visited only by loggers, would depopulate Paradise and Sunrise — **this** would be the visage of The Mountain on every calendar. Well, maybe that's exaggerating a little. But not much.

Drive (don't walk, no matter how your poor car weeps for mercy) road 6000 (see Mashel Mountain) to the saddle between the south and north peaks. Proceed ¾ mile, passing a pair of sideroads right, bending left around the east

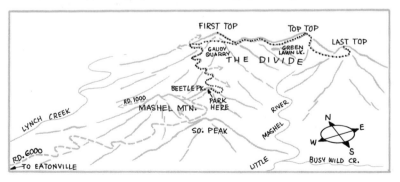

Mt. Rainier from the Divide

side of Mashel, to a 3240-foot saddle. Turn right on the sideroad here, climbing to the top of 3370-foot Beetle Peak, named in honor of the survey vehicle which despite great suffering in 3 days of struggling over miserable Mashel roads bravely conquered this summit at the creaky age of 105,926 miles. Park the car here. In fact, maybe junk it.

84

To the right of the summit knob (views the equal of those from Mashel) find an old cat road adopted by the elk and follow it down the north ridge of Beetle. In a short way, where the rude trail splits, go left. Down more, after a very steep stretch, when the trail splits, go right. And so, after losing some 300 feet in maybe ⅓ mile, congratulations! There in the 3070-foot saddle, step onto a logging road — you have broken through the No Man's Land from the Weyerhaeuser road system to the St. Regis road system. You can now walk continuous road to Kapowsin Lake. But you'll never see a public wheel — St. Regis gates ban them. There isn't even a razzers' cheater path — St. Regis won't stand for them.

Follow the road left, rounding into a tiny-creek draw and a Y; the right is to a 1978 logging show, one of the last there'll be around here until the 22nd century; go left. Ascend around another corner to nice little Lynch Creek and a monster gaudy quarry in the yellowish volcanic rubble. Another sideroad goes right to the 1978 logging; continue straight, bending around another corner, by a smaller quarry. At 1¼ miles from hitting the St. Regis road the way tops the west ridge of The Divide at 3300 feet. At the junctions here, take the first right, along the ridge crest.

Now the eyes turn from the South Puget Plain to the view over Mashel headwaters to Thing Peak and The Mountain. Now begins a classic walk in the sky, following the ridge, high in the air, views everywhere, Rainier framing itself in a series of stunning photographs with foregrounds of googols of stumps and shrubs. At a scant 1 mile, at 3650 feet, the road tops the ridge just past First Top, to whose 3760-foot summit a sideroad leads.

Always on or near the crest, the road proceeds 1 scant mile to a saddle at 3600 feet. In a basin below right is lovely "Green Lawn Lake." Above is a handsome slope of black stumps and white sticks, a masterpiece of geometric desolation. From the saddle are roads left and right — to deadends. Instead take the system of cat tracks between them, staying on or near the crest. In ⅓ steep mile is the 4100-foot plateau of Top Top — and, on the survey day in early June, a glory of blooming beargrass. Continue over the plateau to the east end and a logging road. Pick a spot on the brink to spend a couple hours goggling.

(For variant views even closer to Rainier, continue on logging roads curling around 1 mile to the 4000-foot summit of Last Top.)

Below east is the deep valley of Niesson Creek, which makes The Divide an "island" by connecting the Puyallup and Mashel valleys, evidencing some mystery of a prior drainage. Beyond is the ridge that rises to the climactic box of The Thing, then Deer Creek and scalped Puyallup Point.

Below north is the enormous gulf of the Puyallup, divided from the oddly-wide Ohop valley by the ship prow of St. Paul Lookout. Beyond are Ptarmigan Ridge, from the summit icecap to Spar Pole Hill, and the Mowich Lake Road.

Ah, but the centerpiece. Success Cleaver. Tokaloo Rock. Klapatche Ridge and the in-Park West Side Road. Tahoma Glacier cascading from the bowl ringed by Point Success, Columbia Crest, Liberty Cap. Sunset Amphitheater. Puyallup Glacier. Sunset Ridge. Mowich Face. Mowich and Puyallup Rivers far below, rattling their gravels.

Round trip to Top Top 8 miles, allow 6 hours
High point 4100 feet, elevation gain 1600 feet
May-November

Railroad tracks along Alder Lake (reservoir)

Big Mashel Gorge and Little Mashel Falls (Map — page 87)

Walk lonesome, wheelfree woods past views of a Christmas-card village to a pair of astounding phenomena, one sponsored by the Mashel River, the other by the Little Mashel.

From Highway 161 in Eatonville turn southeast at the stoplight onto the Alder Cutoff. In ½ mile, at the city limits and Paul Kreger Memorial Field, turn north on a road with a "High Yield Forest" sign. Drive ½ mile to the railroad tracks and park, elevation 890 feet.

Hit the tracks south ½ mile to the high-in-the-sky bridge over Mashel River. (Though not dangerous if no trains are around, and they aren't very often on this log-haul line, the bridge won't be every stroller's bowl of cherries; for a bridge-dodging approach, use the alternate starting point, below.) Across the bridge, skid down right to river level and follow a woods road to the gorge. Lordy. If one has walked over the bridge, now, looking up to it in consternation, one may wish one hadn't. But the river and its walls are the superstar. Downstream it widens to pools, becomes just a nice wild river. Upstream, though, it issues from a slot gorge through which mountain tea flows in black deeps as narrow as 4 feet wide under vertical cliffs 200 feet high. Sit on water-carved slabs and admire.

Return to the tracks, pass a path down left (to the head of the gorge), and emerge from woods into a huge, recent, Second Wave clearcut. At 1 scant mile from the bridge, where the tracks round a nose of lichen-black rock, a garden of alumroot, ocean spray, and goatsbeard, is a fine prospect. Ever seen a town nestle? That's what Eatonville does, in the Mashel valley, amid its hills. Look across to the fabulous Ohop Wall, the other way to Hugo Peak, and down to the moldering Eatonville sawmill that closed some 20 years ago but still poses picturesquely, wasteburner and all, beside the ducky old millpond. And look out over lowlands to Bald Hills and Black Hills. Humming "O little town of Eatonville" proceed ¾ mile to where the tracks pass under a bridge of the Alder Cutoff at 2¼ miles from Eatonville; just before the bridge is a wide parking space and alternate start, elevation 1100 feet.

In ⅓ mile is the second feature. A short, no-sweat bridge over Little Mashel River is the overture. From both sides find paths down the mossy, flowers-in-spring, rock slot the river has sliced to the uppermost of three falls. Carefully pick a slick way down by potholes to the plungebasin.

Now for the real action. Return on the tracks 150 feet from the bridge and spot a dirt track up the cutbank. Follow the trail along the gorge rim. Rude paths go off left to poor looks down to the middle falls, but they're nothing much. The main tread leads to the top of the lower falls. They're something, okay. Arched over by maples, the stream flows on lichen-dark, water-rounded, exquisitely-sculptured rock, down a small cataract into a black pool of foam-flecked mountain tea. There it gathers itself and hurls over the brink — to a preliminary drop, then out of sight in the forbidding chasm. Gracious. At one time or another Eatonville got water from here and toyed with a ridiculous hydroelectric scheme, but now much of the falls area is preserved in Pack Forest (which see).

The bottom of the lower falls — actually a double falls totalling about 150 feet — can be reached by a perilous skidway. Exploration of the ½-mile gorge in which the Little Mashel drops 270 more feet was not carried out by the surveyor, stricken with terror.

From the upper falls a closed-off backdoor leads to the Flying M Ranch

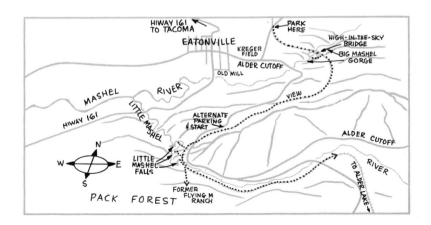

section of Pack Forest, an excellent sidetrip. The railroad is worth walking another 1 forest mile up the pretty little river. Then farms start, changing the mood from wildwood to pastoral. But that's nice too. For one so minded, it's another 6 miles or so to Alder Reservoir.

Round trip 8 miles, allow 6 hours
High point 1200 feet, elevation gain 600 feet
All year

Pack Forest (Map — page 90)

At the interface of lowlands and foothills, on a "mountain island" enclosed by Mashel and Nisqually Rivers, is Pack Forest, a 3000-acre laboratory of the University of Washington's College of Forest Resources. Miles and miles of lonesome footroads wind around hills and valleys in woodland and meadow and views from Rainier to Puget Sound, a walker's paradise. Snowline-probing and animal tracks in winter, flowers in spring and summer, colors and mushrooms in fall. And — peace be with you — on weekends the gates are closed to public wheels, but not feet. Ah, quiet!

Aside from pedestrian pleasures, Pack offers a unique opportunity to observe a wide range of forest-management techniques and experiments. Tree-farming was pioneered here, including some of the earliest plantations in the Northwest. Thinning began in 1930, and in the 1940s the first forest-fertilization studies anywhere. Through the years there have been programs in forest nutrition and in harvesting methods, clearcut and shelterwood. Presently in progress is a project using forests to dispose of METRO sewage sludge and wastewater and studying the effect of these on forest growth and groundwater purity. It was for such purposes that Charles Lathrop Pack made the initial gift of land in 1926, establishing a teaching and research laboratory for teachers and students, a demonstration area for the forest industry, and, for the general public, a living textbook.

The andesite ridges of Pack, glaciated and drift-covered down low, rock-outcropping up high, were thoroughly burned about 1800, only a few relict trees escaping. Some of this 1800 forest survived the big Eatonville Fire of 1926 and other blazes of the period. Recently a management plan has been adopted to make for greater age diversification of Pack's forest groups and thus enhance the educational value: 10 percent of the land, including the 33-acre relict-tree Ecological Area, will be reserved in a natural state; 14 percent, including the 94-acre Hugo Peak Transect of 1800 forest, will be specially managed with only limited salvage logging of fire-damaged trees; and 76 percent, including the almost two-thirds of Pack burned since 1920, will be intensively managed on a conifer rotation of 80 years, approximately 30 acres to be harvested annually. On a single walk a person thus can see trees from seedling age to centuries old, and a variety of planting and tending and harvesting methods.

Drive Highway 161 through Eatonville to Highway 7 (or drive 7 direct from Tacoma). At ⅓ mile south on 7 from the junction is the Pack Forest entry. Enter past the gatehouse, proceed 100 yards to the first intersection, and follow signs left to the public parking area, elevation 800 feet.

Giant cedar at Pack Forest

Management-road construction during the next decade will change things from those of 1978 described here, but not basically. Each year some 30 acres of new clearcut will open new views — as the growth in plantations is closing old ones.

A person could wander Pack for days (but not nights — no camping allowed) on modern management roads and old farm lanes and CCC roads dwindled to trails; everywhere are routes for shortcuts or trip extensions or independent explorations. The basic introduction is the "1000 Loop" (Lathrop Drive), with three mandatory sidetrips. The energetic can tack on the "2000 Loop," with the added sidetrip of the "Canyon Loop." The "Flying M-Bethel Ridge Loop" can be tacked on or done separately. And you can do inside loops and outside loops and loop-the-loops until thoroughly looped.

1000 Loop (Lathrop Drive)

Walk the main entry road by the gate, open to public vehicles 7:30 to 4:30 weekdays, permitting advanced starts for shorter walks, but closed to wheels (not feet) weekends, creating a sort of de facto wilderness area. Ascend to the headquarters area and pass between the administration building and the greenhouse-nursery where are grown the 55,000 seedlings planted each year

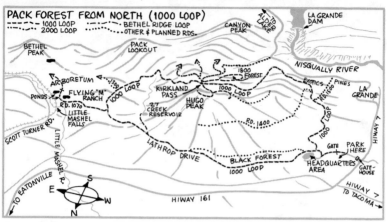

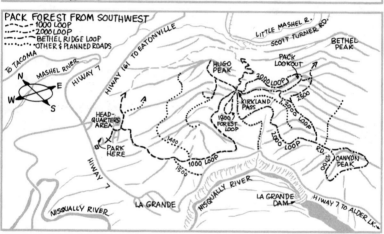

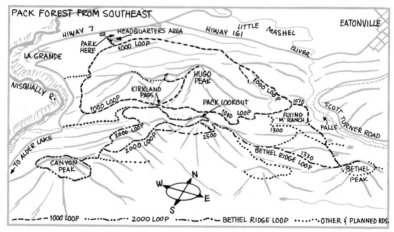

on the Forest. Just beyond, at ⅓ mile from the parking area, is a T with road 1000, Lathrop Drive.

Go left. heeding the sign, "Forest Roads and Trails," and pass above the millpond of the former sawmill. In 1½ woodland miles is the sideroad right a scant ¼ mile to 27 Creek Reservoir, intended by the CCC to provide water for fighting fires, but now abandoned, a moody black pool. In a scant ½ mile more is a Y at the forest edge, 1160 feet, and the takeoff of the first mandatory sidetrip. (Or, bag the loop and spend the whole day here.)

Flying M Ranch-Little Mashel Falls-Arboretum. As soon as you've recovered from the stunning impact of Rainier's white hugeness, go left on road 1070, out in broad pastures of 650-acre Flying M Ranch, famed in the 1960s for rock concerts, acquired by Pack Forest in 1975. In ½ mile, where the farmhouse used to be, is the former ranch entry road from the Alder Cutoff; descend it to the railroad tracks and Little Mashel Falls (which see). Returned from that astounding adventure, continue through fields to the two fish ponds, now devoted to floating ducks and providing foregrounds for photos of The Mountain. Scheduled to be started in 1979, just past here will be the site of a major arboretum, 200 tree species on 80 acres, featuring not only Northwest forest species but also exotics from around the world grown for comparison. **Sidetrip total, 2 miles.**

Proceed onward and upward on road 1000, passing road 1300 (when it's built) left to Bethel Ridge (see below). Forest grown up since the 1926 and other fires abruptly yields, at the edge of the burn, to wonderful big trees of 1800 forest, plus a few older relicts. Note fire damage to the big trees, many of which are dying — thus the salvage logging. In 1¼ miles, gaining 460 feet, is the Forest hub, Kirkland Pass, 1593 feet. Five roads come to the pass, so watch it. Two mandatory sidetrips take off here.

Ecological Area. The pass is surrounded by 1800 forest, tall trees and deep shadows. And in the heart of it are relicts from a more ancient past. Walk the Trail of the Giants down the valley of usually-waterless Newton Creek. The trail branches, forming a loop. Don't go fast, take your time — time to feel the dimensions of big hemlocks and cedars, and especially of the Douglas firs up to 9 feet in diameter, 250 feet tall, maybe 450 years old. **Sidetrip total, ¾ mile.**

Hugo Peak. Located at the exact abrupt front of the Cascades, since being partially clearcut in 1974 to salvage trees rapidly dying from fire damage Hugo is the classic grandstand of the Forest. Walk road 1080 a scant ¼ mile from Kirkland Pass to a T. To the right is the summit of Hugo, 1740 feet. To the left is a 1720-foot second summit — and a 1693-foot third summit to be reached by a future road. Each has, or will have, views. Below is the Mashel valley, the Ohop valley joining from the north. Beyond are the Nisqually, Bald Hills, and woods and farms and lakes of the South Puget Plain, over which Nisqually and Deschutes Rivers run to Nisqually Reach and Budd Inlet, respectively. Beyond saltwaterways rise Black Hills and Olympics. The St. Regis steam plume marks Tacoma. The Issaquah Alps point to Seattle. **Sidetrip total, 1½ miles.**

The way home is short and downhill. Descend from the pass on road 1000, leaving the 1800 cathedral. From a clearcut is a smashing view down to the drowned Nisqually Canyon and the La Grande Dam that done it. Shortly after is a plantation of exotics established in 1927, including Japanese red pine, redwood, Oriental cedar, Port Orford cedar, Korean pine, Arizona cypress, and big-cone spruce. Off left a bit on road 1500 are Ponderosa pines grown from seeds gathered in a dozen areas of the West. The Hugo Peak trail shown on old maps is passed but no longer really exists. Just past a service area is a Y; go left the last bit to the closing of the 1000 Loop at 2 miles from Kirkland Pass.

Loop trip with all sidetrips 10½ miles, allow 7 hours
High point 1740 feet, elevation gain 1200 feet
All year

2000 Loop: Lookout Peak, Canyon Loop

From Kirkland Pass walk road 2000 to Pack Lookout, alternating between 1800 and 1926 forests, a textbook illustration of how fingers of fire follow natural flues up the slope. In a scant 1 mile is "Lookout Peak," 2034 feet, highest point of Pack Forest's "island." But at present, no views. Unless you climb the tower, which even if and when renovated should only be done by superfluous children. Built in 1929, it may be preserved as an historical artifact, a laudable notion. But the surveyor freaked out at the third level, three or four below the tree tops, when he found each step causing the entire structure to shudder and sway. Once it gave Pack's only views but now there is daylight in the swamp and vistas that don't risk your nerves.

Descending from the peak, one notes a resumption of wonderful 1800 forest — and an old lane wandering off in it to the right. To make a short loop of this trip, follow the old lane, in glorious big trees the whole way, down the ridge crest ½ mile to Kirkland Pass. But for the standard loop, continue on road 2000, passing another management road right, then road 2500 left (see Bethel Ridge).

Canyon Loop. At 1700 feet, 1 mile from Lookout Peak, go left on road 2300, which follows a spur ridge up and down and then circles 1855-foot "Canyon Peak," with views from clearcuts to Alder Dam and Reservoir, Stahl Mountain, and the Little Nisqually. **Sidetrip total, 1½ miles.**

Road 2000 ascends 1¾ miles to close the loop at Kirkland Pass.

Loop trip from Kirkland Pass 5¼ miles, allow 3 hours
High point 2034 feet, elevation gain 500 feet

Flying M-Bethel Ridge Loop

As of the survey in late 1978, the easternmost spur of the Pack "island," Bethel Ridge, offered a long wildland walk on roads so old as to have dwindled to mere game trails. It is described here as surveyed. However, when construction is completed of the 1300-series roads the walking will change; the new routes (see map) will be less trail-like but more scenic as clearcuts open up the forests.

Walk 2⅓ miles from the entry gate on road 1000 to Flying M Ranch and go left on road 1070 over pastures to the fish ponds. Continue on an old farm lane that climbs the pasture to forest edge and becomes an old woods road. At 1500 feet, 1 mile from road 1000, is another dammed reservoir, a lovely secluded pool now so greenery-invaded as to be mostly a marsh. From this

Entrance display at Pack Forest

pretty bowl the road-trail climbs to a 1650-foot saddle in Bethel Ridge and splits. The left fork climbs ¼ mile to the 1824-foot highest point of "Bethel Peak," which when sawed open will give famous views to Mashel and Nisqually valleys.

For the loop go right on a wildwood trail that will become road 1330. Dodge branches that descend left and right (or why dodge? why not explore?), stick with the ridge, and at 1¼ miles from the pretty bowl-pond hit road 2500, precisely at a 1790-foot saddle where a new cut has opened a delightful picture of Eatonville.

Follow road 2500, passing a clearcut with a sublime vista of Rainier over a middleground of Mashel, Thing, and Busy Wild, rounding slopes of Lookout Peak, in ¾ mile reaching road 2000. (An easy shortcut can be made on an obscure old road, as noted on the map.) Turn right on 2000 and follow it 1¾ miles up to Lookout Peak and down to Kirkland Pass. Return the 2⅓ miles on road 1000 to the administration building and the Pack gate.

Loop trip 10 miles, allow 7 hours
High point 2050 feet, elevation gain 1500 feet

Looking north from Dobbs Mountain

Dobbs Mountain (Map — page 94)

The long ridge between the Mashel and Little Mashel is mostly hairy with second-growth. However, Second Wave clearcuts have shaved a slope, opening a view over Mashel country to Rainier and out to Puget Sound.

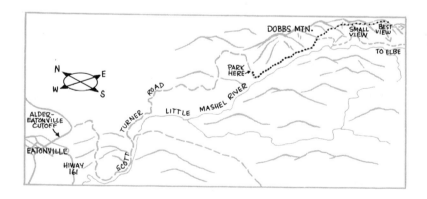

From the stoplight on Highway 161 in Eatonville turn east on the Alder-Eatonville Cutoff, confusingly signed "Elbe." In 2¾ miles turn left on paved Scott Turner Road. Drive through fields and forests toward the jutting 2761-foot prow (wooded, viewless) of Dobbs, then bend right on its lower slopes. The last ranch is passed and at 5½ miles from the highway is a School Bus Zone. A bit beyond, a lesser road takes off downhill right. Park on the turnout here, elevation 1700 feet.

Or drive on a mile or so. But be warned: beyond the limit of school busses the way is an old CCC road that may abruptly go sour and swallow up your car, as it nearly did that of the surveyor. Yet the four-wheelers love the "mud run" over the hump to National. Best label this trip "Never on Sunday."

The nice footroad (when razzers and sports are absent) goes through 50-year-old second-growth mixed forest. Second Wave clearcuts open a little vista down the secluded valley of the Little Mashel to lowlands. The way climbs to the ridge crest and at 2750 feet, 4 miles from School Bus Zone, comes to a turnout with a view over the Mashel. However, there's better ahead. Continue a scant ¼ mile to a Y; go right another ¾ mile to a clearcut and open views from Rainier to Mashel to The Divide to lowlands.

Round trip 9 miles, allow 6 hours
High point 2900 feet, elevation gain 1200 feet
February-December

Nisqually Vista (Map — page 96)

Serene whiteness of The Mountain contrasts with dun starkness of totally-clearcut Busy Wild ridges. But the unique specialty of the walk is the preeminent vista of the upper Nisqually River, from the national park to the mountain front.

Drive Highway 706 east from Elbe 6 miles and turn left on the road signed "Elbe Hills ATV Trails" (gasp, grumble). Stay on the main road 2½ miles to a Y where the Eatonville-National Road goes left (to Dobbs Mountain); go right, signed "Elbe Hills 4WD Trail System" (it is time, O Lord). In a scant ½ mile is another Y, the left being the Busy Wild Road leading to the ATV dreamland; go right. Continue about ¾ mile, passing logging spurs right and a deadend road left, sticking with road 1520, to a big bend right, around a corner, at 2800 feet. BAM. Park here or you might get hurt. (For a great snowline-prober in March or earlier, park sooner and walk here.)

The views start here, naked valley of Busy Wild Creek below, naked slopes of Wild Peak above. Busy Wild Mountain becomes prominent as the way goes along, then The Thing, their foreground of reddish-brown brush inscribed with yellow-brown roads setting off the virgin green of Puyallup Ridge, the white of Rainier, looming huge. West out the Busy Wild-Mashel valley are Dobbs, Mashel, Ohop, and lowlands.

The road climbs to the ridge crest and the second chapter — the south views. Proceed to a Y at 3375 feet, at the foot of the next sharp step in the ridge. The left fork, not surveyed, climbs the step and proceeds east, probably hooking up with Copper Ridge (see Busy Wild Mountain). For the best vista go

Mt. Rainier from Nisqually Vista

right on a spur that quickly dwindles to trail, contouring ¼ mile to a promontory landing.

The broad, deep Nisqually valley is seen, upstream, coming from the Tatoosh Range, continuing by Ashford, directly below, to Elbe and onward to the mountain front and over the South Puget Plain to the sea. River and highway and towns and farms. Plus the South Cascades from Goat Rocks to Adams and St. Helens in the distance, and, close across the valley, High Rock, National Lookout, the "Highway 7 Valley" via which the Nisqually once, when ice-dammed, apparently flowed to join the Cowlitz, Storm King, Round Top, Ladd, and Stahl.

Round trip 4 miles, allow 3 hours
High point 3375 feet, elevation gain 600 feet
April-November

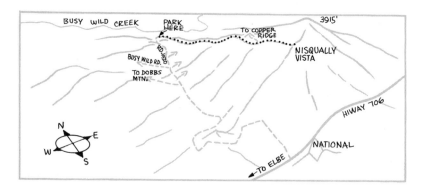

Busy Wild Mountain (Map — page 97)

What! Not yet another brain-spinning vista of Rainier? Yes, but more too. As a foreground for The Mountain That Was God, there is the awesome bleakness of the Kapowsin Tree Mine, offering some of the most staggering clearcut scenery in the Cascades. The drama is explored on a five-destination melange of overlapping hikes.

Drive Highway 7 to Elbe and continue on Highway 706. At 3 miles past Ashford go left on road 159 (the small sign is hard to see). Climb climb climb on this narrow but solid road, at all junctions sticking with 159.

The first destination, on a snowline-prober of winter or spring, depends on where you start and how long you walk. Wherever, it's great. The road leaves the highway at 1850 feet in virgin forest, climbs by lovely Copper Creek and others, proceeds through big old second-growth to more virgin, passes a broad vista of the Nisqually valley, crosses pretty Christine Creek, and swings into the newly-naked logged-to-the-last-stick upper valley of Copper Creek, with wide views.

For the second destination, drive 5¾ miles from the highway, to where the road makes its first switchback to climb from Copper Creek onto Beljica Ridge. Park here, 4200 feet.

Ascend a linked succession of cat roads up the clearcut near the fringe (1978) of virgin forest. Razzers are halted by St. Regis barricades as the way leaves Mt. Baker-Snoqualmie National Forest. In ½ mile is a hillside landing at the end of a road coming from Copper Ridge. Go left on this road to a saddle, then up to the 4520-foot southernmost high point of the ridge. The specialty of the walk is the look straight down to silver-shining braided channels of the Nisqually River, and hamlets and highway. But there is a goodly share of the sights described for subsequent destinations.

Round trip to Copper Ridge 3 miles, allow 2 hours
High point 4520 feet, elevation gain 350 feet
May-November

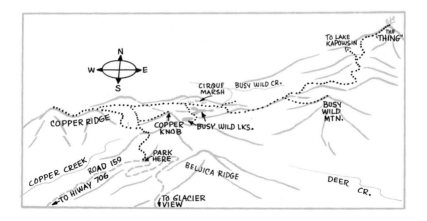

Mt. St. Helens from Busy Wild Mountain

For the third destination, shun the road from Copper Ridge and continue straight up from the landing on a cat track ¼ mile to the ridge crest. To the north ¼ mile is the 4850-foot summit of Copper Knob, still forested as of 1978. Until that defect is remedied, the great view is just where the crest is attained. Walkers who wish to spend hours simply ogling need go no farther. Rainier is the big news, but there are also Adams and St. Helens, the cliff of High Rock, Storm King, The Rockies, Stahl, and Bald Hills. The tree-free Copper Creek valley. The Mashel valley out past Mashel and Dobbs to Ohop.

**Round trip to Copper Knob 2 miles, allow 1½ hours
High point 4850 feet, elevation gain 650 feet**

To rest is not to conquer. A cat track drops 200 feet in a scant ¼ mile to join a major log-haul road — just about the end of the long tortuous line from Kapowsin Lake. Turn right and gently descend the sidehill of stratified lavas, crossing a divide to headwaters of Busy Wild Creek.

Glaciers were once here, briefly. After a long ½ mile on the road, having dropped to 4300 feet, look down left to a meadow-marsh in a cirque. And look right in virgin forest (1978) to shallow, reed-grown Lower Busy Wild Lake. Strike off in open woods, perhaps on vestiges of ancient trail, and in ¼ mile find Upper Busy Wild Lake, 4320 feet, a tiny, cool-shadowed nook of virgin-forest serenity, ringed by hellebore and beargrass and huckleberry.

But, back to the sun-blasted outer bleakness, exclaiming at the satanic beauty of yellow-white road gashes curving around yellow-brown basins green-dotted with fir shrubs. The last scraps of virgin forest should be liquidated by 1981 or so. Then the call of the Yellow-Shafted Talkie Tooter will be heard here no more, a great silence will enwrap the land for centuries — because that's how long it'll be before another crop is ready up here. One hopes the back-country poet who named Busy Wild Creek was not doomed to see his world destroyed.

At a Y where the logs flow left, downhill, turn right, uphill, to the ridge crest. Round a subsummit to a spur shoulder and where the road contours left, leave it for a cat track and walk the naked crest between Deer Creek and Busy Wild Creek. At 1½ miles from Busy Wild Lakes, attain the 4850-foot summit of Busy Wild Mountain.

Whoopee! Settle down for a minimum 1 hour of swinging the horizon. Trace every feature of Rainier from Ptarmigan Ridge to Success Cleaver. In front of it, look down to Deer Creek and across to virgin green of the Forest Service portion of Puyallup Ridge, and to Beljica and Wow. North are Echo and Observation, Tolmie, Park Boundary Peaks, Carbon Ridge. Westerly are Mashel, Dobbs, Ohop. And saltwaterways. South are Goat Rocks and Adams and St. Helens and Bald Hills. In season, blooming amid summit stumps, are glacier lilies and lupine.

Round trip to Busy Wild Mountain 6 miles, allow 4 hours
High point 4850 feet, elevation gain 2000 feet
June-October

The route to the final destination is obvious to any eyeball. Where the route to the top of Busy Wild turns onto the cat track, stick with the road as it gently descends, joins another major log-haul road, and contours around to the saddle between Busy Wild and Big Creeks. When the road to Kapowsin Lake swings left, turn off right and climb to the summit of Thing Peak, 4930 feet. Visiting The Thing, and perhaps having your blood curdled by radiation, are extra added attractions.

Round trip to Thing Peak 11 miles, allow 8 hours
High point 4930 feet, elevation gain 3000 feet

Glacier View (Map — page 100)

Incredibly few people know this place. Those who do know it as not merely one of the supreme views of Rainier but a religious experience. The glory of God's creation is the more exalting because in the other direction is an equally awesome panorama of Man's devastation, a clearcut that extends westward miles and miles. To visit here is to be convinced that the park boundaries must be pushed out to take in this point and the entirety of Puyallup Ridge.

Drive road 159 (see Busy Wild Mountain) 7 miles from Highway 706 to a Y at 4560 feet atop the clearcut ridge between Copper and Deer Creeks. Brace yourself — here is the first look at The Mountain. Recover, if you haven't driven off the cliff, and go right on 159C. In ¾ mile, after the road has bent sharp left and just before it bends sharp right, is a saddle crest a few steps from the road. Spot a footpath, perhaps unsigned. Park here, elevation 4720 feet.

The first scant ½ mile of trail, relocated through a mid-1970s clearcut and losing some 300 feet, can be confusing. The path first contours huckleberry hillside, joins a cat track from the right, is joined by a cat track from the left, and drops a bit to cross another cat track, this spot maybe marked by a rock cairn on a stump. Just below is virgin timber, to which the trail switchbacks. At forest edge, where a former path goes straight, drop off steeply left into trees and to a small oozy meadow. This open green is visible from the road so use it as a guide — it will remain even if more logging is done here on Mt. Baker-Snoqualmie National Forest.

No more route problems. Simply tramp on and enjoy. Another clearcut is skirted but the trail stays in splendid big old firs and hemlocks, lichen-draped, and the understory of black huckleberries and all. At ¾ mile is a signed junction.

The right leads ¼ mile to Beljica Meadows, 4440 feet, a charming, cozy marsh-meadow at the foot of the rock horn of 5475-foot Beljica. The trail continues to Goat Lake at 2 miles, Mt. Beljica at 2 miles, Rainier National Park at 3 miles, and Lake Christine at 3 miles.

The left is signed "Glacier View 3." The trail runs the forest crest of the ridge between Deer Creek and Beljica Creek, coming within a spit of a 1978 extension of road 159, providing a possible shortcut, but who needs it? Now the trail climbs the divide and swings around the side of Peak 5419 to the saddle beyond. Sometimes in meadows and rock gardens, the way climbs and contours around crag-topped Peak 5507. At the saddle beyond is a Y, the

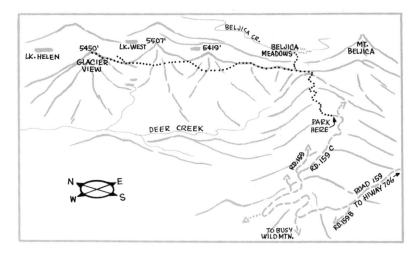

Telephoto view of Gobblers Knob and Tahoma Glacier from Glacier Vista trail

right dropping to Lake West (and a St. Regis clearcut) and Lake Helen (and another St. Regis clearcut — or better say, **the** clearcut that extends from the park boundary to Kapowsin Lake). The left climbs a final ⅓ mile to the 5450-foot summit, site of a long-gone lookout cabin. As the summit, a flat-top, cliff-sided, narrow cleaver of andesite, is reached, trees abruptly yield to rock garden and the whiteness that has tantalized emerges in total dazzling hugeness. To your knees.

Plan to spend at least 2 hours here — it takes that long to recite the names of all the features in sight. Yes, you'll want to digest the West, over naked Deer Creek and naked Busy Wild, Thing, The Divide, and Mashel to where all those missing trees went, the lowlands and saltwaterways and cities. But for the worship services, turn to the East. Over the foreground of the South Puyallup valley is the in-park West Side Road, close enough for tourist's cars to be heard. Above rise Kapatche and St. Andrews Parks, then Tahoma and Puyallup Glaciers, to the summit icecap high in the sky. The whiteness of The Mountain's face is wide, from Sunset Ridge to Success Cleaver. Swing the eyes left, past skinned Puyallup Point to Puyallup and Mowich valleys, St. Paul Lookout, Ptarmigan Ridge, Carbon Ridge. Swing the eyes right, past Gobblers Knob and Wow and Beljica to peaks south of the Nisqually — High Rock, Storm King, Goat Rocks, Adams, St. Helens.

In season, scenery must compete with blossoms, which even on the survey day in late September, amid patches of fresh snow, included (in forest and meadow and on summit rock garden) coolwort, pyrola, coralroot, lousewort, raspberry, grouseberry, beargrass (in seed), hellebore, valerian, kinnikinick, silverleaf, arnica, lupine, phlox, penstemon, paintbrush, yarrow, stonecrop, and bluebells.

Round trip 6 miles, allow 5 hours
High point 5450 feet, elevation gain 1500 feet
July-October

Stahl Vista (Map — page 102)

From a low-elevation, long-walking-season clearcut on the tip of the ridge between Nisqually and Little Nisqually Rivers, a big-sky, broad-horizon panorama stars the valley-drowning arms of green-milky Alder Reservoir, but also features a skyline from Bald Hills to saltwater to The Mountain rising hugely whitely above the Nisqually valley.

At Elbe turn south with Highway 7 over the Nisqually River. In 2¼ miles turn west on Pleasant Valley Road, signed "Recreation Area 4 miles," and drive to the DNR Alder Lake Campground, the last part, past a Y just before the camp, on road 147. Continue on 147 some 3 miles, in reservoir views, to where the road cuts through the spur dividing Nisqually and Little Nisqually valleys. Just before the cut, at 1650 feet, a rude logging road climbs left into an enormous clearcut on the end of Stahl Ridge. Park here.

The only confusion is at ⅓ mile, at a Y in a ravine at 1800 feet; go right, up, and thereafter just stay with the forks that lead most promisingly skyward. In ever-growing views the way meanders up a spur ridge, little bothered by sports. At about 1½ miles, where the main road, such as it is, proceeds a short bit to a ridge-crest plateau, then onward to Peak 2922, abandon the ascent, which leads to gentling slopes and less-good views, and turn off left a few steps to Plenty Far Landing, 2670 feet.

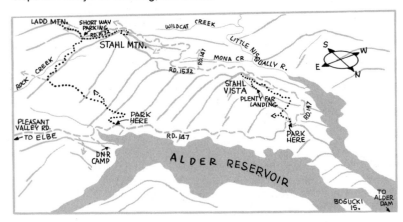

Icicles on Stahl Mountain

Spread the picnic lunch, get out the maps and cameras and binoculars. Rainier is grand but must share top billing here with the reservoir, rock-milky waters a pale, bilious green, shored by dark-green forests and brown clear-cuts. Trace the banks from Alder Dam (below can be seen La Grande Canyon and its reservoir) to Bogucki Island to Reliance Hill. Look westerly over the Little Nisqually to Bald Hill East, Deschutes valley, Porcupine Ridge, Black Hills, lowlands and saltwater. Look northerly to Hugo, Dobbs, Mashel, and Busy Wild. On the October day of the survey the whole world was afire, smoke from burning slash blue-hazing fall-colored slopes to the texture of a dream.

Round trip 3 miles, allow 2 hours
High point 2670 feet, elevation gain 1000 feet
February-December

Stahl Mountain (Map — page 102)

An old fire lookout gives an unusual, unfamiliar view of nearby Rainier over the Nisqually valley, plus two other volcanoes and a bushel of other peaks and valleys of the South Cascades. Two routes lead to the top; a long, steep climb

103

Mt. Adams from Stahl Mountain trail

in splendid virgin forest of a lovely wildwood valley — that won't last, of course; but there will still be the short ascent to the scenery.

The Good Old Long Way

Drive road 147 (see Stahl Vista) a scant ½ mile past Alder Lake Camp to the takeoff left of a newly-rebuilt (1978) road. Park here, elevation 1250 feet.

Walk (or, if open to wheels, drive) this new road as it climbs about ⅓ mile to a Y just past a creek at 1450 feet. The new road climbs right; contour left on a little old woods road (1978). The logging-railroad grade of some 40-odd years ago goes through fine second-growth, floored with wood sorrel; it'll be soon logged. Pass two stock gates of a Pleasant Valley rancher. At about ¼ mile from the second gate, or about 1 mile from the Y, look sharp. Here, at 1575 feet, on the left is a large green-lawn turnout; on the right is a sideroad, marked by a 2-foot-long blaze on an alder. This is the route. If you reach Rock Creek you've gone too far; back up.

Used recently for alder-logging, the sideroad shortly ends and for 30 feet is littered with logs, seeming definitely end-of-the-line. However, forge on and quickly find old but unmistakable tread. The first stretch is barely discernible but just proceed up the crest of a low ridge above Rock Creek, left. For years the only maintenance has been by a local brushpicker, who has built a sort of bridge over a gully, sawn a path through a blowout jackstraw. (Only by a chance meeting with picker did the surveyor find the route.) But he has given up cutting salal and huckleberry on high, confining himself to swordfern, so the lower trail is vanishing. And soon will be obliterated — everywhere are ribbons that mean the loggers are coming, the loggers are coming.

The fine old anachronism of a trail becomes obvious and good as it ascends the valley of Rock Creek in spectral-white alders, then big second-growth conifers, and from 2300 feet — my gosh! — virgin forest! Lichen-draped hemlocks and cedars, firs up to 5 feet in diameter, maidenhair fern draped over springs, pipsissewa and pyrola, pinedrops and coralroot and twinflower, ginger and vanilla and violet, solomon seal and twisted stalk. Or, on a fine October day, masses of coral mushrooms and chanterelles. At 2970 feet, perhaps 1½ miles from the trail start, is the saddle between Ladd and Stahl. And — sob — a great spanking-new logging road.

The trail goes left and right. Left, as the surveyor stupidly found by failing to orient himself, is 3920-foot Ladd, and a wonderful 2 miles of old-tree walking before the path starts downhill. Right is Stahl. Telephone wire still hanging from insulators, the lookout trail climbs a final steep 1 mile. One has about concluded glorious trees will be the only reward when — jeepers creepers! — the way breaks out on the flower-garden crest of a lava cleaver thrusting in open air at 3375 feet. Not far beyond is another pillar-and-buttress formation of knobby, moss-carpet andesite, the 3719-foot summit, anchor rods of the vanished cabin sticking from the lava.

In proper season the show of forest flowers here yields to the rock-garden alpine, with phlox and paintbrush and penstemon and alumroot, kinnikinick and manzanita.

Ah, but the views. Beyond headwaters of the Little Nisqually, over ridge upon green ridge of anonymous South Cascades patched by brown clearcuts, are Goat Rocks and Adams and St. Helens. Far below are pastures of Pleasant Valley. East is "Highway 7 Valley," now used by Roundtop Creek and Tilton River, but presumably once the course of the ice-dammed Nisqually River south to the Cowlitz. Rainier, of course, steals the show, the view here one few people know, from Ptarmigan Ridge to the Tatoosh Range to High Rock, the Nisqually valley as foreground, from Alder Reservoir to Elbe to the national park. West of Rainier are Puyallup Ridge, Busy Wild, Thing, The Divide. On a clear day see Spar Pole Hill, Issaquah Alps — and Baker.

Round trip 8 miles, allow 6 hours
High point 3719 feet, elevation gain 2500 feet
May-November

The New Short Way
Probably by the early 1980s this will be the only way.

Drive road 147 (Little Nisqually Road) about 7 miles from Alder Camp, climbing to virgin forest of astounding big trees (1978) of Mona Creek. Just before a crossing of the creek, turn left on road 1532 and stay with it 4½ miles to the saddle at 2970 feet — recognizable as the only saddle touched by the road. Obscured by slash the first few yards, the trail soon becomes evident.

Round trip 2 miles, allow 2 hours
High point 3719 feet, elevation gain 750 feet

Capitol Forest

THE SOUTHERN FRONTIER: BALD HILLS, THE PRAIRIES, BLACK HILLS

At the south end the **Footsore** world rises to heights that may seem home hills only to the Olympia neighborhood. However, though halfway from Seattle to Oregon, they are still familiarly "Puget Sound." Yet with differences, a touch of the foreign. Ah, viva the differences — even folks for whom the frontier is well beyond the Two-Hour Circle, who fear falling off the edge of the world, must come for excitements not to be found otherwise. There's more to walking than exercise.

Ends. The inland sea ends, and its feeder streams; here is a momentous hydrographic divide. From the Bald Hills flows the Deschutes, southernmost river of the Cascades to enter Puget Sound. Also from the Bald Hills flows the Skookumchuck, which turns south to the Rainier-born Cowlitz and thus the Columbia. But also from the Bald Hills flows the Chehalis, joined from the prairies by the Black, the two together nearly enwrapping the Black Hills and then proceeding west to Grays Harbor, augmented on the way by streams from the curious system of little parallel valleys in the gap between Black Hills and Olympics.

Ends. Here ended the Puget Lobe of the continental glacier. A hiker from the north senses a peculiarity in the hills — they remind of the Western Cascades of Oregon, the Ozarks of the southern Appalachians. The reason is that the ice rode up the north flanks (on the east side of the Black Hills, to about 1460 feet) but not over the highest tops; the terrain is not ice-shaped and youthful — as, say, the Issaquah Alps — but mainly stream-sculptured, maturely-dissected.

The Puget-Willamette Trough extends south, but here where it narrows between Bald Hills-Black Hills "portals" are the enigmatic prairies. What is Eastern Washington doing west of the crest? What are Oregon-like oak groves and western gray squirrels doing so far north? Tolmie in the 1840s remarked on the contrast with lush forests of uplands all around; declaring the prairies unsurpassed in elegance, he compared them to the open parks amid forests on artfully-landscaped estates of English nobility. The art, of course, is Nature's (though prior to 1850 aided by regular burning done by Indians to encourage the camas and the deer). The flats are the outwash plains of rivers from the front of the ice in its farthest advance toward Oregon. The soil is composed of river gravels with poor water-retention; no matter that the skies are Puget Sound-drippy — so far as plants are concerned the sites are semi-arid.

Ends. Here the Really Big River carried ice-dammed waters of the Cascades through today's Chehalis valley to the ocean, joined west of the Black Hills by the Really Big River from the Olympics.

Ends. On prairies and their upland counterparts, the "balds," and in adjoining woodlands, are the northern limits of some plant species. And the southern limits of others.

Merely high-graded here, due to the driving time from northern population centers, the Bald Hills are a westward thrust of the Cascades seeming as unrelated to that range as do their northern counterpart, the Issaquah Alps. Logging is just reaching the center of the subrange, the headwaters of Deschutes and Skookumchuck Rivers, but the outer north ridges sampled here, mostly in Weyerhaeuser's Vail Tree Farm, were railroad-logged decades ago; only the now-arriving Second Wave clearcuts are opening views. And what views they are! The outrigger position gives unique grandstand perspectives over the South Puget Plain to Tacoma and Seattle. Elevations are high enough for long vistas, low enough for all-year walking.

Called "Klahle" ("black") by the Indians, the Black Hills are an isolated uplift some 15 by 12 miles in size seeming to belong to neither nearby mountain range. Like the Olympics, though, they are largely pillow lavas and breccias from submarine eruptions of basalts, deeply weathered to a reddish-brown clay soil that when wet and horse-churned and wheel-rutted becomes a boot-sucking red goo. Elevations from 120 to 2668 feet offer walking the year around, though the heights can be deeply white for spells in winter.

Another name for Black Hills is Capitol State Forest. From 1901 to 1941 several cut-and-get-out companies operated here — the Bordeaux brothers' Mason County Logging, Vance Lumbering, and Mud Bay Logging. They progressed from bullteam to "lokie" logging and built more than 100 miles of railroads, the basis of today's road and trail systems. In the mid-1930s a far-sighted State Forester purchased 33,000 acres of logged, burned lands for 50¢ an acre, supplemented these with gifts, and assembled them with trust lands managed by the state for the common schools and counties. Some of the earliest tree-farming was here, seedlings set out by the CCC, then Cedar Creek Youth Camp.

Since the 1960s the successor of the State Forestry Board, the Department of Natural Resources (DNR), has been authorized by RCW Chapter 79.68 to practice multiple-use sustained-yield forestry on the national forest pattern. Formerly a limiting factor was the statutory requirement to consider as paramount the "best interests of the beneficiaries of granted trust lands," which meant short shrift to no-income-producing recreation (and preservation). Nowadays, with state and federal funds distributed by the state Inter-Agency Committee (IAC), DNR has been able to exploit the recreation resource more adequately. It has done so in a distinctive manner, concentrating on satisfying basic needs but not getting fancy. Thus dollars are stretched and the primitive character of the land minimally altered; DNR camps and trails often remind of the good old days (1930s, of course).

The DNR has seven large multiple-use areas: Capitol Forest, 80,000 acres; Tahuya (see Kitsap Peninsula), 33,000; Sultan-Pilchuck (see **Footsore 2** and **3**), 81,600; Yacolt, 73,000; Hoh-Clearwater, 105,000; Ahtanum, 63,000; and Okanogan, 176,700.

Capitol Forest presently is the most developed for recreation. Some 75 miles of management roads, mostly gravel, are suitable for ordinary automobiles, and there are excellent campgrounds, picnic areas, and vista points, all reached by several approaches. The free DNR map (see below) is indispensable.

Since the 1960s conquest of the world by razzers, the Forest has gained an evil reputation among hikers, many of whom have given it up for lost, muttering dark oaths about the perfidy of DNR. Not to here renounce rights of criticism, and certainly to stress that ATV people flock to DNR areas as their native lands, it must be pointed out that state law compels DNR to serve the ATV; opinions should be expressed to the DNR, but the ultimate hope of outraged walkers-horsemen must be the Legislature.

Some 65 miles of ATV routes have been developed by DNR and user

Spider's web

groups, attracting a veritable ATV industry to the Black Hills, including sales and service outlets, rental agencies, and "staging areas" of private clubs. Hollywood Camp is the main wheel hub, and the North Rim Trail from there to Porter Camp the most popular speedway. Bad scene. NOS. However, distance from population centers has minimized the atrocity — there simply are few nearby residents to be harassed. And the DNR has striven to eliminate conflict among recreationists by splitting the Forest into an ATV Zone and a Hiker-Horse Zone, the deadline being the Black Hills Crest. The system isn't perfect because ATVs inevitably are permitted on all roads and from them readily trespass on trails officially banned to wheels. More enforcement is needed to correct the abuse. But the presence of more pedestrians also will help.

Aside from this flaw, Capitol Forest may well be judged a model of how tree-farming, automobile recreation, and backcountry trail hiking can coexist amiably. For obvious reasons the ATV Zone has been meagerly surveyed. But the wheelfree trail system is magnificent and greater by the year. Walks in deep valleys by small streams in second-growth wildwoods. Walks on moor-like broad-view heights with breathtaking vistas from Olympus to St. Helens to Rainier to Baker, from Puget Sound and Hood Canal to the Pacific Ocean. The more walkers who come, the more votes cast by boots, the more attention will be given by DNR, which at present correctly says in a brochure, "Trailbiking is the single most prevalent use of Capitol Forest."

USGS maps: Bald Hill, Lake Lawrence, Vail, McKenna, Yelm, Maytown, Tumwater, Tenino, Rochester, Shelton, Malone

For a free map of the road system on Vail Tree Farm, write Weyerhaeuser Company, P.O. Box 540, Chehalis, WA 98532

For a free map of Capitol Forest, write Department of Natural Resources, Olympia, WA 98504

Bald Hill East (Map — page 110)

On the absolute mountain front, on the tip of the ridge jutting into the angle between Nisqually and Deschutes Rivers, Second Wave baldness of this bump is not yet total, but enough of the scalp is shaved for long views north to Issaquah Alps, south into Bald Hills, west to Yelm and saltwater and Black Hills, and — oh yes — east to Rainier. At least as exciting in the bloom of mid-May are the little balds where grow Oregon white oak and camas.

From Four Corners, east of Yelm and south of McKenna, drive Bald Hills Road about 10 miles to Single Tree Estates at Clear Lake and 1 mile beyond to an intersection with an unsigned gravel mainline (Weyerhaeuser's road 1000). Turn left on it ¼ mile to an unsigned, double-entry road diverging right. Take this ¼ mile to a Y. The left leads ½ mile to Bald Hill Lake, formerly offering an appealing shore stroll, but the formerly famous big trees liquidated

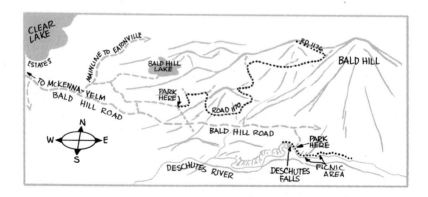

Thistle on Bald Hill East

in 1978; except for pond lilies, herons, and redwing blackbirds, forget it. Take the right a scant 1 mile to a Y. Park here, elevation 830 feet.

Walk (or drive partway if sports are roaring) the left fork, road 1170, dodging lesser spurs and climbing steadily, then dipping into a creek valley. At several spots, apparently due to the dry sites resulting from near-surface, glacier-smoothed, conglomerate bedrock, are prairie-like balds. Groves of Oregon white oak grow amid fields of common camas, poison camas, sea blush, monkeyflower, buttercup, paintbrush, shooting star, strawberry, large bitter-cress, serviceberry.

At 1¾ miles the main road rounds a ridge tip at 1420 feet and the views begin and continue without a break in clearcuts of the middle and late 1970s. Below is the odd cliff of Fossil Rock. In 1 mile more is a saddle at 1700 feet. To the right is the 2026-foot summit of Bald Hill — the goal when it's scalped. Until

111

then turn left on road 1176 a final scant ½ mile, over the tops of two 1740-foot bumps, from pieces here and there assembling a 360-degree panorama.

East beyond the Nisqually River are Ohop Lookout, Hugo, Dobbs, Wow, and Rainier. To the north spot nearby lakes — Kreger, Silver, Cranberry, and Rapjohn — and Ohop Valley, Kapowsin Scarp, Spar Pole Hill, Carbon Ridge. South over headwaters of Deschutes River are Bald Hills — and more of them west, Clear and Elbow Lakes at their foot. Farms and villages and woods dot the enormous sprawl of the South Puget Plain; out there boom Fort Lewis cannon. On a clear day see Olympia, saltwater, Olympics.

Round trip 6½ miles, allow 5 hours
High point 1740 feet, elevation gain 1100 feet
All year

Deschutes Falls (Map — page 110)

Everybody knows the Deschutes River ends in a lovely splashing tumble to saltwater. Few but locals know that near its headwaters is another falls and the supreme beauty spot of the Bald Hills — a big-fir virgin forest where the little river plunges into spooky, spray-billowing depths of a dark deep narrow gorge.

But be warned. The owners, descended from pioneers of the area (none other than the Longmires) and just two removes from the original homesteaders, admit the public to the 290-acre private park only in order not to hog a notable wonder of nature. They do not want crowds, they shun advertising like the plague, even simple signs. Because the park is used to capacity in summer by locals, who come to swim in the river pools, foreigners should confine visits to the off-season. Don't bring your Sunday School class or Scout troop or club outing group. If mobs begin to congregate, the owners, now hospitable and friendly to the occasional quiet, nature-respectful, small parties of walkers, will begin putting up the "Closed" sign more often.

Drive the Bald Hills Road (see Bald Hill East) to the intersection with the Weyerhaeuser mainline. Continue on, pavement ending, a scant 2½ miles to the road-end. If the park is open, as it usually is when the owners are home, pay the modest entry fee, pass the gates, and drive ¼ mile down through sheep pastures to the riverside picnic grounds, elevation 800 feet.

The falls are at hand but for full drama should be approached from upstream. Therefore walk the forest road through the picnic ground to the end in ¼ mile. Continue on trail ½ mile to a general petering-out. Admire the old-growth Douglas firs and understory tangle of this isle of virgin wildness, yearly more precious. Sidepaths lead to the river, rock slabs to sit on and wade from under arching maples.

Returned to the picnic ground, continue downstream on green-mossy buttresses of andesite conglomerate stream-carved in slots and bowls and potholes — and little lazy-green swimming pools safe for little kids, to the alarm of the dippers.

And then — sacre bleu! — the falls! A cable restrains the foolish from too-close looks; even so, folks prone to giddiness often will retreat to get a grip on a tree. The plunge basin is a Darkness far below, a clammy green chasm.

Deschutes Falls

From it extends downstream a slot with 100-foot vertical walls — which at one point virtually touch. The brink path proceeds from one gasp to another, then slip-skids to the gorge bottom. Himmel. A fearful spot. The sky is a thin strip of brightness half-screened by leaning firs and maples. Drips from overhangs flash in the sun. The dank precipices are a saxifrage garden, hung with flowers in crannied walls, draped with ferns, shrubs festooned with old man's beard dancing in the breezes. Slow-flowing river, floating leaves and flecks of foam, issues from the gorge, surges by enormous green boulders, around a sharp corner, out of sight.

Round trip 2 miles, allow 2 hours
High point 850 feet, elevation gain 150 feet
All year

Porcupine Ridge (Map — page 114)

Here is the 50-yard line of the Bald Hills game, the royal box of the scenery opera. From a 1970s clearcut the scarp plummets, nothing to block unique views over the amazing vast expanse of the South Puget Plain, from here appearing table-flat, a sprawling dark green of forests patched with light green of prairie farms. Off right is the monster white bulk of Rainier, off left the dark rise of the Black Hills. Beyond are saltwaterways, Olympia, Tacoma, and Seattle. Fantastic.

From Highway 7 south of Tacoma drive Highway 507 to McKenna. Just out of town, across the Nisqually River, turn left on Vail Loop Road, here signed "Lake Lawrence." In a scant 1 mile cross Bald Hills Road at Four Corners. (If driving from Olympia, reach here on Bald Hills Road from Yelm.) Continue 9½ miles to the outskirts of Vail and just before crossing the Weyerhaeuser log-haul railroad turn left on the unsigned mainline (road 1000) paralleling the tracks. In 1¾ miles, where1000 goes straight and 2000 goes right, park, elevation 450 feet.

Now, a true confession and a sad story. The surveyor, knowledgeable about gates on other Weyerhaeuser tree farms, took a different route to the summit than the one here described. And descended in dusk to find himself locked in. Oh, cruel! Thanks to a sympathetic swing-shift crew at the reload, and a courteous fellow who drove out from Vail to unlock, disaster was averted. But the lesson learned was that due to equipment thefts and vandalism (and few recreationists outside hunting season) gate policy on theVail Tree Farm is undependable. So, even if gates are open, consider them closed. Except in hunting season, and then you are better off someplace else. The upshot is that the following route was eyeballed from both ends and is known from maps to be simple and easy, but was not walked. And thus will not be given a blow-by-blow narration. Until the next edition.

In the angle between big roads 1000 and 2000 is little old gated woods road 1020, the start of the route, which will, however, finish on road 1040. Begin with 1½ steep miles switchbacking up a spur, then a valley, in big second-growth, passing a road right, attaining the Porcupine crest at 1221 feet. At the Y here go left a long ½ mile on the crest to a Y. Go left, upward on the crest, 1

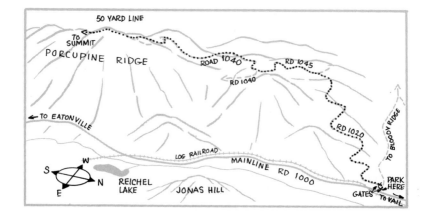

Mt. Rainier from Porcupine Ridge

mile, passing a road left, to 1500 feet. Drop ⅓ mile on the north side of Point 1610 to a Y at 1340 feet. Go right, up, passing a road left, a final ¾ mile to the wide plateau newly shaved clean. Any handy stump on the lip of the north scarp provides the box seat and picnic table, at 1860 feet, about 4¼ miles. You can't miss it.

(Sentimentalists may wish to continue upsy-downsy on the crest 2 miles to the summit of Porcupine Ridge and the site of the old lookout, 2252 feet; the grassy field ringed by 50-foot firs is moody but viewless.)

Just below is the log dump of the railroad-end reload by Reichel Lake. The oddities of Shell Rock Ridge and Jonas Hill interest, and waters of Lake Lawrence, and cows on green prairies. The Deschutes River can be traced over the South Puget Plain to Olympia on Budd Inlet, as can the Nisqually from Rainier to Nisqually Reach. Tacoma is in view and also, pointed to by the long westward thrust of the Issaquah Alps, Seattle. Green and Gold Mountains mark the location of Bremerton. And the horizons include Black Hills, Olympics, Cascades.

Round trip 8½ miles, allow 6 hours
High point 1860 feet, elevation gain 1800 feet
All year

Fenced-in experimental plot on Bloody Ridge

Bloody Ridge (Map — page 117)

From plantations on the westernmost heights of the Bald Hills, the southernmost vista of the **Footsore** world, look down to where the Puget Glacier halted in its Oregonward rush and died. See the hydrographic divide: the extension of the Puget Trough in which the Cowlitz flows south to the Columbia, and the Chehalis also flows south before turning west to Grays Harbor; and the Deschutes and Nisqually flowing over the South Puget Plain to Puget Sound.

Drive to the 1000-2000 junction (see Porcupine Ridge) and park, elevation 450 feet. Gates are often open but always treacherous — don't trust them.

Walk right on big broad road 2000 for 1 mile and reverse-turn right, uphill, on lesser but good road 2020 (unsigned). At a junction in ¼ mile, follow the good road in its switchback left. Continue 2 miles, climbing, swinging around a ridge to the Skookumchuck valley, turning up Baumgard Creek to a Y, 1120 feet. For the full tour, do a loop; for a shorter walk (round trip 10½ miles from the car) take the concluding leg.

Go left for the loop, in and out of beaver-marshy, clearcut Baumgard valley. The old logging-railroad grade enters cool lush second-growth, rounds Miller Hill, and emerges in the recently-skinned valley of "Short Run." Moor-like fields open broad looks over the Skookumchuck valley (and reservoir) to Blue

Ridge. At 3 miles from the 1120-foot Y are the 1400-foot crest of a spur ridge and an experimental plot fenced to keep out deer and elk. In ¾ mile pass a sideroad to Miller Hill, former lookout site now forested but to be a good destination when re-skinned. In 1 more mile, at all junctions going upward, the way attains the plateau crest of Bloody Ridge at 1573 feet.

The road of the route thus far proceeds ahead to Baumgard Hill, probably the best destination in a few years, when once more logged. For now (1979) turn right on a good sideroad which quickly leads to a T, 5 miles from the 1120 Y. The loop return is left, but the immediate job is a sidetrip right, along the crest, in climax views north and west and south. Views don't get better than this but for neatness continue a final 1 mile to a quarry in rotten volcanic rock and through a field to the summit of Bald Hill West, 1750 feet.

There's Rainier, big, white, close, beyond Porcupine, Bald Hill East, Mashel, and Wow. Close below north are Weyerhaeuser headquarters at Vail, the old-timey-whistling-locomotive log-haul railroad, and the Deschutes River flowing to Olympia. And through towns and farms of the plain flows the Nisqually River. See cities, and Issaquah Alps. However, this is distinctively the place to view Bald Hills south, Black Hills west, and Doty and Willapa Hills southwest. And almost Oregon. Just below west, above Tenino, is the bitter end of the Bald Hills and the edge of the prairie province.

For the short concluding leg of the loop, from the ridge-crest T go downhill north, swinging around the head of Baumgard Creek, regaining the Y in 2¼ miles.

Complete trip 15 miles, allow 10 hours
High point 1750 feet, elevation gain 1300 feet
All year

Millersylvania State Park (Map — page 118)

Out in the prairies, on minor uplands rising from flatness, is a miracle wildland of big-tree forest and marshland creeks and pastures and orchards of

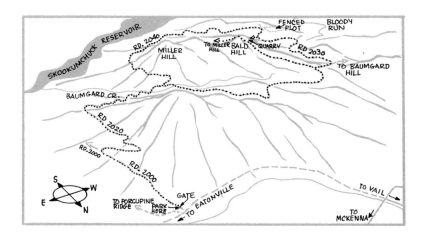

Spruce Creek, Millersylvania State Park

the old homestead going gracefully back to nature. The Miller in question, bodyguard and general of Franz Josef I of Austria, eloped with Princess Anna Barbara and emigrated in 1881 to Washington Territory. Over the years he and his heirs high-graded the forest, but so carefully it retains a virgin appearance; his sylvania was willed to the state in 1924 by his son, on condition it be

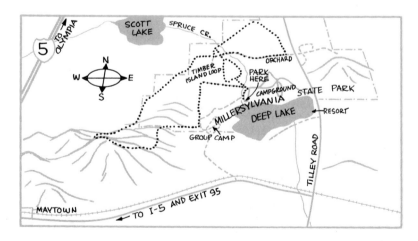

preserved. Now with another half-century of growth, the monster Douglas firs of the 835-acre park are enough to wring a "Himmel!" out of a walker.

Go off I-5 on Exit 95 and follow "state park" signs east 2½ miles on Maytown Road, then ¾ mile north on Tilly Road to Deep Lake and the park entrance. Drive ½ mile by the headquarters and lakeshore camp areas (164 camps, 52 trailer hookups) to the boat-launch. Park by the shore, elevation 195 feet.

Despite miles and miles of trails (officially 5.23, but likely quintuple that) as of 1978 there isn't an organized system and signs are few. Who cares? Precise navigation would demand close attention to map and compass but getting dangerously lost would require dedication — farms and roads surround the wildland. There isn't any "best hike." The question is, how many hours of joy do you want? The surveyor spent half a day tooling around at high speed, not often knowing exactly where he was, but liking wherever he was just fine.

Walk back from the lakeshore to the sign, "Timber Island Ecology Trail," and do that nice little loop along Spruce Creek, the forest-tea outlet of Deep Lake flowing to outside-the-park Scott Lake, and through big trees. The surveyor then took trails at random, looping around, not consulting the map in order to preserve the adventurous confusion. Taking forks that trended generally east, his way came out in scotchbroom fields, rows of gnarled, lichen-covered fruit trees. Beside the campground he swung northward in woods to the rail fence of the park boundary and turned westerly, up a hill to the 373-foot summit of a plateau. His way looped around the hill, down to the broad green plain of the park's Group Camp. A trail at the foot of the hill led back over a wide marsh, then Spruce Creek, to the car. For the life of him the surveyor couldn't follow the exact route again. So what? Getting half-lost is half the fun.

Sample magical mystery tour 6 miles, allow 4 hours
High point 373 feet, elevation gain 200 feet
All year

Grand Mound Prairie (Map — page 119)

A spacious wildlife recreation area, open to public feet, in the heart of the prairie province, is the best place to sample this semi-desert oddity of an ecosystem. Stay away in bird-hunting season. Come any other time of year, especially in the spring flowers climaxing in April and May. If lucky you'll arrive in that brief spell when all the prairies are blue with camas.

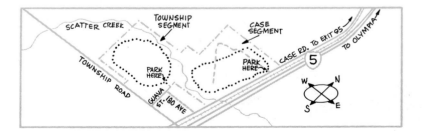

Aerial view of Mima Mounds

From Exit 95 on I-5 drive Case Road south 4 miles to a sign on the right, "Scatter Creek Wildlife Recreation Area." Park here to explore the Case Segment that constitutes about half the 1161-acre area, largely prairie but also woodlands along Scatter Creek and on slopes of the Black Hills. For possibly the best introduction, continue on Case Road another 1 mile, turn right on 180 Avenue, and in ½ mile turn right on Guava Street a short bit to headquarters of the Township Segment and the parking area, elevation 190 feet.

There is no trail system and none needed. One loop samples both the creek and the prairie. Walk west past the headquarters building, the gracious old farmhouse of the Brewer Homestead dating from about 1858. Past the barn trend right, down to Scatter Creek, wide and slow and deep, much of the course through a great dismal swamp. Wonderful. Push through snowberry thickets in fir forests to secret spots where lichen-somber maples and oak lean over the creek. Wild things live here. Birds. Beaver. Golly knows.

Emerge into big sky of Scotch Broom Prairie, views of Rainier and Black Hills and Bald Hills. Stroll through brown straw (winter) or yellow-blue-white-red flowers (spring and summer). At the west boundary fence loop back east. Where burrowing critters (pocket gophers?) have dug it up, note the gravelly soil that makes the prairies. Note a few subdued Mima mounds, the rest obliterated by a century of ploughs. Note the large grove of oak trees whose acorns support the big squirrels — western grays at just about the northern limit of their range. Watch out for acorn-loving bears. A bit off right is the site of Fort Henness, where during the alarms of 1855-56 the 224 pioneers of the Five Prairies holed up for 16 months — and never saw an Indian.

And so back to the parking lot. If more prairie roaming is wanted, visit Case Segment. And/or Mima Mounds Natural Area.

Sample loop trip 3 miles, allow 2 hours
High point 190 feet, no elevation gain
All year

Mima Mounds Natural Area (Map — page 122)

To quote from an old Nature Conservancy postcard, "Mima Prairie is the type locality of the mysterious Mima-microrelief or pimpled plains of western North America. Scientists agree that the spacing of the mounds is a 'squeeze pattern.' Biologists claim that the mounds were built by gophers and (along with beaver dams) are the largest structures created by any mammal. Geologists claim that the mounds are the result of freezing and thawing. In 1966, The Nature Conservancy leased part of the prairie as an emergency measure to save it from damage by grazing, mining, and other commercial uses."

To update the story, geologists have found the same mounds in process of formation, by a complicated process of ice melting and dumping of morainal material, at the toes of stagnant glaciers, and since this is precisely the farthest advance of the Puget Lobe, that perhaps has ended the debate. (And also stilled those giggles about landing pads of Ancient Astronauts.) As for protection, that grew steadily more urgent with burgeoning motorcycle hood-

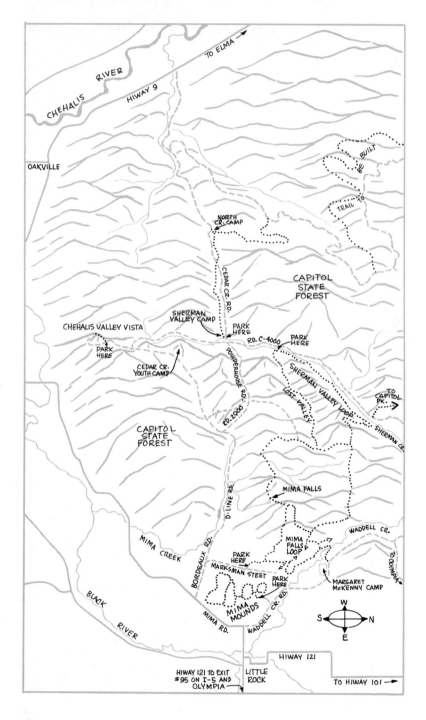

Mima Mounds Natural Area

lumism; of the nearly 1,000,000 mounds originally scattered over some 30,000 acres of prairies, most not already leveled by plows and cows and bulldozers were being ravaged by razzers. In 1967 the site on Mima Prairie was declared by the National Park Service as a Registered National Landmark. Evergreen State College took over the lease for study and protection purposes. Now the land manager, the state DNR, has built a trail system (completion, late 1979) that will preserve the site while permitting public enjoyment of the phenomenon.

Drive I-5 south to Exit 95 and go off on Highway 121 to Little Rock. Go straight through that hamlet on the road signed "Capitol Forest." In ¾ mile is a T; go right on Waddell Creek Road about ¾ mile and at the DNR sign turn left on the entry road a scant ¼ mile to the parking area and trailhead, elevation 240 feet.

Wander the trails any old way, any old how. The natural area, nearly a square mile, is thoroughly sampled, fields, forest, and clumps of shrub-like firs pioneering the fields — has the climate changed in past centuries, growing wetter and better for trees, or is the cessation of regular burning by the Indians responsible for forest expansion? The spring flower show is famous but even on the survey day in late October there was a profusion of bluebells-of-Scotland amid the yellow grass and the airy balls of yellow-green lichen. Birds: little flitterers in the grass looking for seeds and bugs, raptors patrolling above looking for little critters in the grass.

And mounds. Some in the woods, covered with moss and ferns. Some in the prairies, covered with grass and herbs. Contrast those seen from highways, low bumps nearly or completely flattened, to those here, notably pristine, with full original relief.

Don't rush. Take your time. Feel the vibrations. Watch out for Ancient Astronauts.

Round trip about 5 miles, allow 5 hours
High point 240 feet, minor elevation gain
All year

Mima Falls Loop (Map — page 122)

At the edge of Capitol Forest, where the Black Hills rise abruptly from Mima Prairie, are miles of interconnecting trails through a maze of mysterious wildwood valleys. Ease of access gives particular attraction in winter, when higher roads are treacherously mucky or snowy. But on the survey day in early

Bridge above Mima Falls

June the display of woodland herbs and shrubs in bloom totalled 50 species, featuring the inside-out flower unknown north of here.

Drive I-5 south to Exit 95 and go off on Highway 121 to Little Rock. Go straight through that hamlet on the road signed "Capitol Forest." In ¾ mile is a T from which Waddell Creek Road, right, also leads into the Forest; go left on Mima Road 1¼ miles to Bordeaux Road and turn right. In ¾ mile turn right on Marksman Street. In 1 mile turn left to Mima Falls trailhead, elevation 260 feet.

The path ascends moderately in forest ½ mile to a Y. The left, signed "Mima Falls 2," is the loop return; go right, signed "Camp McKenny 1.9," over alder bottom ½ mile to a T. The right is from a private gun club on Mima Prairie, just a spit distant; go left on the "ATV Winter Route," machines banned April 15-October 15, and that's a laugh. In a few steps is a Y. The left is a shortcut but for the full loop go right, signed "McKenney 1." The way swings around a corner and sidehills Waddell Creek valley 1 long mile to a Y about 2¼ miles from the hike start. The loop is left, signed only "ATV Traffic." For a sidetrip go right, dropping ⅓ mile to the bridge over lovely Waddell Creek; just ⅓ mile up the hill are Margaret McKenny Camp, 280 feet, and the Waddell Creek Road, an alternate approach and trailhead.

Returned from the sidetrip, follow the ATV Traffic a short bit to a Y. The right is the motorcycle route, signed "Hollywood ATV Trailhead 8.5, Beware Beware"; go left on "ATV Winter ha-ha Route," signed "Mima Trailhead 3." Cross an alder bottom and climb a scant ½ mile to a T. The left is the shortcut (see above); go right, signed "Capitol Peak." In a long ¼ mile is another T; go left, signed "Mima Falls 1.7" (The right, unsigned, is the starting leg of a longer loop off the loop, unsurveyed, adding maybe 6-8 miles, around through Lost Valley and Mima Creek, past Mima Falls, to rejoin the loop on the present agenda. At the far end is a connection to the Sherman Valley Trail, which see. And from there, connections to the trail up Capitol Peak, which see. But the distances involved make the trip more attractive to horsemen than hikers.)

Did you make sure to go left before those parentheses? If not, you may not get home until tomorrow. Over hill and dale goes the way, reaching the highest point of the trip, some 650 feet, and dropping to a T in 1¼ miles. The left is the way home; first go right, over a marshy creek and around a spur ⅓ mile to Mima Falls, 420 feet. The 30-foot cataract down black-mossy basalt is not terribly exciting.

Returned from the sidetrip, proceed onward through 1½ more miles of fine forest, by some beaver ponds, by sawdust and waste of an ancient sawmill, to the start.

Loop trip with sidetrips 7½ miles, allow 5 hours
High point 650 feet, elevation gain 1000 feet
All year

Chehalis Valley Vista (Map — page 122)

Not much walking — but oh the looking! Do this at day's end after some other Black Hills jaunt.

From Mima Road (see Mima Falls Loop) drive Bordeaux Road ("D Line") 3¼ miles, by the Bordeaux Entrance, to a Y where gravel road D-2900 goes

Chehalis Valley Vista

right to Sherman Valley; stay with the paved road left 2¾ miles and turn left on the road signed "Chehalis Valley Vista." Dodge lesser spurs 1½ miles to the road-end parking area, elevation 1100 feet.

Ascend the path ¼ mile through shrubby trees to a cleared knoll, 1150 feet, on the brink of the plunge to the floodplain 1000 feet below. You are standing on the absolute southern boundary of the **Footsore** world, beyond the limits of ancient ice, looking to Oregon, to the ocean, and a goshamighty more.

See Rainier, Adams, and St. Helens, and the hamlet of Rochester out in Baker Prairie, and Willapa Hills beyond the Doty Hills, and the enormous plume rising from the Chehalis Steam Plant, where stripmined coal is burned to generate electricity.

Directly below, the Black River meanders at the foot of the Black Hills scarp. Across emerald pastures 2½ miles, the Chehalis River meanders at the foot of the opposite scarp. But they didn't dig this valley — that was done eons ago by the Really Big River, several times the size of today's Columbia, the sum of all the rivers of the Cascades dammed from more direct routes to the sea by the wall of Canadian ice.

Round trip ½ mile, allow 2 hours
High point 1150 feet, elevation gain 50 feet
All year

Cedar Creek (Map — page 122)

The biggest stream in the Black Hills, intimately experienced on a foot-only path particularly swell for leading tiny children by the hand, introducing them to splashing-type puddles, throwing-type rocks, and frogs.

From the D-Line (see Chehalis Valley Vista) turn right on D-2900, signed "Sherman Valley Camp 2." Go up to a ridge crest and down the other side to Sherman Valley Y. Go straight ahead on Cedar Creek Road to the west end of Sherman Valley Camp. At the parking area with the sign, "Foot Trails Only," park, elevation 388 feet.

Walk down into the delightful streambank campground to a dandy foot-only bridge over Cedar Creek, which has just received the waters of Sherman Creek. The water seems a dark tea — until one realizes the color is from algae-covered bottom pebbles. Black water for the Black Hills. The path often is precisely beside the water, on a bottom carpeted with thousand mothers, sometimes on an elevated alluvial terrace, sometimes high on the sidehill. Lichen-silvered alders lean over the stream, lacing branches high above the bird avenue. Stare into spooky depths of black pools. Show the kiddies a beaver-gnawed giant cottonwood. Pause to let them play on gravel bars — or, at one point, an outcrop of black basalt where white suds fleck black water.

The trail crosses another bridge the little kids will love and at 2 miles hits Cedar Creek Road; go back the way you came. (Not surveyed, the trail crosses the road and leads ¾ mile to North Creek Camp and thence up North Creek.)

Round trip 4 miles, allow 3 hours
High point 600 feet, elevation gain 400 feet
All year

Sherman Valley Loop (Map — page 122)

The longest and richest valley walk in the Black Hills, following an old rail grade up one stream through skunk cabbage and beaver ponds in splendid mixed forest, then crossing a ridge and switchbacking down firs and ferns and descending another creek in the supreme alder bottom of the area.

From Sherman Valley Y (see Cedar Creek) turn right on Sherman Valley Road (C-4000) 1¼ miles upstream to a trail sign on the right, "Sherman Valley Trail." Park here, elevation 450 feet. (There's a second trailhead 2 miles up the road but in the surveyor's opinion this is the most esthetic start.)

Cross Sherman Creek, wide and black-bottomed and alder-overhung, to a T. The loop, equally esthetic either way, here is described counterclockwise. Turn right, signed "Mima Trailhead," round a corner into tributary Lost Valley, and hit one of the Bordeaux' boys railroads. The little creek is pretty, the huge cedar stumps are crowned by salal gardens, the firs are big, the alders moss-green or lichen-silvery. Rusted ironware and rotten trestlework are passed, and a stump with a cable groove and spikes. Beaver dams. The creek is crossed and recrossed repeatedly. Inside-out flower and foamflower and youth-on-age and trillium and ginger and all.

At 2½ miles, 1000 feet, near the ridge crest at the valley head, is a Y. The right leads 7.1 miles to McKenny Camp via Mima Falls (which see); go left, climb above the creek head in the now-silent valley, ¾ mile to another Y at 1100 feet. The right leads in 4.8 miles to McKenny Camp and 5.8 to Mima Trailhead; go left, signed "Fall Creek Camp 2.1." Now not on rail grade but new trail, sidehill through a saddle, 1150 feet, and leave Lost Valley for another tributary of Sherman Creek. The trail makes long, lazy switchbacks down the steep hill in fine fir and massed ferns, crossing and recrossing trickle creeks. Capitol Peak is glimpsed.

Dry-hillside ecosystem is left for that of lush valley. At 2 miles from the 1100-foot Y is Sherman Creek, 580 feet. A bridge crosses to the road and upper trailhead, which connects to the Capitol Peak Trail (which see), for the long walk from Mima Prairie or McKenny Camp to the summit. Go left, downstream, swinging in and out of tributary valleys, sometimes close by marvelous wide Sherman Creek, sometimes up on the slope with grand overlooks of Sherman Valley and down to the creek in interwoven billows of alders. The way crosses waterfalling creeks and carpets of Oregon shamrock, tunnels thickets of vine maple, with screened views of the Black Hills Crest and Fuzzy Top, just about the only virgin forest remaining in the Black Hills. (How come? It was unhandy for railroading.) At about 2½ miles from the upper trailhead the loop is closed.

Loop trip 8 miles, allow 6 hours
High point 1150 feet, elevation gain 900 feet
All year

Capitol Peak (Map — page 130)

One of the two tippy-tops of the Black Hills, Capitol commands a grand sweep of horizons from Cascades to Olympics, Bald Hills to Willapa Hills, saltwater fingers of Puget Sound to infinity of the Pacific Ocean. The ascent excellently samples the second-growth wildland from green depths of Sherman Valley to wide-sky heights.

Drive to the upper trailhead of Sherman Valley Trail (which see). Across the road is the Capitol trailhead, signed for Camp Wedekind and Porter, elevation 580 feet. The claim is made that Capitol Peak is 3.2 miles. A sign in the woods a few steps away says 4.5 miles. Preposterous. The surveyor's feet added up 5½.

In second-growth fir and Second Wave clearcuts the trail sidehills out of Sherman Valley, passing several alternate entries from Fall Creek Camp. At ½ mile, in cool alder bottom, is the crossing of West Fork Fall Creek. The first of many old logging railroad grades is joined for a lovely passage through alternating alder and fir forest. The grade is left, the trail climbs, hits another grade and contours, leaves and climbs, and so on, the pattern repeated. At 1250 feet, 1½ miles from the creek crossing, C Line Road is crossed. (An alternate start for a shorter ascent — but missing the nicest woods.)

Contouring above the road, the trail passes screened views over Sherman Valley to Fuzzy Top, its dark-green 200-year-old firs prominent in the lighter

The summit of Capitol Peak

green of 50-year-old firs. At 1350 feet, ½ mile from the C Line, is a bridge over West Fork Fall Creek, clear, cool, waterfalling, tasty. In a scant ½ mile, at 1525 feet, is a T with a motorcycle route on a rail grade that goes left to the C Line and right, in maybe 3 miles, to the Capitol Peak Road, suggesting an adventurous (unsurveyed) alternate return. Go right a few feet and then left, leaving the grade for resuming foot trail, signed "Capitol Peak." Then another rail grade, another contour. But at 1650 feet, ½ mile from the motorcycle route, something different.

Switchbacks, by the dozen. And spindly young firs with lots of holes between — views south to the Chehalis valley. For a scant 2 miles the trail alternately climbs and maddeningly contours (for the comfort of horses). A trickle is appreciated on a scorching day. A "meadow" opens up a view over the head of West Fork Fall Creek to — ta! da! — Capitol Peak, which has begun to seem a myth. At 2350 feet the trail attains the saddle between the peak and the long Black Hills Crest (which see) west. And (sob) the Porter Creek Road.

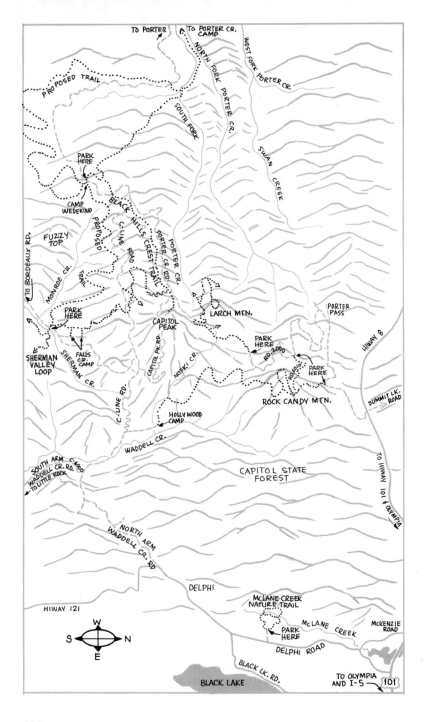

The final long ½ mile is all road. Turn right from the trail a few steps to Capitol Forest Vista and a triple fork. The right is the Capitol Peak Road (see above). The left leads to Big Larch Mountain (which see). Take the middle fork and climb the crest in fir shrubs and flowers to the summit, 2667 feet, 5½ miles. If one comes on a spring Sunday, one realizes the ideal time for this ascent is winter, when at least the family sedans are missing from the vehicle parade, maybe the motorcycles if the snow is deep enough, leaving only four-wheel sports and the regiment of service trucks always here tending the forest of radio towers, testimony to the American revision of Descartes: "I communicate, therefore I exist."

Move from one side to another of the summit plateau, then to the other summit, for the best views in various directions. South: the big valley of Sherman Creek, Prairies (Mima, Baker, Grand Mound, and other), Chehalis valley, Doty and Willapa Hills. Easterly to northerly: the big valley of Waddell Creek, South Puget Plain, Bald Hills, St. Helens, Adams, Rainier, Glacier, Baker. Northerly: the big valley of Porter Creek, Big Larch and Rock Candy, Totten, Eld, Budd, and Henderson Inlets and Nisqually Reach, Black Lake and Olympia, Issaquah Alps, Green and Gold Mountains, Olympics — starring the home of the gods, Olympus. West: what that Spanish chap saw from a peak in Darien.

Round trip 11 miles, allow 8 hours
High point 2667 feet, elevation gain 2300 feet
February-December

Black Hills Crest (Map — page 130)

The five-star scenic supershow of the Black Hills. It ends atop Capitol Peak and has all those views. But in addition are kaleidoscopes from the trail along the crest of the range's longest, highest ridge, between the valleys of Sherman and Porter Creeks. Stroll for miles in bilberry and bracken and alpine-seeming shrubby firs, the sky-surrounded crest eerily moor-like. Enough to make a Scot homesick. Or an Ozark Mountain boy.

For maybe the most expeditious of a half-dozen possible approaches, leave I-5 on Exit 104 in Olympia and drive Highway 101 west 2 miles. Go south on the exit signed "West Olympia, Black Lake" on Black Lake Boulevard 4 miles to a T with Delphi Road. Turn left 2 miles and turn right on Waddell Creek Road. Go from pavement to gravel, pass the Delphi Entrance, and at 3 miles from Delphi Road come to a Y. The left is C-6000, to McKenny Camp; go right, signed "Hollywood 2.2, Capitol Peak 10.9." In 1½ miles is a Y, the right "Hollywood Camp .8"; go left on the C line, the way to go all the rest of the way. The road switchbacks up steeply, then contours slopes of Capitol Peak, 2¼ miles to an intersection with Capitol Peak Road (unsigned) right and Sherman Valley Road left, signed "Sherman Valley Camp 7.2, Fall Creek Camp 3.2" (another good approach — see Cedar Creek). Go straight, signed "Capitol Peak 7.5." Contouring, then climbing, in 5½ miles the C Line tops the ridge (the Black Hills Crest that you'll be walking) at 2150 feet, 19.8 miles from Olympia. Drive left along the ridge 1¾ miles to Camp Wedekind, site of the 1947-65 planting camp from which better than 10,000,000 seedlings were set out amid the stumps. Park at the pleasant little camp, with picnic shelter but no water, in a field in broad-view "Wedekind Pass," elevation 1896 feet.

Walk Porter Creek Road a couple hundred feet and turn right on lesser C-70 toward a quarry. In another hundred feet diverge right on a still-lesser track and ascend to the quarry top and the first trail sign, "Capitol Peak 3.8, Porter Creek Camp 5.1." Ascend gently a long ½ mile to the crest at 2150 feet and a Y. The left, unsurveyed, descends to Iron Creek Road and Porter Creek Camp; go right, signed "Capitol Peak 3.5."

Now, stroll. On wings, almost, liberated from heavy Earth. A little up, a little down, from one "moor" to another. Grass and salal, huckleberry and salmon-berry, old stumps and young firs — including plantations of alpine-appearing nobles. Lumps of weathered basalt columns poke through thin soil. In season the way is colorful with alpine-seeming flowers. Moors fall off right to Sherman Valley and ocean-draining Chehalis Valley, left to Porter Valley and lacework of blue inlets and green peninsulas of South Sound and the Great Bend of Hood Canal. Ahead are the stump ridge of Big Larch and the surreal summit decorations of Capitol — and huge clean Rainier looming whitely beyond.

Twice the road is crossed and twice more can be briefly spotted, but mostly the walker is totally unaware of wheels, so skillfully is the trail placed. The second crossing can confuse. This is at the 2150-foot saddle where the C Line tops the ridge (see above). Take a few steps right from the junction along the C Line and go left on a lesser road obscurely signed "Trail." In a couple hundred feet the trail indeed takes off up left to the crest. After a final grassy, rocky, meadow-like knoll at 2450 feet, the trail drops the short bit to a final 2150-foot saddle, that of Capitol Forest Vista, there meeting the top of the Capitol Peak (which see) trail from Sherman Valley. The final ¾ mile is on the road to Capitol Peak, 2667 feet. But if the razzers are thronging you may not want to go. No matter. You've already had a trip.

Round trip 8 miles, allow 6 hours
High point 2667 feet, elevation gain 1500 feet
February-December

Scheduled to be built in 1979-80 are two other hiker-horse, no-wheel trails that will take instant rank as Black Hills classics, lending themselves to any number of exciting loops; routes are shown on the sketch map. A 12.8-mile trail will start from the existing Porter Creek Trail at Porter Creek, climb to and follow the crest of the 1500-foot ridge that forms the western rampart of the Black Hills, then contour and climb from ridge to valley to ridge to Camp Wedekind. The other new wonder, about 8 miles long, will go from Camp Wedekind along the south slope of the Black Hills Crest, mostly contouring, then drop to Sherman Valley.

McLane Creek Nature Trail (Map — page 130)

Beaver ponds, beaver dams, beaver lodges, and — if you're quiet and lucky — beaver splashing about their business oblivious to the audience. And an encyclopedia of woodland plants and marsh plants and swamp plants, on a mere 41 acres of DNR land that seem ten times that.

McLane Creek Nature Trail

Drive Black Hills Boulevard to Delphi Road (see Black Hills Crest) and turn right 1 scant mile to the DNR sign and access road leading to the trailhead parking area, elevation 150 feet.

A self-guiding pamphlet and interpretive signs aid understanding of sights along the way, the most spectacular of which are three beaver ponds, the centerpiece broad and strewn with lily pads and wiggling with salamanders; view platforms are comfortable spots to lie in wait for the beaver. The path proceeds on plank walks through marshes and swamps, on bridges over McLane Creek. Partway along the 1.1-mile outer loop is a shortcut connector along an old railroad grade, passing close by one of the two beaver lodges. There are skunk cabbage and devils club, alder and fir — including at least one monster "wolf" disdained by the loggers. Ancient cedar stumps nurse young cedars. A two-legged maple arches over a trail "tunnel." Picturesque snags house bird families.

Complete trip 2 miles, allow many hours
High point 175 feet, elevation gain 25 feet
All year

Dogwood

Rock Candy Mountain (Map — page 130)

Northernmost of the three highest peaks of the Black Hills and giving the choicest view straight down to petering-out saltwaterways of Puget Sound, Rock Candy cannot be ignored. Nevertheless, because it lies in the ATV Zone it must be "Never On Sunday" for hikers. Unless it's a winter Sunday with snow deeper than a wheel.

From Exit 104 on I-5 turn west on Highway 101; where it diverges right, stay left on Highway 8. At an intersection about 13 miles from I-5, where Summit Lake Road goes right, go left on Rock Candy Road (B Line), which immediately dwindles to a gravel lane mainly following old logging-railroad grades. Just off the highway it goes left, then bends gradually right, crosses an enormous powerline swath, and starts uphill in woods.

(At about 840 feet, 1½ miles from Highway 8, a bit past Rock Candy Entrance, a woods road, perhaps distinguished by a length of rusty culvert lying on the ground, heads uphill. Not surveyed, this is a motorcycle trail up Rock Candy, useful for hikers when snow not only bars motorcycles but forbids driving much farther.)

At 1150-foot Porter Pass, 2½ miles from the highway, is a Y; go left along the powerline to a second Y on the other side of the pass; again go left, signed "Capitol Peak." Staying with the obvious main road, twist in and out of valleys

3½ miles from the pass to where the main road, B-2000, continues straight and lesser B-2010 goes left. Park here, elevation 1700 feet.

On quiet days 2010 is a lovely footroad tunneling second-growth, gently ascending on a grade to the liking of a locomotive as it completely encircles Rock Candy. The first big views are from a promontory out over Porter Pass to the ridge marking the northwest end of the Black Hills, and out Porter Creek, and to the Olympics. Tunnel resumes. At 1¼ miles is a Y. From the road left, downhill, the winter route (see above) comes in. Go right, uphill. At the Y spot a track straight up the cutbank; this leads to a decent path, a shortcut to or from the summit. Just above the Y on the road is a splendiferous promontory view out north and northeast over Highway 8 and Summit Lake to Olympics, saltwaterways, and Rainier.

Walk on, reflecting that the ghosts of old railroads are much better walking companions than the too too solid metal of motorcycles. At a scant ¼ mile from the Y note an unsigned razzer track coming up out of the woods left.

(Not surveyed except by eyeballing from various points, this motorcycle trail, one of a maze, climbs some 5 or 6 miles from Hollywood Camp, 425 feet. On a quiet winter weekday it would make a fine walk. Drive Waddell Creek Road to where the C Line goes left — see Black Hills Crest. Turn right a scant 1 mile to the trailhead. Hollywood Camp, site from the 1920s until 1947 of Mason County Logging Company's Camp 4, is worth a visit in its own right, though now not even a ghost town remains. The name was given by brush apes honoring the sybaritic magnificence of railroad-car bunkhouses; the same humorists named Rock Candy Mountain, reputed to have, among other hobo's dreams, bulldogs with rubber teeth and cops with wooden legs, cigarette trees and hens that lay softboiled eggs, and a lake of booze where you can paddle around in big canoes.)

Continue. As the grade rounds the mountain, windows open on different vistas, from east to south, then again west and north. A final steep switchback leads to the summit ridge and through salal and little firs to the summit, 2364 feet, about 2½ miles.

A fringe of trees blocks views north but these were well-seen on the way. The dry south slopes of the basalt-rocky summit are open, with horizons from Rainier to Adams, Stahl, Bloody Ridge, Tenino in the prairies between Bald and Black Hills, and St. Helens. Directly below is the Waddell Creek valley, site of Hollywood, above which rise Big Larch and Capitol. Out there in the Puget-Willamette Trough are the plume of the Chehalis Steam Plant, and the Cowlitz draining to the Columbia.

Round trip 5 miles, allow 3 hours
High point 2364 feet, elevation gain 700 feet
February-December

Big Larch Mountain (Map — page 130)

The highest peak in the Black Hills (by 1 foot, according to the USGS), Big Larch is also the best of the lot. Though in the heart of the ATV Zone, it's the only high summit that's wheelfree. And it has neither trees (larches or any other) to block views nor radio towers to clutter — and to spawn parades of

Logging road on side of Big Larch Mountain

service vehicles and razzers. At the end there's no trail, just game traces through a garden of silver stumps and logs, little shrubs and pretty flowers. And the views! Actually, the other peaks have the approximately equal. But the surveyor is prejudiced because he came to Big Larch on a crystalline day of late October and for the first time in all his **Footsore** travels saw, grandly ice-chiseled in the depths of the Olympics, none other than Olympus. And by golly, out west was none other than the really-truly ocean. Boy.

Drive past the turnoff to Rock Candy Mountain (which see) 1¼ miles to the 1650-foot saddle between Rock Candy and Big Larch. At the Y there, go left, signed "Capitol Peak 2.9." Easy enough for nimble little cars, this road is not for the masses, most of whom will have conniption fits if they meet another vehicle — one or the other in the confrontation will have to self-destruct. It is thus recommended that at 1750 feet, about ¼ mile from the saddle, where a promontory parking area is on the right, the car be halted, the walking begun.

Not only does the road become steep and rocky-rough and narrow, it's on the side of a precipice above Waddell Creek, nerveracking to drive. But breathtaking for views, which are continuous, the planted firs decades from pushing up to eye-level. In 1¼ miles a new sideroad climbs steeply right to the 2596-foot east peak of Larch, which the US Government warns you not to trespass against, having in 1978 decorated it with two tall towers. Be a dutiful citizen and continue on by ¼ mile to the 2200-foot pass between Noski Creek (to Waddell Creek) and South Fork Porter Creek. From the Y here the left climbs a scant 1 mile to the west ridge of Capitol Peak; this thus is an alternate driving approach (see Black Hills Crest).

But walk right. And if you've driven to here, park now. The way is a lousy wheelroad, tremendous footroad in steep-slope big-view clearcuts. A little dribble is passed, headwaters of Porter Creek, and a collapsed railroad trestle. At a Y 1 mile from the pass take the lesser, uphill, right. Walk by in-place rotted remnants of railroad ties ¾ mile to the ridge crest at 2475 feet.

Having rounded the U-turn of the road, at the second of two bulldozed turnouts spot, up to the right, obscure tracks made by trucks a few years ago during the setting out of seedlings. Follow these and when they fail pick an easy way through shrubs and salal on a network of interwoven game trails. Stick on or near the hogback and ascend gently ¾ mile to the summit plateau.

Ah, the stump garden, the sculptured silver wood. So sun-scorched and wind-blasted is the crest, so hot and so cold, that even though noble fir has been planted, trees won't grow big here for a long time. As grace notes to stumps and alpine-seeming shrubs are a myriad alpine-seeming flowers (in season, not October). Peace! No wheels! Stumps and chunks of weathered basalt contrast with the mess on Capitol. To enjoy the views, walk to edges of the plateau, 2659 feet, for separate panoramas.

What's the view? See the catalog for Capitol Peak. Big Larch has all that, in a different perspective, and more. Bring a big lunch. Maybe dinner, too, for the evening light show.

Round trip (from parking promontory) 8 miles, allow 6 hours
High point 2659 feet, elevation gain 1000 feet
February-December

Union Station in Tacoma

PUGET SOUND TRAIL: TACOMA TO OLYMPIA TO ALLYN

Walkable the whole year, close to homes of nearly everybody, the Puget Sound Trail is Puget Sound City's single most important walking route; even if their various governments don't, Puget Sounders know it. Folks flock to exchange the gloom and clutter of dank winter forests for the freedom and simplicity of the sands, hobnob with ducks and admire pretty boats, open eyes and souls in panoramas of waves and islands and mountains and sky.

The way begins in Tacoma, where the steam plume is the showiest, the smelter stack the tallest, and Point Defiance the greatest city park in the Northwest, arguably the nation. Two parallel strips of steel lead through The Narrows, skinniest section of the Sound's main channel, under the most esthetic bridge in the region, past some of the most enormous gravel mines. Then commences the longest stretch of the most utter wildness on the entire Trail, the triple sequence of Fort Lewis Military Reservation, the old and empty Dupont explosives-making preserve, and Nisqually National Wildlife Refuge on the delta of the Nisqually River. And here is a twin controversy, one of the ragingest: Weyerhaeuser at the Dupont site and Burlington-Northern at the old and empty Atlas Powder explodery on the other side of the Nisqually plan construction of twin heavy-industry complexes and ports that would bracket the wildlife refuge (some refuge), foreclose the opportunity for the most magnificent public park system on the inland sea, and radically alter the character of the South Sound.

The "South Sound." What's that? How does it differ from the "North Sound"? The boundary is less a line than a zone of transition, but the Nisqually may be said to complete the change that starts at Tacoma.

North is Main Street carrying traffic of the world. South is lonesomer, with few ships, some tugs-barges, mainly pleasure craft. North is where the glaciers came from and stayed the longest. In the South the Vashon Glaciation, the most recent, was relatively brief and its drift is more mixed with the older Salmon Springs deposits, the gravels partly iron-cemented to conglomerate, the sands nearly sandstone, the blue clays often iron-stained and compacted to rubbly shale, forming quite vertical walls — but not so tall as North, usually less than 100 feet and often mere banks that let houses crowd the water.

South is the hotbed of history: the historical museum in Tacoma; the reconstruction of Fort Nisqually at Point Defiance; old homes of Steilacoom; the site of Fort Nisqually, first European settlement on Puget Sound; Treaty Tree where were signed the Medicine Creek Treaties that started the Indian Wars; and Tumwater, first American settlement on the Sound.

North is characterized by broad sweeps of water and wind, long views and violent storm surfs, high bluffs, often of naked drift, and wide beaches beaten from the cliffs; drama.

South is what Vancouver called "the sea in the forest." A complexity of bays and spits, a maze of passages and inlets and reaches and islands. Estuaries lovely to look at, delightful to boat, appalling to boot, the intermingling of muck and brush and water often forming absolute route-stoppers. Birds enjoy the protected waters — everywhere in winter are small flocks, vast fleets — and the population of great blue herons and kingfishers may be the largest in the world. Seals, too, are happy here. So are people who appreciate the intimacy, the coziness, of narrow waterways where waves are feebler and thus beaches narrower. When trees slide down the bluff and topple to the sands they are not, North-like, battered to driftwood in a winter and carried away by longshore currents; they just lay there growing seaweed and barnacles, awful to crawl through. Vegetation grows to the very edge of the beach, swordferns rooted in the sands, and maples and alders lean far over the gravels, enclosing green-lit alcoves of waterfalls and maidenhair fern; if they lean too low they give a walker the brushfits. The shallow bays drain at low tide to become enormities of mudflats, seeming alternate routes and brush escapes, but often sucking in boots, knees, thighs, maybe entire hikers. It's a whole new beach-walking game, brandnew to the explorer from the North. Worth the learning. South is different. But good.

The mile-by-mile description of the Trail ends at Tumwater Falls. Puget Sound, though, goes on and is traced through its fascinating frittering away into long, narrow fingers (let it be noted, with few public put-ins, and little evidence much will be preserved from subdivision) to its westernmost waters at Shelton, its northwesternmost at Allyn. But, you say, the Sound has another shore. Yes. For that see following chapters.

USGS maps: Tacoma South, Tacoma North, Gig Harbor, Steilacoom, McNeil Island, Fort Lewis, Nisqually, Lacey, Longbranch, Squaxin Island, Tumwater, Shelton, Potlatch, Mason Lake, Vaughn, Belfair

Mile 0-7½: Union Station-Old City Hall-Bayside Trail-Historical Museum-Garfield Gulch Park-Puget Park-ASARCO Smelter-Point Defiance Park (Map — page 141)

The fitting commencement is Union Station, superb example of the 19th-century Railroad School of architecture, preserved in all its beautiful ugliness, reminding that Second City began as a rail promotion when Seattle's principle industry was real-estate speculation. The Trail proceeds along Pacific Avenue ½ mile to 11 Street, then a long ⅓ mile through downtown, which quits before it gets tiresome, to Old City Hall at South 7 Street. Here Pacific splits. The right fork is the new Schuster Parkway, with a splendid sidewalk at the foot of the drift bluff that separates up-high downtown Tacoma from its down-low commercial waterfront. Take the left fork, atop-the-bluff Stadium Way, a scant ¼ mile to the start of the Bayside Trail.

Most city trails are purely of local interest; this one, some 2¼ miles long, is worth coming a distance for; with sidetrips, it can richly fill a day. The trail has a half-dozen easy accesses served by buses and several convenient parking areas, the first on Stadium Way at the trail start at South 5 Street, via a stairway down from the sidewalk. The path contours upsy-downsy along the wildwood bluff, sometimes in a fantastic "ivy forest," often in great views to the St. Regis steam plume, waterways and industry of the Puyallup flats, ships in Commencement Bay, Cascades and Olympics. Five rustic picnic shelters are nice spots to get out of the rain and eat your kipper snacks. Soon after the third shelter is a sidepath uphill to the Washington State Historical Society Museum, worth days of browsing; parking at North 4 Street and Stadium Way. Also notable here is the natural amphitheater, the stadium, famed in the pre-electronic era for its acoustics, letting Fourth-of-July oratory reverberate. Another wonder is Stadium High School, housed in a majestic old railway hotel in French Provincial, replete with spires and turrets and garrets. What a crazy place to go to school! Past the fifth shelter, and around a point above old red sheds of Sperry Ocean Dock, the way swings into Garfield Gulch Park. A short path drops to the gulch mouth. A longer path swings up the gulch to Garfield Playground (street parking on Borough Road at North D Street) and a view of rambling Annie Wright Seminary, then descends the gulch to the end of the Bayside Trail on sidewalk of Schuster Parkway. No parking just here.

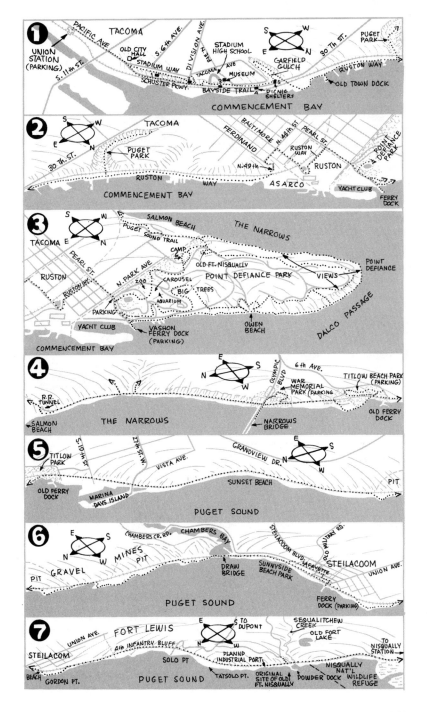

St. Regis pulpmill on Commencement Bay, from Bayside Trail

Cross under the parkway skyway, over the tracks, and walk the seawall to a park strip (with parking) leading to McCarver Street, where Schuster Parkway ends, the arterial becoming Ruston Way. Have a fresh seafood lunch: shop at Ocean Fish Company, go out on the public Old Town Dock, sit on a bench, and peel shrimp while watching the fishermen, human and feathered, and enjoying views down Commencement Bay to Mount Tahoma. First seen by Europeans (Vancouver) in 1792, named in 1841 by the Wilkes Exploring Expedition, which here commenced its work, the bay was first settled in 1852. In the 1860s Job Carr homesteaded at Chebaulip (Old Town, Old Tacoma). On behalf of the railroad, McCarver renamed the projected metropolis for The Mountain and moved the center up the bay.

Parking is plentiful as Ruston Way proceeds by a picturesque old derelict sawmill on a pier, a fish and chips bar (oh the aroma!), site of the Top of the Ocean restaurant (one of innumerable Tacoma houses of refreshment and entertainment burned by arsonists in the 1970s), Harbor Lights, and a boat company. A paved bikeway-footpath comes in from Alder Way and goes along beside the seawall.

For a sidetrip at Alder Way, walk the trail 1 mile up the green ravine of Puget Park, a fine wild scene.

At 49 Street a monster sign, "ASARCO TACOMA," announces entry to the City of Ruston, a chunk of Butte plunked down by the Sound. An interestingly-cruddy industrial beach gives a great view back to Commencement Bay and the Cascades and down the Sound to Vashon and Maury Islands and Glacier Peak. The public highway to Point Defiance tunnels through the smelter — too dangerous to walk. Actually, few folks will wish to walk from here on. This spot, 5½ miles from Union Station, makes a nice day's tour — with the option of riding back on the bus.

But, for the purists, a detour continues the Trail. From Ruston Way climb the bluff on North 49, switchbacking up Waterview to Ferdinand. Turn right on 48th, cross Huson to the hilltop, to Baltimore. Turn right, downhill, passing the very foot of the gigantic masonry heap of the smelter stack, visible from Cascades to Olympics. Stand a while, struck dumb. But not too long a while because standing here has been adjudged by the EPA as harmful to your health. At the bottom of the hill, in the mill area, turn left on Ruston Way and continue along streets and sidewalks to the entrance to Point Defiance Park.

Bus: 13, Oakland, to Historical Museum; 11, Point Defiance, to the park

Point Defiance Park (Map — page 141)

The greatest city park in the nation? On the nomination list, anyhow. The greatest in the Northwest? No contest. The average city park is dandy for the folks for whom it's handy, but nothing to justify a long trip. Here's no average park. Acquired from the Army in 1888 (formal title transferred in 1906) this peninsula ¾ mile wide and nearly 2 miles long juts out between The Narrows and Dalco Passage, providing some 3 miles of mostly-wild beach from which drift cliffs leap to an upland of big-tree virgin forest interwoven with 50 miles or more of trails. There also are gardens, zoo, and aquarium — and Camp Six and Fort Nisqually, by golly. Second-largest municipal park in America, exceeded only by New York's Central Park, this is not merely a city asset but a regional treasure.

All roads (and a bus line) lead to Point Defiance. The easiest way for foreigners to get there is to leave I-5 on Exit 132, follow Highway 16 toward Narrows Bridge, and turn right on Pearl Street.

Five Mile Drive, looping the perimeter, has numerous parking areas to permit short walks on blufftop or in forest. For the beach walk, up to 6 miles round trip on a low-medium tide, drive to parking at the Vashon ferry dock or Owen Beach; the walking is discussed below, when Trail narration resumes. A good introduction is a perimeter survey. For this, park at the first opportunity, just inside the Pearl Street entrance, elevation 100 feet.

Not to overburden with elaborate and unnecessary instructions, the plan is to head for the water but stop short, atop the bluff, and except for one deviation, stay there all around the peninsula. The trail system is not signed and there are a dozen times more paths than shown on maps — just take the outermost (nearest the bluff) path and, that failing, walk the road or cross into forest to find a path there. Following are sights along the way:

Overlook of Vashon Island ferry dock, the black-slag (from the smelter)

A Shay locomotive at Point Defiance Park

peninsula on which is built the Tacoma Yacht Club, Commencement Bay, Cascades. Japanese Gardens. Job Carr home, moved here from Old Tacoma, built 1864, the settlement's first post office. A sign on Five Mile Drive, "Big Tree Trail — This is the Forest Primeval," leading on a ¾-mile loop up one side of a ravine, down the other, sampling glorious old Douglas firs and other splendid wildland vegetables. Rhododendron Gardens. A major ravine, one of several slicing the bluff, this one carrying the road down to Owen Beach; for perimeter purposes it is best to follow the road down to the beach and on the far side of the ravine find meager paths up the bluff to more formal trails. Vashon Island Viewpoint. Another superb green-riot ravine, with the loop's last decent trail down to the beach. The Mountaineer Tree, a fir 220 feet tall, a circumference of 24 feet, about 400 years old. Another great viewpoint, up Colvos Passage. Point Defiance Viewpoint, atop a sand-gravel cliff above the light, with views across to Gig Harbor. Here, in 1841, Lieutenant Wilkes declared that with a few cannon he could defy the fleets of the world; in 1868 President Johnson signed the order reserving the site for coast artillery, but guns never were emplaced. Walking distance to here, about 4 miles. Onward to:

Madronas leaning over the bluff brink. Eagle-perch fir snags. Narrows Bridge Viewpoint. Never Never Land, a Mother Goose World (optional). A viewpoint noting the camp made May 20, 1792 by Peter Puget, when detailed by Captain Vancouver to explore this "sea in the forest."

Fort Nisqually — allow at least an hour here. The first fort, built in 1833 by Hudson's Bay Company, was destroyed by Indians and little is known about it except the location near the beach just north of the Nisqually River. The second fort was built in 1843 at a more inland site at Dupont, 17 miles south of here. Remnants were moved here in 1933 and the entire fort faithfully reconstructed. Among the fort's firsts: first white settlement on the Sound, first cattle, sheep, and chickens on the Sound, first white marriage, first white child, first religious instruction, first murder. The only original buildings are the granary, the oldest surviving building (1843) in Washington, and the factor's house, now a museum, open afternoons, featuring rooms with pioneer furnishings, other relics, and a small souvenir shop. Replicas, displaying pioneer artifacts: blacksmith shop, two lookout towers, kitchen, washroom, Nisqually House (the warehouse that was located on the beach below the fort). Also original is the boiler of the wood-burning **Beaver,** launched in England in 1835, arrived at Nisqually in 1837, the first steamship on the Northwest Coast, initial vessel of the mosquito fleet that ruled the inland sea for a century, wrecked off Vancouver, British Columbia, in 1888. Onward:

From a group camp just below the fort, bluff-near paths lead to the Salmon Beach community and the Narrows Bridge (see Puget Sound Trail below).

Camp Six — allow another hour, especially if you've spent a lot of time in second-growth forests among evidences of railroad logging, for here are a logging railroad complete with locomotive, a Shay No. 7, invented 1880, a huge Lidgerwood Skidder, a Dolbeer Donkey, a loaded log car, other donkeys, yarders, and loaders, a 110-foot fully-rigged spar tree, and two complete logging camps, one (formerly Camp 7 near Kapowsin) resting on the ground, the other (Quinault Car Camp) on flatcars. Onward, now inland, the bluff having been left at the fort:

Northwest Native Gardens. Via a detour left, the zoo (the owls are particularly outstanding); the aquarium, best on a rainy winter day when the seals are lonesome and will stage a swimming show for your solitary benefit; and the 1906 carousel. Rose gardens. Pond full of islands, bridges, and ducks. Waterfalls. And so back to the Pear Street Entrance, some 3 walking miles from Point Defiance.

Perimeter loop 7 miles, allow 7 years
High point 300 feet, elevation gain 800 feet
Bus: 11, Point Defiance

The Tacoma Narrows Bridge from War Memorial Park

Mile 7½-14: Point Defiance Park-Vashon Ferry Dock-
Dalco Passage-Point Defiance Light-The Narrows-Salmon Beach-
Bennett Tunnel-Narrows Bridge (Map — page 141)

From the park entrance walk road or path down ¼ mile to the Vashon ferry dock and follow the shore on an old, closed-off road a scant 1 mile to Owens Bathing Beach. From now on the beach is wild, and wilder, beneath the 200-foot jungled bluff of sand and blue clay, views over Dalco Passage, north to the Issaquah Alps. In 1 mile is the last path up the bluff — the last easy beach escape in the park. In a long ½ mile more the shore curves around to Point Defiance and the light, at the base of a great sand precipice. An exciting place — Dalco currents colliding with Narrows currents, fishermen, boated and winged, clustered at the rip, views over the water to Gig Harbor and up and down the Sound.

It's a good spot for thoughtful, cautious folk to turn around. The next section of Trail — to Bennett Tunnel — is recommended only for the doughty, and maybe a little dumb. The saving grace (and what saved the surveyor's neck) is that a person needn't hike the stretch twice in a day but can loop back to the start by Tacoma bus. Actually, at low tide the 1½ miles south of the point, to park's end, are safe and partly easy — and the most rewardingly wild section of the park. And though there is no safe way up the bluff, a rude path of sorts blunders along the bluff foot, through the clumps of alder forest riding sand blocks down to block the beach with brush; an explorer doesn't risk drowning, only exquisite suffering, with the possibility of cracking wide open, as happened to the surveyor, who at last said the hell with it and went wading in The Narrows, water to his waist.

At the park's end (unsigned) begins Salmon Beach, offering the most Alternative life style south of Fish Town. Ever-menaced by the unstable sand precipice above, on a southwest shore open to storms, beside The Narrows which at change of tides runs river-swift, with boat and trail access only, are some 50 residences built on pilings of driftwood and scraps stacked and tacked together, ingeniously designed, gaudily painted. Crazy, man. And to attempt to describe the 1 mile by Salmon Beach to Bennett Tunnel also is. On the ground, though, the route is self-evident, and goes something like this: From the start of the shanties find a path up the bluff to the main access trail and ascend a scant ¼ mile to a turnaround with garages sized for cars of the 1920s and with (late 1977) 44 mailboxes. (Note trails in the woods north — for chickening-out purposes, these lead to the Fort Nisqually section of the park.) On the south side of the turnaround circle, by the bluff edge, find a fairly decent trail climbing a scant ¼ mile to a gravel road, 260 feet. The road goes left to civilization, right down toward the beach; go straight on a woods road along the flat near the bluff edge a scant ¼ mile to a turnaround with parking area. Find a good old trail dropping off the lip into confusion. The next scant ½ mile is beyond description. Paths go everywhere in the largest, finest madrona forest in the surveyor's experience. Avoid those that go inland to civilization and those that drop to houses of Salmon Beach. If you get onto poor trail, or dangerous, retreat, because there is at least one easy, safe way. At last find a path that drops directly onto the top of the mouth of Nelson Bennett Tunnel, and thence to the railroad tracks. Fun, wasn't it?

Now the way is plainly marked by the two parallel strips of steel. Above left, the wildland bluff continues — a 6-mile jungle from Point Defiance to Titlow Beach that would make a famous trail, and indeed doubtless has a network of paths familiar to many local residents under the age of 16. Below right is the water — and rarely any beach, due to the railroad invasion. The view is south to Narrows Bridge and across to Point Evans and Point Fosdick. Grebes ride the currents, and gulls on bits of driftwood, apparently for the sheer thrill of the speed.

At ¾ mile from the tunnel is a little waterfall-creek and a trail up the bluff — to where? A bit south is a large creek valley and a woods road — from where? Here are square miles of in-city wilderness, guaranteed by the bluff's treachery to remain so. The way passes under powerlines carrying Lake Cushman electricity to Tacoma and at a long 2 miles from Bennett Tunnel crosses under the awesome Narrows Bridge. In the wonderful wild valley just beyond is (what else? you maybe expected a park?) another sewage plant. The service road winds up the bluff ¼ mile to parking at War Memorial Park.

Bus: 11, Point Defiance, to Vashon ferry dock; 12A, University Place, to 6 Avenue and Jackson; walk ¾ mile to War Memorial Park

Abandoned docks in front of Titlow Beach Park

Mile 14-21½: Narrows Bridge-Titlow Beach Park-Days Island-Sunset Beach-Chambers Bay-Sunnyside Beach Park-Steilacoom ferry dock (Map — page 141)

From I-5 take Exit 132 and drive Highway 16 to the Narrows Bridge. Just before the bridge turn right at the former toll plaza and park at little War Memorial Park, elevation 120 feet.

Walk out on the bridge for views up and down The Narrows (skinniest segment of the main channel of Puget Sound) from Point Defiance to Steilacoom. It's exciting as trucks cross and the entire monstrous structure **bounces.** The Pictorial Center in the toll plaza tells that The Narrows are 4600 feet wide, 120 feet deep, with 12-foot tides running as fast as 8mph. A campaign begun in 1923 culminated in the 1940 completion of the first bridge. Called "Galloping Gertie," it never rested, but walked and trotted in breezes, at winds of 35mph galloped, and on November 7, 1940, at 42mph, snapped, killing a hysterical dog. On October 14, 1950, was opened the present bridge, "Sturdy Gertie."

From the park walk the switchbacking road down to the Western Slopes Treatment Plant and onto the railroad tracks. In ½ mile begins Titlow Beach Park, ¾ mile long and extending inland as much as ¼ mile, mostly wildwoods on both sides of the tracks, a maze of paths everywhere. Leave the tracks for ⅓ mile, walking the beach or the top of the low clay-till bank in forest of fir and madrona, a picnic ground. Then follow the top of the seawall on an old, closed road some ½ mile to park's end at 6 Avenue, in the community of Titlow. Inland from the tracks is the developed section of the park, with playfields, duck ponds — and if a sidetrip is wanted, the 1½-mile or so Fit Trail looping over the greensward, around Titlow Lagoon, up the hill and through the woods. At each of 20 stations the pedestrian is commanded to halt and do pushups or situps or jumpups or leaps over bars or swings across creeks on rings. This gives the ducks fits, and thus the name.

Titlow, with plentiful public parking and a bus line, is reached by driving Highway 16 to where it curves right to the Narrows Bridge and keeping left on 6 Avenue down to the water. Remnants remain of the pre-bridge ferry dock.

Walk the tracks south from Titlow 1 mile through boatworks and marinas in the bay sheltered by Days Island, which is totally covered with houses. In the next 1¼ miles the bluff rears up, keeping houses at a respectful distance atop, the route a strip of wildland. Sunset Beach interrupts, a row of outside-the-tracks cottages on a bulkhead fill. Wild shore resumes for a long ½ mile.

Now for something completely different. The next 1½ miles are one of the most gigantic gravel-mining operations on the Sound — probably in the world. Two gigantic "cirques," of Pioneer and Glacier, gouge the bluff. One looks into the big holes, up the mountains of sand, and expects to see a Foreign Legion patrol ride over the skyline, pursued by a pack of snarling camels. The gravel factories fascinate, with clanking rumbling conveyor belts and washers and sorters, and hoppers for loading rail cars, and docks for loading barges. Let it be noted, though, that the noise and machinery are confined to two spots and most of the 1½ miles is empty and lonesome, and most is excellent sandy beach, a favorite place for private swimming and whatnot.

Views have been over the water to Fox Island, now left behind, yielding to McNeil Island, whereon appear the penitentiary buildings. At the end of the gravel mines the way crosses a drawbridge over the mouth of Chambers Bay, an estuary in the canyon of Chambers Creek, a long wilderness strip in the midst of suburbia. Marina, lumber yards, and pulpmill steam clouds at the inlet head are picturesque. Just south of the bay, on the shoulder of the Steilacoom-Chambers Creek Road, is public parking.

Now begins the outside-the-tracks bulge of land occupied by Steilacoom's Sunnyside Beach Park, featuring (where else would you put it?) a sewage plant. Parking beside the highway, here named Lafayette Street. Soon comes the ferry dock.

Bus: Tacoma 12A, University Place, to Titlow and to within ¾ mile of Narrows Bridge

Mile 21½-24½: Steilacoom ferry dock-Gordon Point-Cormorant Passage-Solo Point (Map — page 141)

From I-5 take Exit 129, signed "Steilacoom," and drive a tortuous and confusing route by a thousand stoplights, all red, past Steilacoom Lake and Western Washington State Hospital, to Steilacoom. Before reaching the ferry dock turn right on the closest-to-the-water street, Commercial, and park somewhere between the dock and Pioneer Orchard Park, on the hill north at Main Street.

Devote an hour or more to touring the town, one of the earliest white settlements on Puget Sound, incorporated 1854, and never growing to such size as to wipe out all the old buildings. From here to Bellingham ran the Military Road built in the Indian Wars (or, as Indian historians would call them, the White Wars). Numerous houses have plaques identifying them as built in the 1850s. Pioneer Orchard Park is the site of a log cabin used as a school and an Indian Wars refuge. Visit the museum in the Town Hall on Lafayette and Main (1-4 p.m. Tuesday-Thursday, 1-5 Sunday).

Another thing to do at Steilacoom is ride the little ferry to Anderson Island (which see). The shuttlings of the vessel now enliven the water traffic, which south of Tacoma consists mainly of tugs-barges and pleasure craft; this is still Main Street, but down at the lonesome end.

From the ferry dock hit the tracks south. In a long ½ mile is Steilacoom Bathing Beach Park on Gordon Point, and Steilacoom Marina. Walk out to scan the view north to Narrows Bridge, Fox Island, and Carr Inlet, westerly over McNeil Island to the Olympics, and to Ketron and Anderson Islands.

Proceed along Cormorant Passage, separating the mainland from little Ketron Island (which see). Bluff rears up to keep houses from the tracks — and soon there are no houses because ¾ mile south of Gordon Point begins Fort Lewis, reserved for warfare and wilderness. Little creeks cut ravines through the jungle of 4th Infantry Bluff. What wildwoods are up there? What walks?

At some 2½ miles from Gordon Point wild solitude is briefly interrupted by the public road at Solo Point.

Mile 24½-30½: Solo Point-Tatsolo Point-Dupont Powder Dock-Sequalitchew Creek-Nisqually Delta-Nisqually Station (Map — page 141)

Go off I-5 on Exit 119, signed "Dupont, Steilacoom." Turn right at the interchange stoplight to a Y and take the right, signed "Steilacoom." At 2¼ miles from the exit spot on obscure fish symbol on the left, denoting a Game Department public access to water, and signs saying "Ft. Lewis Water Pollution Control Plant" and "Solo Point." In ¾ mile, at an unsigned intersection, go right, in 1½ more miles passing the sewage plant and winding downhill to a ravine and the large parking area on Solo Point. (Just before the sewage plant

Beach near Ecology Park south of Solo Point

is Scout-built Ecology Park, with a self-guiding nature trail, a fine view over the Sound, and a path of sorts down wildwoods to the shore.)

Head south on the tracks, in views to Anderson Island, in the most total solitude of any stretch of the Puget Sound Trail. Something else new: the forest changes from the usual alder-maple mix on clay-sand-gravel-till bluff to Douglas fir on a moderate slope of loose gravels — outwash from the final push south of the Puget Glacier. Inland begin the prairies, and here their notable flower shows extend to the very shore. Tatsolo Point is rounded and views open south past the tip of Anderson Island to the Black Hills — and to the Nisqually Delta. Old pilings are passed, and an old wagon-like road down the bluff, perhaps a settlers' landing predating the fort, maybe even the railroad.

At 2 miles from Solo Point the long pier of the old Dupont powder dock juts out. Fort Lewis has been left for the even more complete wilderness of the 3200 acres where formerly explosives were manufactured, beginning in 1909, an activity that required much empty land around, just in case. Weyerhaeuser Company has acquired the property and is planning to build a major — an enormous — log-and-lumber-products warehousing and shipping port, and perhaps mills as well, and perhaps a major "industrial park" with other companies as tenants. Environmentalists oppose the project for reasons: immediately south is the Nisqually National Wildlife Refuge, crucial to the survival of wildfowl migrating on the Pacific Flyway, as well as resident wildlife; plentiful shipping facilities are available at Tacoma and north and elsewhere in the state, rendering unnecessary a major port on the South Sound, which ought to be left free of the risk of pollution catastrophes; this is the wildest, most peaceful section of the Puget Sound Trail; Sequalitchew Creek's canyon, down which would come the truck highway to the docks, is the largest and most magnificent wildland gulch on the entire Puget Sound Trail; the site is among the most historical in the Northwest, with a major village of the Nisquallys for eons, Nisqually House built in 1832 and the first Fort Nisqually in 1833, both at the canyon mouth, an American church mission in 1840, the second Fort Nisqually (see Point Defiance Park) in 1843, up on the bluff where are planned a truck road and rail spur. Weyerhaeuser intends to proceed. The Nisqually Delta Association, if it can raise the funds from public contributions, intends to carry on the contest wherever necessary. Even if unopposed, the company could not start building until 1980 or so. In view of the opposition, estimates are 1985, 1990, and never.

A few steps past the powder dock a pilings jetty juts out at the edge of the vast muds of the Nisqually Flats; here is the boundary of the Wildlife Refuge, where oil and organisms should never mix. Fir forests and "normal" mucky-cliff deciduous forest resumes. Tracks leave shores of Nisqually Reach and swing into 2-mile-wide Nisqually valley. Above are wildwoods. Below are delta sloughs and marshes and pastures and continuous NO TRESPASSING signs; in future there may be an entrance here to the Refuge. Mounts Road is crossed on a bridge, then the twin torrents of I-5, and at 3¾ miles from Solo Point is the concrete foundation of vanished Nisqually Station.

To get here for walks north to Solo Point and all, go off I-5 on Exit 116, signed "Mounts Road, Old Nisqually." Drive a scant 2 miles from the interchange toward Old Nisqually and shortly after crossing the railroad tracks spot the foundation. Ample parking here, elevation 60 feet.

Mile 30½-38: Nisqually Station-Nisqually River-Medicine Creek-Nisqually Head (Map — page 153)

The next segment of the Trail is not recommended at present, though it has history and scenery in the first stretch and farther along might become great in a future development of the Nisqually Wildlife Refuge.

At Nisqually Station leave the tracks and walk the Old Pacific Highway, crossing the Nisqually River, going from Fort Lewis to the Nisqually Indian Reservation; downstream a bit is Frank's Landing, scene of opening battles in the Indian (White) Wars of the 1970s.

Just beyond the river turn east on 6 Avenue SE a long ¼ mile to a Game Department public access on the river banks. A woods road-trail leads upstream, and a dike downstream by houses; a person could put together a walk of 1-2 miles, mainly interesting for watching Indian fishermen speed up and down the stream in motorboats, tending nets.

Proceed along Old Pacific Highway to cross Medicine Creek, now called McAllister Creek. At a Y by a grocery store is a monument commemorating December 24-26, 1854, when Governor Stevens hornswoggled the Indians into signing the Medicine Creek Treaties that triggered the Indian Wars of the 1850s. Nearby is the Treaty Tree where the signing took place.

At the monument turn right on 7th, then right again on Steilacoom Road to I-5 and Nisqually Plaza. A trail could be developed from here along the wild-jungled 3-mile wall above McAllister Creek to Nisqually Head. As things

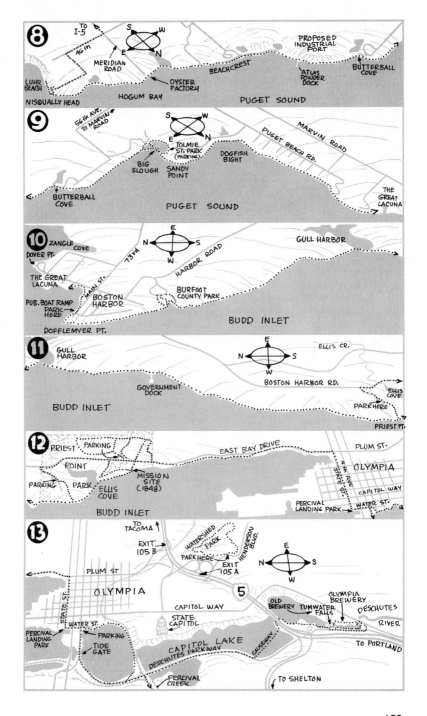

153

Nisqually National Wildlife Refuge

stand, if some knucklehead really were determined to walk every step from Tacoma to Olympia he'd have to do it via Martin Way and Meridian Road (which is north-south on the Willamette Meridian) and onward to Nisqually Head.

Nisqually National Wildlife Refuge (Map — page 155)

The last major unspoiled estuary of its kind on the Pacific Coast of the United States, and an important stopover on the Pacific Flyway for migratory waterfowl, the Nisqually Delta has recorded some 50 species of mammals, 200 of birds, 125 of fish, and 300 of higher plants in its ecosystems of open freshwater and saltwater, mud flats, freshwater marshes, salt marshes, mixed coniferous forests, deciduous woodlands, shrubs, grasslands, croplands, and the tidally-influenced fresh waters of Nisqually River and McAllister Creek. On one winter trip the surveyor saw a coyote dive from a dike into a slough, swim across, and run a mile over fields; he also saw (and was closely inspected by) a group of three otters; deer were numerous, and more birds than he knows. Led by the late Margaret McKenny and the Nisqually Delta Association, in 1974 a movement culminated in the establishment of a Nisqually National Wildlife Refuge, managed by the U.S. Fish and Wildlife Service, authorized for an ultimate 3780 acres.

Go off I-5 on Exit 114, signed "Nisqually." Cross under I-5 and turn right ¼ mile to the refuge gate — no hunting, no pets, foot traffic only, daylight use only. Park at the gate, elevation virtually nothing.

Visitors are asked to have patience during the period of facilities development — most of which, however, will be complete by the mid-1980s. Visitors also are asked to understand that "Closed" signs may be posted here and there to protect the public — or the wildlife. The plan envisions an ultimate four entrances to the refuge, a Twin Barns Environmental Education Center, five trails totalling 10½ miles, observation-photo blinds, and interpretive stations.

Opening in late 1979, starting at the Main Entrance, will be the ⅔-mile Nisqually River Trail. From it will be the ½-mile Bulrush Trail, designed for the handicapped, to be built in the 1980s. Tentatively proposed for the other side of the Nisqually, presently privately owned, are a Mounts Road Entrance and

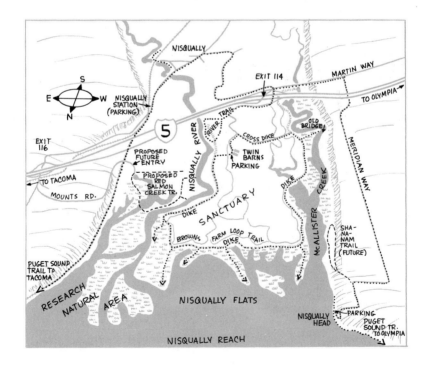

a 3-mile Red Salmon Creek Trail. For the other side of McAllister Creek, a West Ridge Entrance and 1¾-mile Sha-Na-Nam Trail of major archaeologic interest are planned to be built perhaps in 1983.

The classic walk long has been the perimeter loop around the Outer Dike. Now named the Brown Farm Trail, remembering what the delta used to be, it remains the big show. But please keep in mind: until a controlled hunting program can be instituted, the dike will be closed — for the safety of walkers — during the waterfowl hunting season. To avoid disappointments during the development period, visitors are encouraged to call in advance, (206) 753-9467.

From Twin Barns walk to the river and the dike, which follows the Nisqually, gray-green with rock milk from Rainier's glaciers, 1½ miles to the vicinity of the mouth, where diked freshwater marshes yield to salt marshes open to the tides. Look north to Ketron Island, Steilacoom, Narrows Bridge, ASARCO Smelter. Over Nisqually Reach to the Olympics. Turn around and — holy cow! — that's Rainier!

The dike turns left (west). Salt marsh reaches out in long, inviting fingers. The wildfowl display depends on the season. Nearly always there are clouds of peep — by the hundreds, the thousands.

In a long 1 mile, at McAllister (Medicine) Creek, the dike turns left (south), following the slough back into the delta, the sluggish water meandering through tidal marshes. In 1½ miles the trail leaves the Outer Dike and turns east on the Cross Dike, which leads in 1¼ miles back to the refuge entrance.

And what besides walking are you doing all that way? Watching herons blunder out of bulrushes into the air, hawks circle above, waterfowl feeding and flying, little birds flittering. And maybe coyotes swimming, otter diving.

Brown Farm Trail loop trip 5¼ miles, allow 4 hours
High point 10 feet, minor elevation gain
All year (presently, except bird-hunting season)

Mile 38-41: Nisqually Head-Hogum Bay-De Wolf Bight-Beachcrest-Butterball Cove-Big Slough-Tolmie State Park (Map — page 153)

Go off I-5 on Exit 114, signed "Nisqually," and drive Martin Way west 1 long mile from Nisqually Plaza. Turn right, north, on Meridian Road 2½ miles. Turn right on 46th and in ¼ mile turn left and ¼ mile more turn right, following "Public Fishing" signs to the Game Department picnic and boat-launch site at Luhr Landing.

South is a research facility of Evergreen State College and an unsafe old dock that looks like a ferry slip. Luhr Beach is an entry point to Nisqually National Wildlife Refuge.

The beach west is formidably private and there is no walking except in the high-toleration season (winter weekdays, small, quiet parties) at low-medium tides. A few beach-near bank-top houses are passed and in ¼ mile is an enchanting spot, the first of several tidal lagoons in creek estuaries; sneak up on gangs of floating waterfowl. The bluff lowers, permitting beachside houses, and in another ¼ mile a "point" of oyster shells juts into Hogum Bay. See the conveyor belt bringing shells from the "opening" room. See the oyster dredge working offshore, bringing in cargoes, picking up shells for dumping on the

Tolmie State Park

oyster beds, as nowadays is required by law. Oysters may be purchased from the factory's retail outlet.

Unusual for this area, there now is ½ mile of beach mysteriously wild. In the middle is another valley, another estuary lagoon in a cove behind a grassy baymouth bar, wild-tangled forest ringing the waters. Wildness ends in the first of two private beaches of Beachcrest community. Each beach is a little valley; the second has another dandy lagoon. The scant ½ mile of Beachcrest ends in a third valley-estuary-lagoon, this a boat moorage. At low tide one can go inland, leap the mucky creek, and battle brush to regain open beach.

Now comes another long ½ mile of wilderness — this one no mystery. In the middle is a derelict dock led to by a woods road from the bluff top. Up there, in the middle of the large emptiness usual for such business, Atlas Powder manufactured explosives. Burlington-Northern has acquired the property and is planning an enormous industrial and port complex, the twin of the Weyerhaeuser complex on the other side of the Nisqually National Wildlife Refuge, which thus straddled and menaced would not be much of a refuge. When moves are made toward fulfilling the plan, the Nisqually Delta Association will be on hand to express an opinion, you bet.

What is presently a great stretch of wildness, potentially a magnificent park, ends in another great valley, baymouth bar, and lagoon at Butterball Cove, with two cute little houses on the bar sharing the beauty with the ducks. At the south end is a 50-foot cliff of wavy-banded, yellow-brown riverbar sands; this handsome cliff, and a companion north of the cove, block walking at all but rather low tides.

The bank is crowded with houses, some by the bulkhead-invaded beach, the final ½ mile to the cove of Big Slough and Tolmie State Park.

Mile 41-73: Tolmie State Park-Sandy Point-Dogfish Bight-The Great Lacuna-Henderson Inlet-Dofflemeyer Point (Map — page 153)

Go off I-5 on Exit 111, signed "Yelm, Marvin Road," turn right on Marvin Road, and drive 5 miles, following signs that lead relentlessly to Tolmie State Park. Park either in the bluff-top lot or down in the valley near the beach.

In an area so densely subdivided the public hardly can glimpse the water, this new little park is a jewel beyond price, much worth a visit even in the bright, warm season when toleration of trespassing is zero and walkers must stay strictly on public property. A delightful stroll of maybe 2 miles can be put together from these materials: the ¼ mile of beach to Sandy Point; the woods trail to Sandy Point; the grassy baymouth bar that nearly closes off charming (little) Big Slough; the path down a ravine from the bluff to the beach; a path up the lush-green, wild-tangled valley of Big Slough Creek. A historical display tells about Dr. William Frazer Tolmie (1812-1866), who spent 16 years with Hudson's Bay Company at Nisqually House and Fort Nisqually as physician, surgeon, botanist, and fur trader, and on his botanizing tour of 1833 was the first white man to set foot on slopes of Rainier.

But to proceed on the Trail. A scant ¼ mile from the valley parking lot is Sandy Point, the start of private beach and almost continuous houses. In ½ mile more is the splendid slough of Dogfish Bight, the enclosing bar solid with houses. So is the shore north 2 miles to Mill Bight, an estuary that means business, a boot-stopper. And so the Great Lacuna . . .

The hiker's pal, the beach-guarding bluff so nearly omnipresent on the inland sea, relents, permitting houses near the beach, even on the beach. And the sheltered, feeble-wave beaches are narrow, often brushy. And the beach repeatedly is interrupted by impassable estuaries. And the privates have rigidly fenced out the publics.

The surveyor spent hours probing roads and rarely even saw the water, so expertly is it guarded from alien feet and eyes. The very concept of a Puget Sound Trail is tenuous here and is maintained only from stubborness as an expression of faith in the future. In this generation, only for residents and guests and roving sailors are the 7 miles from Tolmie State Park by Mill Bight and Baird Cove to Johnson Point, and the 8 miles to the head of Henderson Inlet, first of the frittering-away fingers of the South Sound, and the 10 miles up Henderson Inlet by Woodward and Chapman Bays, where Weyerhaeuser's log railroad dumps the bay full of wood, booming grounds where are assembled rafts of logs, to Dana Passage, and the 7 miles by Dickenson Point and Big Fishtrap and Zangle Cove to Boston Harbor and Dofflemyer Point, at the mouth of Budd Inlet.

Mile 73-78: Dofflemyer Point-Budd Inlet-Gull Harbor-
Burfoot County Park-Priest Point Park (Map — page 153)

Drive Boston Harbor Road via East Bay Drive from Olympia (see Priest Point Park) to the cozy old village of Boston Harbor. Turn left on Main Street ¼

Inlet north of Burfoot County Park

mile to an unsigned public boat-launch and parking area.

Though solidly populated, the shore can be strolled the 1 mile to Dover Point at the mouth of Zangle Cove; the route was not surveyed beyond there but might continue.

Olympiaward the shore of Budd Inlet is just about all private, but the level of toleration is high if you are quiet and polite and leave the shellfish alone. For the hiker from the north this second of the frittering-way fingers, the first to be walked, is a new experience — what from now on is the standard experience. Here is the "sea in the forest," seeming more a lake than an arm of the ocean. Rarely any surf here. The water snuggles.

Dofflemyer Point, with a little old light, is immediately rounded and Budd Inlet entered. In ¾ mostly-wild mile is Burfoot (Thurston) County Park. From Boston Harbor Road the park entrance leads to parking areas, elevation 80 feet. A trail system twists and loops around in lovely woods on the bluff slope and descends a cool green ravine to a tiny cove nearly closed off by a little baymouth bar.

The 1½ miles south from the park have a drift bluff 60-100 feet high that keeps all but a couple houses away from the beach. The dome of the Capitol is glimpsed. Once in a great while a ship passes, to or from the Port of Olympia. Beyond the waters rise the Black Hills. A naked till bluff, bright in season with yarrow and vetch and lupine (and poison oak!), announces Gull Harbor. But it's not a used harbor, rather a wonderful little wilderness of forest and estuary lagoon and birds. A baymouth bar nearly closes off the harbor — only at low tide can the channel reasonably be hopped-waded. This makes a good turnaround for a pleasant walk from the park.

Though a few breaks in the bluff permit waterside houses, the next 2¾ miles are mostly in solitude. After 1 mile of just about perfect wilderness are a dock and some sort of small federal-state port and research facility; on the day of the survey, the lightship **Relief** was docked. Beyond is a wooded bluff down which a few staircases come from unseen houses. A picturesque group of floating boathouses, with other houses nearby atop a 30-foot bluff, nourish a fleet of moored sailboats. Pretty. Then a point is rounded and Priest Point Park begins.

Priest Point Park (Map — page 153)

Forests of big firs and lush ferns, very deep and greenly wild ravines, a cozy little duck and heron harbor, and a mile of beach with views to ships in the Port of Olympia. And like most everywhere around here, some history, too.

Go off I-5 on Exit 105-B and turn right on Plum Street, which at the shore becomes East Bay Drive; continue on it straight north. Where houses yield to forest, spot an inconspicuous park sign on the median lawn of East Bay, which bisects the park, and turn right on the entry road, which winds uphill a bit to a parking lot, elevation 100 feet.

With proper design the 254-acre park easily could hold a weaving, looping trail system of 5-10 miles. Presently, despite a maze of paths and service roads, there isn't a coherent lengthy walk. But there are a mess of nice little ones. However, the two gorges of Ellis and Mission Creeks have no paths at all. Nevertheless, a person can spend a few hours poking around in the park's hillside-forest and bluff-top, beachside-forest segments. No route description is needed. Just go.

For an alternate starting point, at the north end of the park go off East Bay Drive on Flora Vista Road and in several feet turn left on an unmarked gravel road. Where the road becomes a private driveway is a small turnaround-parking area from which a path descends a gully to the beach at Priest Point, just south of where houses mark the boundary. At a low enough tide the beach can be walked south and Ellis Cove, at high tide always floating a flotilla of birds, squished across on mudflats to the main picnic-area portion of the park.

Though no traces remain, at the mouth of Mission Creek the Oblate priest, Father Pascal Ricard, in 1848 built his mission to the Squaxin Indians.

Introductory loops 3½ miles, allow 2½ hours
High point 140 feet, elevation gain 200 feet
All year

Mile 78-83½: Priest Point Park-Olympia-Percival Landing Park-Capitol Lake Park-Deschutes River-Tumwater Falls Park (Map — page 153)
Not with a whimper but a bang-bang-bang ends the Puget Sound Trail. The

Telephoto of Olympia from Priest Point Park

individual bangs can be separately visited from any number of parking areas or linked together on an 11-mile round trip from Priest Point Park that will render you shell-shocked with ecstasy.

From Priest Point Park the way is on the sidewalk of East Bay Drive, pleasantly viewful over the beach houses, and then if desired on low-tide sandflats. Across waters of Budd Inlet are the fill peninsula on which is built the Port of Olympia, and the Black Hills rising beyond. In 1½ miles is State Street, which leads west ½ mile through beautiful downtown Olympia to Water Street.

Here is Percival Landing Park. (Go off I-5 on Exit 105-B, turn right on Plum, then left on State. At Water turn right to limited parking or left to very large lots by Capitol Lake. And if these are full there's a ton of parking along Deschutes Parkway.) Walk the promenades of Percival Landing. Look at the pretty little boats, out past big boats and ships along Budd Inlet to Washington, The Brothers, Constance.

Urban park is continuous from here to the end of the Trail. Walk Water the 2 blocks to Capitol Lake Park. Formerly Budd Inlet did at low tide what comes naturally for these long skinny fingers of the South Sound — it became a mudflat. For years this gave state politics a distinctive reek. In 1949, to bring the Legislature the odor of dignity, a dam was built to let the Deschutes River maintain a lake. Partly ringed by lawns, partly cattails, partly wild tanglewood bluff, it provides a postcard/calendar foreground for the Capitol dome rising from green forest into clouds of circling gulls. The ducks love it. And the joggers.

Proceed on sidewalk and waterside path over the dam-tidegate, where in season salmon and steelhead can be seen coming upstream to spawn, and beside Deschutes Parkway. Directly across the lake from the Capitol is a new peninsula-park with ample parking, pretty views of the skyline of downtown Olympia. (Across the bridge at the park end a cheaters' path rounds the fence to the railroad tracks for a shortcut return.) Past the park Percival Creek enters the lake; railroad tracks lead up the valley, which was not surveyed but appears to offer a 1-mile wildland, worth a sidetrip.

At 1¾ miles a new (1979) causeway-trail goes from the Parkway over the lake and under I-5. Beyond is as-yet-undeveloped park, a wide mucky flat partly occupied by an ancient orchard. Informal parking and a public boat-launch of sorts. (All this will change as the park is completed; for now, get here via Grant Street from Deschutes Parkway.)

The history begins to get thick. Up Grant Street from the lake, which here narrows to become the mouth of the Deschutes River, is a handsome antique dwelling, a registered Historic Place, built in 1854 by Nathaniel Crosby III, Bing's grandfather. Find a path to the riverbank and look across to noble brick bastions of the original Olympia Brewery, built in 1905, converted to other purposes with the coming of Prohibition to the state in 1916. The new brewery, on the hill above, was opened with Repeal in 1933.

Here, too, are the first looks at the lowermost falls of the Deschutes, called Tumwater Falls, partly retaining the Indian name, "Tumtum," for the throb of the heart suggested by the sound. Walk the road uphill, parallel to the river, to Deschutes Parkway, and past the entry road to Olympia Brewery and past Falls Terrace Restaurant enter Tumwater Falls Park, ¾ mile from Capitol Lake. (To drive to the park, leave I-5 on Exit 103 and follow signs to Deschutes Parkway and the park entrance.)

Soak up the history. The headquarters exhibit has a huge granite erratic from Hartstene Island with a petroglyph of mountains, sun, bow, arrow, a bear and assorted other animals. A panel of photos shows scenes of the falls in olden times and buildings that were here: Horton Pipe Factory (1872), the first power plant (1890), Ira Ward house (1860), George Gelbach Flour Mill (1883), Tumwater Falls Powerhouse (1904), and so on. A monument tells the story of Colonel Michael T. Simmons arriving here in 1845 with 32 companions and establishing the first American settlement (which they called Newmarket) north of the Columbia River.

Soak up the scenery. Southernmost of Cascades rivers to enter Puget Sound, here the Deschutes got hung up on a stratum of hard rock precisely at tidewater; a series of foaming cataracts strung along a slot of spring-dripping, fern-and-moss-hung rock cliffs, drop a total 115 feet. In the ¼-mile length of the gorge are trails along both sides, artfully placed to experience the clouds of spray billowing from plunge basins, smaller falls of tributary creeks cascading off the walls into landscapings of native shrubs. Sidepaths lead to rock outcrops scoured and potholed by the river, view platforms of the falls and fish ladderways, where in season spawning salmon and steelhead can be watched battling up the torrent. So, walk up and down both sides of the gorge, crossing at lower and upper ends on quaint bridges, in ¾ mile doing the whole park. But better plan on doing it twice or more. And don't hurry.

The imposing structures atop the cliff ought not be ignored. The large sign announces daily visiting hours. So, climb the cliff trail, here in Tumwater, where begins the Inland Passage to Alaska, and thus end the Puget Sound Trail. It's a long walk from Bellingham. Makes a person thirsty.

Watershed Park (Map — page 153)

Walking shores of Capitol Lake, one admires wildwoods on the far shore. No simple connection presently makes a sidetrip, but the 150 acres of Olympia's old watershed on Moxlie Creek are worth a separate visit.

From Exit 105-A or 105-B on I-5, drive Henderson Boulevard southeast to a small trailhead parking area. Elevation, 100 feet.

The volunteer-built, foot-only path drops into the fine wild ravine to a Y; do the loop in either direction. The way winds through big cedar and fir and hemlock, fern-draped maples. It crosses and recrosses the creek on neat little bridges, weaves through soggy alder bottoms on plank walks, climbs and descends the sidehill, tunnels through shrubs of the valley floor, and generally extracts all the juices from the in-city wilderness. Still to be seen are miscellaneous machinery and wire-wrapped wooden pipes that until the 1940s diverted Moxlie into city faucets.

Loop trip 1½ miles, allow 1 hour
High point 100 feet, elevation gain 100 feet

Eld Inlet (Map — page 163)

Third in sequence of the ice channels (then), inlets (now), Eld is formidably privatized most of its length and where not, at the head in Mud Bay, is unattractive for energetic walking, though fascinating to poke about in saltgrass and mudflats. However, on each shore the survey found a gap in the defenses against public feet, a way to the water.

Evergreen State College

Our newest state college has the state's largest campus, more than 1000 acres, mostly second-growth wilderness, and 3300 feet of natural waterfront. A splendid trail samples trees and waves.

From Exit 104 on I-5 drive Highway 101 for 3 miles and exit on Evergreen Parkway. In about 2 miles enter the campus, turn left at the sign, "Campus Plaza, Parking," pay the small fee, and park just beyond the booth in Lot B (left) or C (right). Elevation, 190 feet.

Walk through the campus core, first over the plaza to the library, then

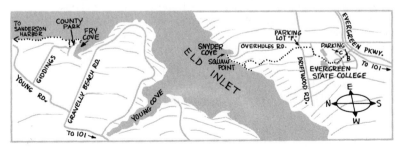

between the latter and the Activities Building, by the Recreation Center and Residence Halls, and cross Driftwood Road to Parking Lot F. Bear left and on the far side of the lot, about ¾ mile from the start, spot a sign, "Nature Trail." The path expertly savors the varied systems of the wildland: great big old stumps from the long-ago logging, alder bottoms with gurgling creek, a pond, an old pasture, ferny-mossy maples, handsome stands of cedar and fir and hemlock.

At ¾ mile from Lot F is a T. The left leads a few yards to the beach and a little baymouth bar enclosing a little lagoon. In the season when the woods are bright with blossoms the beach should only be visited by the liberal-minded, since students come here to gain overall tans; on the survey day the flowers of snow were coldly blooming and the only waterside sport was snowballing the ducks.

The right leads ¼ mile along the slope in fine firs and madronas, salal and twinflower, to Geoduck House, the college's marine ecology studies center, on Squaw Point. Sit on the grassy lawn under a big old fir, look to the college's boats in Snyder Cove, and across the inlet to Young Cove and Flapjack Point, and to Black Hills and Olympics.

Round trip 4 miles, allow 3 hours
High point 190 feet, elevation gain 190 feet

Frye Cove County Park

An excellent Thurston County park, undeveloped, virtually unknown.

Drive Highway 101 a scant 2½ miles past the crossing of Eld Inlet (Mud Bay) and turn right on Steamboat Island Road. In 1 mile turn right on Gravelly Beach Road. In a scant 2 miles turn left on Young Road. In ⅔ mile turn right on Giddings Road and follow this woods lane ¾ mile. As it narrows more and prepares to quit altogether, a sign announces the park, "no public facilities — held for future development." Park at the sign, elevation 100 feet.

Descend the trail, at its bottom taking either the left or right fork to the beach. For the gem experience, walk south to the mouth of Frye Cove, uninhabited and lonesome, one of those charming estuaries appalling to boot but intriguing to gaze into, wondering what would be found around the sinuous corners, deep in forest, if one had a boat. Firs lean over the water, framing the scene.

At a low-medium tide, head north along the inlet, under a steep forest that roofs the beach and often blocks it with logs and branches. A glorious maple extends 35 feet over gravels and waters. A Douglas fir 5 feet in diameter grows out of the very beach! Duck into a green-dark alcove of overhanging alders to find springs dripping down a clay cliff hung with maidenhair fern. Climb patiently over seaweedy, barnacled logs — or, at low tide, squish around in boot-swallowing mud. Look out the inlet to its mouth at Cooper Point.

Though several houses are hidden up in the woods in the first 2 miles, scarcely so much as a trail betrays their presence. Beach-near houses then begin and continue the 1 mile to Sanderson Harbor, which halts progress.

Round trip 6 miles, allow 4 hours

Frye Cove County Park

Totten and Skookum Inlets (Map — page 166)

There simply aren't enough people yet to fill all the many miles of waterfront; as a consequence, though choice spots are inhabited, wildness grows more common on the fourth of the "seas in the forest" and its offshoot, the fifth.

Kamilche Point
A walk from the tip of the stubby peninsula separating two inlets permits a peek into Skookum and a fine sampling of Totten.

Drive Highway 101 past the head of Totten Inlet (Oyster Bay). Where Highway 108, signed "McCleary, Aberdeen," goes left up Kamilche Valley, go right, signed "Kamilche." Proceed through this hamlet, over the railroad, and turn left on Kamilche Point Road, which in 4 miles runs into the water and ends at a private dock. Park on the public road. Beach access is by toleration, at a high level on lonesome winter days, absent on sunny weekends.

Walk left a bit to the mouth of Wildcat Cove. Look into it, and across narrow Skookum Inlet to Deer Harbor. Three cute little waterways in one view. But mucky no-beach shores prevent exploration.

Then walk right, round Kamilche Point, with two houses atop. Beyond, however, Totten Inlet beach is secluded by a 40-foot wooded bluff, the houses there mainly out of sight. Blue clay is exposed on the beach. A ruins of an old dock is passed, then a huge erratic, a big modern dock with anchored boats, and a small oyster factory on a grassy point. Wildness resumes, marvelous maple canopies thrusting 30 feet over the beach. A creek dribbles from a terrific, wild-tangled valley. At 1¼ miles the shore bends into Big Cove, with a couple houses on the waterside flat. Wild beach resumes to Deepwater Point, at 2 miles. The survey proceeded no farther but perhaps could have continued 2 more miles into the head of Totten Inlet, Oyster Bay, before being stopped by tideflat muck.

A surveyor who previously has spent hours driving around seeking ways to the opposite side of Totten Inlet, without success, now is chagrined to see that for miles that shore is wilderness only sporadically molested by humanity. But how would one get at it? Well, by driving Steamboat Island Road (see Frye Cove County Park) and its sideroads, when population thins out finding an unguarded stretch of water-near woods, and striking off in the brush.

Round trip 4 or 8 miles, allow 3 or 6 hours

Arcadia Point

At the tip of the peninsula separating the fourth and sixth of the finger seas begins an excellent, long-as-you-like exploration of Totten Inlet.

Drive Highway 101 past Kamilche 1 mile and turn right on Lynch Road, which joins Arcadia Road, which at 10 miles from 101 ends at Arcadia. A block before the end is a public parking lot for the boat-launch. Access to the beach is public but walking requires toleration, normally at a pretty high level way out here in the sticks.

Left a few feet is the light on Arcadia Point, where a palatial home and a moat-like yacht basin prevent exploration into Hammersley Inlet. But there is a busy view of many nice things: "Hammersley Point" (which see), Pickering Passage, Squaxin and Hope Islands, both appearing perfectly housefree and wild, and cute little Steamboat Island, attached to peninsula-tip Sandy Point by a bridge and totally housed.

The walk is right, southerly along Totten Inlet. In ⅓ mile are a till point pocked by bird caves and a mudflat cove; at middle tides the channel can be walked across but at high it's a swim, so watch it. Above the grassy baymouth bar are bluff houses but soon the way is wild, though at intervals the top of the 100-foot bluff is cleared, indicating unseen houses. Old, unused concrete bulkheads are passed, old unused roads to the beach, and remains of a boathouse-on-pilings overwhelmed by a clay slump. The sliding-bluff forest sometimes pushes out on the beach, making mean struggles through weedy,

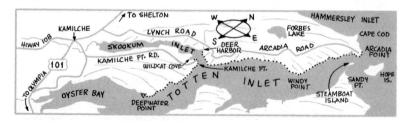

Poison oak

barnacled logs. Steamboat Island is passed. A double-trunked maple leans 40 feet over the beach. Creeklets dribble out of green-delicious gulches. Sands are tracked by deer and raccoon.

With only a couple houses encountered beside the beach in all this distance, at 2¾ miles is Windy Point. Views are long down Totten Inlet and to its mostly-wild far shore and to the Black Hills. Though not surveyed, the way appears open and pleasant and little-inhabited another scant 4 miles to the mouth of Skookum Inlet and Deer Harbor, which surely would halt progress.

Round trip 5½ or 13 miles, allow 4 or 9 hours

The Hammersley Inlet shore of this peninsula has long wild stretches — the 2 miles from Cape Cod to Mill Cove seem totally pristine (and the opposite shore equally so, the lonesomest of all the "seas in the forest"). But there is no public access except by boat. However, a person could drive Arcadia Road to some point about ½ mile from the water, park unobtrusively, and thrash through the woods. The surveyor cannot help you. Way out in the boondocks he was preparing to undertake such an expedition when, in a farmhouse at the limit of his vision, he spotted a pair of binoculars trained on him; as he hoisted rucksack, pickup trucks materialized from all around and began converging. He decamped, realizing even here there are defenses against vagabonds, especially those suspected of being oyster rustlers.

Hammersley Inlet (Map — page 168)

The last of the six finger seas has many claims to being the best. Virtually river-narrow most of its length, with odd little capes and secluded little coves, then opening to the big surprise of Oakland Bay and the two thundering-loud mills of Shelton, it's a stimulating mixture of industry, residence — and pure wilderness. Not to forget another element that can be exceedingly stimulating — poison oak.

Walker Park

Where Highway 101 veers left to bypass Shelton, go right on Highway 3 to the south part of town and turn right on Arcadia Road. In 1½ miles turn left at signs for Walker (Mason) County Park, reached in ⅓ mile.

The pleasant, big-fir-shaded preserve affords a pleasing prospect westward to Eagle Point, which hides Shelton, and Munson Point, beyond which opens Oakland Bay. Tugs tow log rafts. Ships carry lumber.

Walking toward Eagle Point is made impractical by bulkheads and homes; the other direction, though populated, has an amiably high level of toleration. How far to go? In 3 miles is Skookum Point and 1 mile beyond is trip's mandatory end and trip's glory, Channel Point at the mouth of Mill Channel, at the mouth of Mill Creek. After all his travels of the South Sound, this is the surveyor's nomination for the champion of charm.

Beyond the foot-stopping channel are the greatest 2 miles of this inlet, perhaps of all the inlets. All the way to Cape Cod the shore appears pristine, and so does the facing shore, to Cape Horn. But how to get there? See Arcadia Point and "Hammersley Point."

Round trip 8 miles, allow 6 hours

Shorecrest Park

Farther from Shelton in commuting miles and thus only now being built on at all, and that largely with summer and retirement homes, this shore of the inlet has views equal and superior to the other.

Drive Highway 3 north from Shelton past the head of Oakland Bay. (Let it be noted that Shelton and its lumber mills are the westernmost point of Puget Sound and thus Oakland Bay is among the ends of this arm of the inland sea. For that reason an indefatigable collector of waterways may well wish to savor it. This is readily done by parking on the shoulder of Highway 3 and dropping to the beach, open and walkable much of the distance from bay-head saltgrass and mudflats to open water by the mills.) Just after crossing Deer Creek turn right on Agate Road and drive 3½ miles to the crossroads/grocery store of

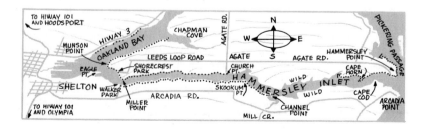

Shorecrest Park

Agate. Turn right a long 2 miles and then left on Crestview ¾ mile to tiny but luscious Shorecrest (Mason) County Park.

Walk both ways, one at a time. Though the bank of iron-stained glacial drift is too low to keep houses away, most are tucked discreetly in the dry-country rainshadow woods of fir and madrona. The trees lean picturesquely over the beach. From the bank hang picturesque festoons of poison oak, shiny green (Oregon grape-like) in summer, shades of red in fall.

From the park itself is an excellent view of steaming-clunking-humming lumber mills (Simpson and Rayonier) and beautiful downtown Shelton, famed far and wide as the native land of Bob and Ira Spring. For closer, better views walk east ½ mile to Munson Point. Continue on for expansive views up Oakland Bay to the head. Not surveyed, at 2½ miles is the mouth of Chapman Cove.

In the other direction the shore quickly rounds the low gravel cliff of Miller Point, the beach easy-walking sand and pebbles under arching firs and madronas, by scattered houses. In a succession of vistas over the cozy inlet, barely ¼ mile wide, a lake in the woods, to houses and yards and dogs barking, children playing, the way proceeds 3 miles to Church Point light. Here is public street-end parking, an alternate start. Bulkheads and such make the route less attractive beyond.

Round trips 5 and 6 miles, allow 3 and 4 hours

"Hammersley Point"

Of all the undeveloped land on the inlets, "Hammersley Point" at the inlet mouth cries out the loudest to be made a state park. What a glory! But chances are that unless you hurry the NO TRESPASSING signs will be up when you arrive.

Drive east on Agate Road (see Shorecrest Park) or south from Hartstene Island bridge (see Pickering Passage). At the big right-angle turn, go off on Benson Loop Road, which immediately forks; take the left. In a scant ¾ mile, where the Loop turns sharp right, go straight on a narrow gravel road ¼ mile. Four or five or more driveways go off left to shore homes. At the last one park, out of everybody's way, elevation 100 feet.

Walk the partly-overgrown, undriven, log-blocked (but as of mid-1978 unposted) woods road straight ahead. It curves left atop an alarmingly-overhanging 40-foot shore cliff and descends to end at ¼ mile in a field and orchard of an ancient farm. What a spot! Gnarled fruit trees compete with scotchbroom and tall grass. At just one place the formidable bank of old tills and "baked" clays dips to the beach. The views here at the mouth of the inlet are busy. Northward runs Pickering Passage, beyond which is the wilderness forest of Squaxin Island. Across the inlet mouth is Arcadia Point, with mansions and yachts, and beyond that is Hope Island (wild) and picturesque Steamboat Island at the mouth of Squaxin Passage and Totten Inlet.

North from the point (whose till cliff can only be rounded at low tide) the bluff above Pickering Passage has scattered houses atop, but the toleration is easy 1 mile for sure and an unsurveyed distance farther.

The other direction is the dazzler. Just down Hammersley are "the narrows," over which George Washington might easily hurl a silver dollar. Guarding the far shore is the formidable forest bluff of Cape Cod, and this shore the incredible bare-till cliffs of arrete-skinny Cape Horn. Needless to say, no houses anywhere near. Wild! The tip of the Cape Horn cleaver is a scant 1 mile distant. What's beyond? High tide prevented the surveyor from checking it out afoot, but evidence of maps and cross-inlet views and sideroad explorations suggests wildness pure or near it the 2½ miles to (populated) Libby Point — though an estuary 1 mile past Cape Horn might be a boot-stopper.

Even if tides prevent walking, the views are worth the trip. Poke around the old farm, amid flowers from a long-gone garden, smelling mint crushed by boots. Clamber the till cliff of the point, admiring wall-hangings of manzanita and poison oak.

Round trips 2 and 4 miles and more, allow 1 and 3 hours and more

Pickering Passage (Map — page 168)

On the other side of giant Hartstene Island is the main channel of Case Inlet. On this side, canal-narrow and woodsy-secluded, is Pickering Passage. Population is low, toleration high.

Drive Highway 3 to 8 miles northerly of Shelton, 10½ miles southerly of Allyn, and turn east on the road signed "Hartstene Island." Drive 4 miles to the bridge and park on the shoulder. Or better, ¼ mile north at the former landing of the old Hartstene ferry.

Walk both ways. South ½ mile from the ferry is walk's end at the mouth of

Graham Point Bay; look south along the Passage to Slalom Point at the tip of Squaxin Island, a wildwood Indian reservation. North 1½ miles is walk's end at the mouth of Jones Creek estuary.

Round trips 4 miles, allow 3 hours

Case Inlet (Map — page 171)

One of the twin fishhooks-terminii of Puget Sound, Case Inlet curls so far north as nearly to join the fishhook of Hood Canal and make Kitsap Peninsula an island. No student of the Puget Sound Trail can fail to be intrigued by the geographical significance, compelled to come pay homage. Mainly for the meditation — there's better walking elsewhere. Population is dense, meaning no wildness and requiring toleration, not always high.

North Bay

Here is the Momentous Spot — the most northwesterly waters of the Sound, reaching within 2 miles of the most southeasterly waters of Hood Canal, Lynch Cove.

Drive Highway 3 from Olympia or Bremerton, or Highways 16, 302, and 3 from Tacoma, to the hamlet of Allyn. Park at the Port of Allyn dock and boat-launch.

The shore south is too many-housed to interest. So, do the meditation walk north, where houses are few along the mudflats. Persisting through guck and clams and the rich reek of salt decay, in 1½ miles the pilgrim attains the saltgrass marsh-meadows of the bay head. Turn around and start back to Bellingham.

Round trip 3 miles, allow 2 hours

Rocky Bay

On the west side of North Bay, at the mouth, is walking less momentous but also less ooky and more scenic.

On Highway 302, at ¼ mile north of the right-angle turn at Rocky Point, park on a broad shoulder.

Drop the several feet to the beach and walk north ½ mile to a point for views to Allyn and the bay head. Then walk south ½ mile to Rocky Point for views down Case Inlet to Reach and Stretch Islands and beyond, and around the corner into cute little Rocky Bay.

Round trip 2 miles, allow 1½ hours

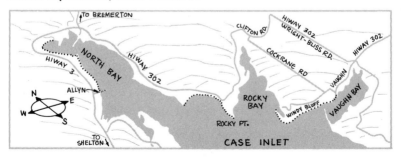

Seaweed on Vaughn Bay

Vaughn Bay

Nor should the connoisseur ignore the next-door bay.

At 1¼ miles west of Key Center on Highway 302 take the sideroad ¾ mile to Vaughn and park at the public boat-launch.

Vaughn Bay is another of the cozy estuaries in which the vicinity abounds. The highlight of this one is the splendid long baymouth bar. Walk west (many houses, toleration required) ½ mile to within a pebble's toss of the bar tip, inaccessible across the channel but good to look at. Continue another ¼ mile to upthrusting naked gravels of Windy Bluff, with another spit pushing into Rocky Bay.

Round trip 2 miles, allow 1½ hours

ISLANDS IN THE SOUND

Psychologists have written about the "island personality" and poets the "island psyche" and publishers recognize a dependable market for the "island book." Sales around the world of Hazel Heckman's **Island in the Sound,** the Anderson story, symptomize the nigh-universal longing to be an islander, safely circumscribed by guardian waters on a tight little isle. More's the pity that addled vandals ever are permitted to build de-islanding bridges. More's the honor to Vashonites who have defended their way of life against the attempted benevolence of engineers — even to the extent of opposing "better" (worse) ferry service. Make islands easy and they'll be subdivided, that's the Bainbridge lesson.

The pedestrian yearning to go on pilgrimage to a water-surrounded shrine and not owning a boat finds most such are so far from easy as to be impossible. Still, he is by no means shut out.

Blake is virtually the walker's definition of island perfection — entirely a park, almost entirely a wildland, a joy of a beach and a delight of a forest interior. (This is the only interior surveyed; on the other islands attention is confined to the shores.)

Though so close to crowded urbia, Vashon and Maury, the two nowadays connected by a dry-land (formerly low-tide-only) isthmus, retain a rural character despite being largely a suburbia. Thus is demonstrated the value of a ferry bottleneck. Except when somebody tries to foist a hydrofoil on them, the folks tend to be more relaxed than neighbors across Main Street, more tolerant of trespassers — at least those who scrupulously observe the Trespassing Code (see Introduction, **Footsore 1**).

Fox illustrates the relationship of man and glacier. Where drift bluffs lower, giving residents easy access to the water, the rascals cuddle up, invade the beach with bulkheads. But when a noble scarp of vertical (and/or slidey) till-gravel-sand-clay leaps high, they sit atop and enjoy the view and let wildness rule the waves. Most of the Fox shore is sinking under the weight of money, and the bridge has reduced it to an appendage of the Kitsap Peninsula, but ah that one fine southwest stretch of bluff peace. . .

McNeil is the future — and what a brilliant future it can be if we play our cards right — a Blake Island writ large.

Anderson has been somewhat modified from the Heckman-portrayed past; one enormous retirement-and-vacation development is underway. But the future will not destroy the pastoral-rural-wild mode while the ferry service is straight out of the 1920s. Long live the 1920s!

Hartstene no longer is protected by a ferry yet still has remoteness, which for now is doing the job. So large that a developer hardly knows where to start, so distant from anywhere that customers are hard to net, the interior is mostly farms scattered in a great second-growth wildland and the beach has more wild miles than all the other islands combined.

What's so different about islands? Not much, really. Uplands and beaches are about the same as on nearby mainland. The getting there is the most of it. Evil spirits, so wise men said of old, cannot cross water.

USGS maps: Duwamish Head, Bremerton East, Vashon, Olalla, Des Moines, Tacoma North, Gig Harbor, Fox Island, Steilacoom, McNeil Island, Nisqually, Longbranch, Squaxin Island, Vaughn, Mason Lake

Indian longhouse at Tillicum Village

Blake Island (Map — page 175)

In the middle of Main Street, ferries rushing this way and that, big ships and little boats and tugs and barges tooling around, jet airplanes booming and propellor jobs clacketing, cities and suburbs humming on every side, are 475 acres of green peace. The beach, and the big-tree forest, are as wild now as when Chief Seattle (reputedly) was born here, and tribes gathered for parties. Bought by William Pitt Trimble in 1904 and kept by him as a summer home until 1929, in 1957 the sanctuary became Blake Island State Marine Park.

For non-boaters, access is by craft of Seattle Harbor Tours serving Tillicum Village, an Indian-longhouse restaurant on 4½ leased acres. The **Goodtime** leaves from Pier 56 in Seattle, at the foot of Seneca Street just north of the ferry terminal and just south of Waterfront Park and Seattle Aquarium, attractions suitable for combining with a Blake trip while awaiting the boat. Park in an Alaskan Way lot or on the street, or come by Metro Magic Carpet Bus 25. On a vessel reminding one of the mosquito fleet, the trip from Blake to Seattle takes 45 minutes, with long views up and down the open Sound, north to Whidbey Island, south to Rainier, then threading through Elliott Bay traffic. The trip to Blake is 60 minutes, including a waterfront tour.

The boat schedule dictates the hike itinerary. To learn the current schedule and make (required) reservations, call Tillicum Village Tours, 329-5700. Round trip (1978) is $4.50. To note only the trips (1978) of interest to a walker: On Sundays from May 1 through October 15 the boat leaves Seattle at 1 p.m., docks on Blake about 2:00, pulls out at 5:15; this 3¼-hour stay permits either a complete circling of the shore with sidetrips in the woods, or a complete circling of the perimeter trail with sidetrips to the beach. Daily except Sunday, June 1 through July 15, there are two daily trips, the first leaving Seattle at 11:15 a.m., the second leaving Blake at 9:45 p.m.; by combining them a hiker has 9½ hours on the island and can do the whole trail system plus the entire beach, and then lazy around watching the sunset and eating a picnic supper — or buying the salmon dinner served at Tillicum Village, Indian-baked, with dances performed, and crafts displayed. Daily from July 15 through the first week of September another trip leaves Blake at 7:15 p.m., giving a 7-hour island stay. Of course, the supreme plan is to combine any trip of one day with any trip of the next, camping at one of the three beachside campgrounds, marveling at the all-around skyglow of the billion-eyed megalopolis. (From October 15 to April 30 you must have your own boat, though for a group of 50 or so Tillicum Tours Service will run a charter; call for information.)

At any but high tides the circuit of the longest purely-wild beach so near downtown Seattle is the first priority. Walk up the dock toward the longhouse, turn left, and go. (Left is advised in order to do the largely-cobble east-south-west beach first, saving the mainly-sand north beach for the end.) Village, picnic area, and campground are soon left behind, East Point rounded, and solitude attained — since few of the **Goodtime** crowds venture far from the longhouse. Grand fir, madrona, and maple overhang the beach. Views are to West Seattle and the Fauntleroy-Vashon ferry, Rainier and Issaquah Alps, Space Needle and grain terminal and Magnolia Bluff. At 1¼ miles Madrona Point is rounded and the view shifts down Colvos Passage between Vashon and Point Southworth, then across Yukon Harbor to Colby and Colchester. South End Campground, on a spur from the perimeter trail, is passed; the jungled bluff of glacial drift rears up 200 feet from the beach; fleeing herons go "gark! gark!" The elevated terrace of a fossil beach begins, and on it is West Point Campground. Then the noble sandspit thrusts out in the waves, driftwood line and dune line enclosing a (usually) dry lagoon. At a scant 2 miles from Madrona Point is the tip of the spit, the climax delight; plan to sit a long while watching Seattle-Bremerton ferries dashing through Rich Passage between Orchard Point and Bainbridge Island. See the Olympics. A final 1¼ miles leads back under an alder canopy, in views to the Seattle-Winslow ferry and the metropolis, to the longhouse, completing a 4½-mile loop.

That's the half of it. Now, inland. Logged in the 1850s (except for some wolfish Douglas fir on the south side), the island has regrown a mixed forest that offers every variety of Puget Sound woodland experience — and meetings with some of the island's puny, half-starved 120-odd deer, striving to

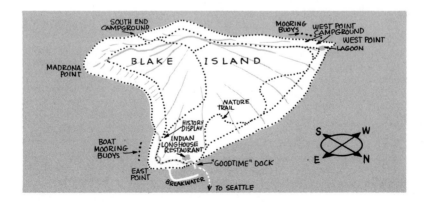

survive in a habitat that can support only 50 or so. To start the perimeter counterclockwise, walk by the right side of the longhouse to a bridge over a little gulch. To do it clockwise, meander through the campground any old way and near its end turn inland on the old road to the foundations of the Trimble house. A few steps beyond is a Y; left is the island loop trail, right is the cross-island trail. The loop is the basic trail but the cross-island trail offers additional green mystery, as do the nature trail and various lesser paths. Frequent spurs lead to the beach, permitting easy switches from one Blake mode to the other.

Beach loop 4½ miles, allow 3 hours
Perimeter trail loop 4 miles, allow 3 hours
High point 200 feet, elevation gain 500 feet
May 1-October 15 (if you have your own boat, all year)

Vashon Island (Map — page 177)

Occupying a lot of space — 13 miles long and up to 4 miles wide — near the center of Puget Sound City, Vashon serves Tacoma, Seattle, and Bremerton as suburbia-exurbia. The scene strikes a visitor as rural, most settlements being moderate expansions of farming crossroads or summer-home colonies from mosquito-fleet days. To long-time residents the situation seems different; bumper stickers say "Vashon Is Sinking." The prevailing mood might be described as a genial xenophobia. Recreational visits tend to be discouraged — there is no tourist industry, no big park system, and virtually all beaches are private. Nevertheless, except in the summer season and other times when large numbers of residents are actively using their beaches, trespassing is generally tolerated by small groups of quiet, clean, polite foreigners — so long as they lay off the clams and don't picnic in somebody's front yard. Few are the signs saying "Keep Off"; many say something firm but courteous such as "Private Beach — Do Not Loiter," or "No Clamming," or "No Fires." Leave your dog home, haul away your garbage, and eat your lunch on the long wild stretches. Behave so and your meetings with locals are likely to be pleasant — they'll tell you about island history, give information on that classic beach walk, the 35-mile around-the-island loop.

Precisely because it is so centrally located, so quick of access, Vashon "belongs" to a great many people, whether or not they ever so much as visit. The existence of islandness is a potential opportunity enriching all of us. Those walkers who do visit must perforce become active Defenders of Vashon. And one way to do that is by not contaminating the island with your personal wheels, unless of bicycles. There's no need for it. Bus, ferry, feet, that's all you need.

East Shore From Vashon Heights

Walk the entire east shore, for miles in wildness, in ever-changing views across Main Street traffic to Seattle shores and mountains beyond, on a beach that is easy-open at all but the highest tides.

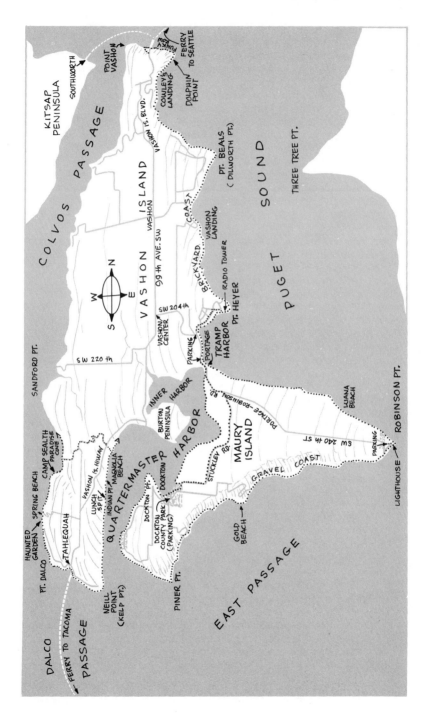

Only one bus a day (and it doesn't run Sundays or some holidays) permits the ingenuity. In downtown Seattle catch Metro 118, the "Harlan Special" (Harlan drives it and always has) leaving 7th and Blanchard at 8 a.m. Alternatively, drive to the Fauntleroy ferry terminal in West Seattle and park, walk on the 8:35 ferry ($1.10 to get on Vashon, nothing to get off, and there's a message in that), and on the ferry board 118, which transports you to the south end of the east shore at Portage, arriving 9:20.

Should the water still be too high on your arrival for the beach to be easy, the first 1½ miles around Tramp Harbor to Point Heyer can be walked above the tides, the first ¾ mile on road shoulder atop the seawall to Ellisport, the next ¾ mile on public road climbing above the shore, then dropping to cross the lagoon onto the Point Heyer spit, site of the KVI radio tower but aside from that in a natural state of lagoon, dune, driftwood. Much time can be whiled away out here amid waves and gulls, looking to Rainier, watching jets land and take off at Sea-Tac Airport. When the water has lowered to 10 feet or so, head north.

The 3½ miles to Dilworth Point (Point Beals) are virtually all wild beneath a tanglewood bluff as high as 300 feet. The cozy trail-access cottages of Klahanie briefly interrupt, and a mansion at ancient Vashon Landing, and cottages in the valley-cove just north, but mainly the people are atop the bluff with not even trails down. Creeks flow from jungle over gravels — which by the unusual abundance of red-brick pebbles and cobbles tell of a past when the island had nine or more brickyards. Across Puget Sound is the thrust of Three Tree Point.

Dilworth Point (where in the 1930s, while swimming, the surveyor watched an airplane fly over, carrying Wiley Post and Will Rogers to Alaska and eternity) is a logical turnaround; it's 4¼ miles back to Ellisport, where the 2:33 or 4:48 afternoon bus can be taken to the ferry dock. No time or energy is saved by turning back here, but more of the day is spent in wildness, because Dilworth itself is densely populated, as is the entire shore for a mile north.

In good toleration season, though, the next 3½ miles to Dolphin Point have much interest. The architectural tastes of beachdwellers entertain, especially in those constructions dependent not on tons of money but on beachcombing, scavenging, and do-it-yourself handicrafting. At 1¾ miles from Dilworth wildness resumes for nearly 1 mile; then, at Cowley's Landing, is a vision of the past — a nearly-intact dock and gangplank from the era of the mosquito fleet. Just beyond, on beach-invading riprap, is a short stretch that cannot be passed without wading at above 7 feet of water — the only such obstacle on the route.

Dolphin Point, thoroughly civilized, is yet a marvelous viewpoint. Ferries shuttle to Fauntleroy, Southworth, Bremerton, Winslow. Look south on the Sound to where you came from. And north to Blake and Bainbridge Islands — and Whidbey. The Seattle shore is distinguished by the wild gap in solid habitations, the Green Mile of Lincoln Park.

The final ½ mile is quaint along cabins-cottages of Funky Row, home-made and homey. The escape from the beach is blocked by their bulkheads and requires less than 7 feet of water: walk under the ferry dock and easily off the beach onto the far side of the dock. If the water is above 7 feet, either wade or stand there shouting, "Help!" Somebody may let you walk through their yard.

One-way trip 9½ miles, allow 7 hours

Tahlequah ferry dock

If the east shore can be so neatly done, why not the west, which an eyeball survey from across Colvos Passage shows to be a succession of wild delights, only intermittently interrupted by tidy little villages? Reason No. 1: walking from the ferry dock down the west shore, in less than ½ mile one bumps against a great jutting beach-blocker fill that cannot be passed at more than 2 or so feet of water. Reason No. 2: the bus route is such that from it one would have to walk 2 miles or more of country roads to get on the beach. The west shore thus is best sampled by walking from Paradise Cove (see below).

South-End Loop From Tahlequah

Of all the beach walks in this book, here perhaps is the richest in combining solitude of wild beach beneath green-jungle glacial-drift bluff, views over busy waterways to the metropolis of Second City, and poignant memories of the grand old days of the mosquito fleet.

Drive (or take the Point Defiance bus from downtown Tacoma) to Point Defiance Park (which see). Walk on the nice little ferry for the 15-minute voyage over Dalco Passage to Tahlequah, an old village in and around the valley of Tahlequah Creek, the weathered houses grown comfortably into the landscape.

To loop is not compulsory. A person can stroll up the west shore, along Colvos Passage; Camp Sealth at 3 miles is a good turnaround. Or the other way around Neill Point to Quartermaster Harbor; "Lunch Spit" at 3 miles is a fine goal. For each of these round trips, 6 miles each, allow 4 hours.

The loop is the classic if time, tides, and energy permit. To do it clockwise (use wristwatch for orientation) walk off the ferry dock, turn left to Tahlequah Grocery for nostalgia and some extra lunch supplies, and from it scramble down to the beach. In the first ½ mile are Tahlequah Creek, continuous bulkheads, and cozy homes. Views are east to Commencement Bay, downtown Tacoma, St. Regis steam plume, ships and mountains.

Rounding Point Dalco shifts the mood to wildness, the jungle-drift wall rising a steep 260 feet. Views focus now on the greenery of Point Defiance, the mouth of The Narrows, and the mouth of Gig Harbor. New vistas open north up Colvos Passage, with tugs hauling log rafts, fishermen dragging lines. At 1 mile from the point is a wild valley where grow, mysteriously, tall poplars. Step in a bit from the beach and find by the creek a haunted cottage, flowers and beanstalks of a garden gone wild, overgrown by hellberries. A bit farther up the beach is a larger valley where part of a mosquito-fleet dock still stands, old houses line sides of the valley, and one on a bulkhead by the beach bears faded lettering, "Miramar — Board and Room — And Lunches." This is Spring Beach; close your eyes and see the excursion steamer docking, hear the singing around the beachfire.

Revert to the wild mode 1 long mile to a wildland protected by the Seattle-King County Council of Camp Fire Girls. Here is Camp Sealth, a wonderland fondly remembered by generations of girls and more than a few boys; it was in the spring of 1939 that Troop 324 voyaged here on the **Virginia V** to perform, as was the troop's wont, a Good Deed, working on trails. But the trail system must be left alone by the public; while walking rapidly by on the beach, admire the nature preserve and the snug buildings tucked in and around the valley.

"Sealth Point" is rounded to Paradise Cove. Houses start. At ¾ mile from the point, 4 miles from Tahlequah, a public street-end at an old boathouse provides a take-out for the loop.

(As noted above, here is about the only practical approach for a foreigner to the west shore of the island. North 2 miles, houses and wildness alternating, is Sandford Point, a 12-mile round trip from Tahlequah. Beyond are splendors unsurveyed.)

Walk the county road up a lovely forest ravine to the island top, 480 feet. Turn left on 131 Avenue a short bit, then right on 248 Street. At an unsigned Y go right, downhill, to Vashon Island Highway. Cross to a public lane that deadends at the water on Magnolia Beach. This cross-island walk on quiet country roads totals 2¼ miles.

(If a sidetrip is wanted, turn left over a wide sand delta, round the shore to the tip of Burton Peninsula, a long 2 miles, and look into Inner Harbor.)

But watch the tides — ahead lie feeble-wave beaches overhung by alder and maple, cool retreats on hot days, but not so lovable when full of water, demanding that a person swim or fight hillside brush. The first 1½ miles south along Quartermaster Harbor, by Indian Point and Harbor Heights, with views to Dockton on Maury Island, are mostly bulkheaded and populated, many boats moored.

In ½ mile more is "Lunch Spit," a tiny jut of sand enclosing a tiny lagoon. To the south 2 miles can be seen Neill (Kelp) Point, and in all that distance, no sign of man. A second little spit is passed, several inviting ravines. Then houses do indeed exist but up in the trees, no interruption of the mood. (And providing emergency escapes to an overland return if, as happened on the survey, the beach is totally swallowed up.) Piner Point on Maury Island is

Lighthouse on Robinson Point

passed and the water panorama widens, climaxing at Neill Point with a prospect east and north on the Sound to Redondo, Tacoma again, and Rainier. A final 1 mile beside bulkheads and houses leads back to Tahlequah.

Loop trip 11 miles, allow 8 hours
High point 480 feet, elevation gain 480 feet

Maury Island (Map — page 177)

Miles of beaches varying from purely wild to scatteredly populated, a Coast Guard lighthouse built in 1915, some of the most stupendous gravel mines in the world, and changing views across ships and barges and sailboats of East Passage to the Puget Sound Trail from Three Tree Point to the ASARCO Smelter, plus Cascades. Three public parking-beach accesses permit trips short or long — up to a complete circuit of the island. Or better, leave the car on the mainland and travel solely by ferry, bus, and shank's mare.

Bus first. Take Metro 118 (see Vashon Island), arriving at Portage at 9:20 a.m. on a day of good walking tides. (But never on Sunday or some holidays — no bus service.) Plan the itinerary to be back at Portage at 2:30 or 4:45 p.m. to bus back to the Fauntleroy ferry.

Otherwise, drive Vashon Island Highway from Vashon Heights or Tahlequah to 1¾ miles south of Vashon town and turn east on SW 204 Street, which in 1 long mile descends to the beach. Turn south on Ellisport-Portage Road ¾ mile and park anywhere on the wide shoulders near Portage Grocery (1910).

Walk the high-toleration shores of Tramp Harbor, leaving behind the low isthmus that connects Maury to Vashon, looking over boat-busy waters to Issaquah Alps. Though several gulches and benches permit houses near the beach, most of the way a 100-foot wildwood bluff keeps the peace. Stubs of pilings speak of the mosquito fleet. Bulkheaded dwellings of Luana Beach break the greenery for ¾ mile, then solitude resumes to the jutting spit and grassy fields of Robinson Point.

Here, 3½ miles from Portage, is a scenic climax and satisfying turnaround. The lagoon is filled but not otherwise intruded, the open fields grow wind-waving grass and wildflowers. Water views are unsurpassed. The lighthouse and keeper's house are picturesque; inquire at the office for possible touring of the light station, with a past dating to 1893.

To put in at Robinson Point for hikes south, drive (no bus) from Portage ¾ mile to a Y. The right leads in 3 miles to Dockton (King) County Park (see below). Go left on Robinson Point Road, descending in 3 miles to a parking area by the keeper's house.

Rounding the corner, the pilgrim's vistas open southward past Des Moines Marina to Tacoma. Now begins the famous Gravel Coast from which a substantial portion of the mass of Maury has been removed. Two barge-loading docks are active, two are in a condition of handsome dilapidation, and others are reduced to piling stubs. The two active pits are awesomely vast desolations. Those recently abandoned have grown up in grass and madronas; in early summer, with poppies, vetch, yarrow, and ocean spray in orange-blue-white-cream bloom, they are winsomely California-pretty. The oldest abandoned pits are so wooded one wouldn't know from a quick look they aren't mysterious features of a natural landscape.

The first half of the 6 miles from Robinson Point to Piner Point is mostly uninhabited, partly due to on-going mining and partly the imposing 300-foot bluff that plunges from the island plateau. The second half alternates between scattered houses and solid homes, notably at Gold Beach, where the removal of the primeval bluff by excavation has created a landscape ideal for subdivision. Piner Point is a wildwood bulge with views across to Dash Point and Commencement Bay, downtown Tacoma and Rainier, and the cruel finger. A nice spot for lunching and turning around.

If stubbornly intent on doing the total Maury, proceed the 4 miles to Dockton County Park. The bluff drops to naught, a hodgepodge of dwellings rich and poor push close to the water, but the narrow waters of Quartermaster Harbor have charm. Dockton Point is rounded; the protected cove is full of pretty boats and cruddy garbage that impedes feet. The park is a good spot to contemplate the heavy-industrial past. The cove once was the site of a floating drydock employing 400 workers, another 200 at other shipyards; many a vessel of the mosquito fleet was built here.

The surveyor gazed upon the narrow, tree-obstructed, boot-sucking beach leading past Burton Peninsula to the Inner Harbor and decided he wasn't stubborn enough to stick by the water the last 3 miles back to Portage; the road is by the shore and has nice views.

Round trip from Portage to Robinson Point 7 miles, allow 5 hours
Round trip from Robinson Point to Piner Point 12 miles, allow 8 hours
Maury loop trip 16½ miles, allow 10 hours

Fox Island (Map — page 183)

A wide, clean, weather-shore beach, walkable at all but the highest tides, is securely wild for miles beneath one of the truly great naked-gravel bluffs, topped by perilously-overhanging madronas. Views are continuously exciting over the water road.

Drive Highway 16 from Tacoma Narrows Bridge to either of the two exits to Gig Harbor and follow "Fox Island" signs intricately but infallibly some 5 miles to the bridge that in 1954 replaced the ferry over Hale Passage. On the island proceed on the main highway, Island Boulevard, some 2¼ miles to a T with 9th. Turn right ½ mile, then left on Kamus a short bit to a Y; go right on Mowitsh 1½ miles. Here the public road turns right and becomes 14th; stay on it a long ½ mile to the end in a turn circle, elevation 40 feet.

No signs bar the way, which has the look of a public street-end and in any event is a much-used beach access. Ignore the obvious road continuing from the circle and walk around a gravel heap blocking a wide trench dug through the glacial-till bluff; a trail descends the trench the short bit to the beach, where presumably was once a boat landing (mosquito fleet?). Just left, toward Fox Point, is an elaborate but long-unused dock on massive concrete piers. Houses are beyond, nigh continuous, so don't go there.

Instead turn right, in a few steps round Toy Point, and pass a small cluster of houses. Then the splendid bluff leaps up 100, 200 feet, so formidably steep the unseen people atop have only a couple trails down. Wildness rules. Vertical jungle alternates with vertical gravel in foreset beds. In 1 mile is the glorious tip of light-marked Gibson Point. Views north to Narrows Bridge and Titlow Beach and smelter stack yield to views south to gravel mines, Chambers Bay, and Steilacoom. Tugs and fishing boats ripple the waters. Iron

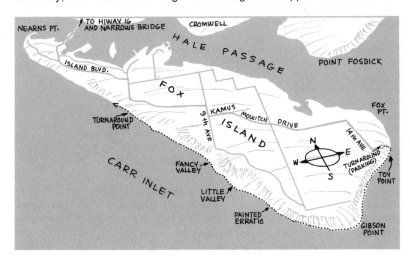

Abandoned dock on Fox Island

horses sound horns on the Puget Sound Trail. Army guns boom at Fort Lewis. Rainier rises high. From here the way rounds into Carr Inlet and the views extend over to the penal colony of McNeil Island and beyond to Anderson and Ketron Islands.

At 1 mile from Gibson Point is Painted Erratic, a monster hunk of granite brightened by children's spray-can art. For a short walk this is the proper turnaround; the solitude, previously total, now becomes intermittent.

Yet still considerable. A little valley with a handful of cozy cottages is followed by a wild stretch. Beyond a bulge to which several trail-access cabins cling is Fancy Valley, a wide beach terrace crowded with houses small and enormous. Wildness resumes and views up Carr Inlet grow, reaching to the tip of Fox Island, the mouth of Hale Passage, and Green Point on the other side. Across Carr are Still Harbor, on McNeil, and tiny Gertrude Island, site of the seal rookery.

At "Turnaround Point," the bulge of an old terrace at 2 miles from Painted Erratic, the survey was terminated by deepening winter twilight and the onset of a storm that took to thrashing the beach with oceanic waves and the surveyor with sideways rain. However, the shore is lonesome ¾ mile more to another fancy valley and appeared attractive beyond, around a bulge 1¾ miles to Nearns Point.

Round trip to Turnaround Point 8 miles, allow 5 hours

McNeil Island (Map — page 185)

Since 1875 there has been a federal penitentiary on McNeil and since 1932 the entire 4413-acre island has been federally owned; the last non-prison-connected resident left in 1936. The facility now is tentatively planned for closure by the mid-1980s. What then?

One may be excused for hoping the entire island is kept in public ownership, a magnificent multi-purpose region-serving park, perhaps with room for other compatible activities, educational and the like. State Parks has pre-filed a request for 1000 acres including Still Harbor, Gertrude Island, and Wyckoff Shoal.

As it happens, over the generations McNeil has become a de facto wildlife sanctuary — and the last major harbor-seal rookery in the South Sound, where are nurtured most seals seen in the region, is precisely on Gertrude Island and Still Harbor. Here too are bald eagle nests and a great blue heron rookery. The Audubon Society recommends that the crucial habitats be assigned to the U.S. Fish and Wildlife Service as a national wildlife refuge.

The debate has begun. The surveyor intends to visit as soon as that is possible without committing a federal crime, possibly as early as 1981. (On one occasion, while walking an opposite shore, he was eyed askance by a group of locals, but at length they conceded, "Well, I guess you're headed the wrong way to be escaping.")

Whatever else is done, the entire 16-mile beach must be kept open to public feet — except where they would interfere with wildlife, which must have absolute priority. Boats have got the whole rest of the Sound; seals deserve one corner to themselves.

Anderson Island (Map — page 186)

Candidly, the charm of Anderson is better savored in pages of Hazel Heckman's books than from roadside views. And the beaches are good but not exceptional. Ah, but the ferry! There's the trip!

Drive to Steilacoom (see Puget Sound Trail) and park as near the ferry dock as is easy. To mention those of most interest to walkers, as of 1979 there are runs to Anderson each morning at 7:40, 9:15, and 11 and each afternoon at 2; returns from Anderson each afternoon at 2:50, 4:45, and 6:30. Arrive a half-hour early to have plenty of time to park and buy a ticket at the restaurant on the dock. Passenger fare (1979) is $1 to get on the island, nothing to get off.

The 30-car **Steilacoom,** built in 1936 at Bath, Maine is the proper scale for the inland sea and takes the properly sedate pace, requiring 30 minutes for the 3½ miles over Main Street — more if there are barges or log rafts to dodge. It's the happiest, old-timiest ferry ride left on the Sound. But to locals it's the new ferry, only acquired from the U.S. Navy in 1976, put in service the summer of 1977. The former ferry, now the standby tied up at the Steilacoom dock, is the

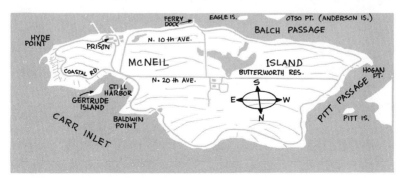

18-car, wooden-hull **Islander,** even old-timier and better. Its backup was the 9-car **Tahoma,** and we're sorry we missed it.

An inch-by-inch survey of the island shore found no public access except at the ferry dock, from which a staircase leads to the beach. So, two choices:

South

Due to a beachside road the first scant ½ mile to Yoman Point, then a 200-foot wall of wildness, trespassing is rather readily tolerated to Sandy Point, 2 miles from the dock; in fact, ½ mile of tidelands are public. The bluff of gravel and varved clay and jungle is nice, and the trickle-creek waterfalls down through masses of maidenhair fern. The view is the feature: the cute ferry shuttling to McNeil Island and past cute Ketron Island to Steilacoom; barges and boats on Main Street; iron horses charging along the Puget Sound Trail; north to Fox Island and Narrows Bridge, south to the wilderness of Fort Lewis (boom-boom-boom) and the Weyerhaeuser chimerical superport and the Nisqually delta; over all, lofty white Rainier.

Just past the new dock of Riviera Country Club is Sandy Point, from which aliens are sternly warned by an old sign. A single house stands on the splendid spit in lonely grandeur. On a bleary November, quiet foreigners might be tolerated the 1½ further miles around the tip into a lonesome cove with a tidal lagoon cut off by a baymouth bar, to Cole Point and its fine tall wall of sand and clay, and the next, nameless point at the mouth of East Oro Bay. From there one can view a bit of the "old island" — pastures edging the bay, farmhouses and barns from another century.

Round trip to Sandy Point 4 miles, allow 3 hours

North

Strictly for misery weather of winter weekdays is the other direction, thickly populated at the start, only gradually progressing to wildness. The beach is

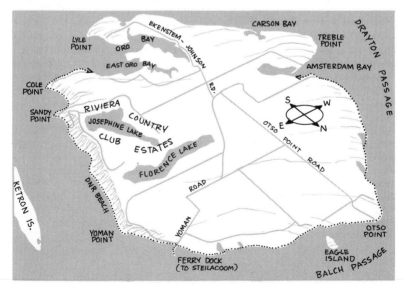

Anderson Island ferry

broken by a series of pretty and amusing little estuary-gulches, and the solitary walker is likely to accumulate a pack of companions, friendly dogs who take the excuse for a jaunt, harassing gulls and herons. Directly across Balch Passage is the McNeil ferry dock and the penitentiary. Aside from that, McNeil appears mostly wild except for seameadow-like pastures and one-time farmhouses now used for penal purposes. The wildlife sanctuary of tiny Eagle Island is passed, and then at 1¾ miles Otso Point is rounded and the intimacy of Balch Passage yields to the wide-openness of Drayton Passage, across which are Pitt Passage, Filucy Bay, and Devils Head, the tip of Longbranch Peninsula, beyond which lies Nisqually Reach. The way now becomes wild and is embellished by the two largest and best estuaries of the route (watch those tides, folks, or be prepared to wade channels on your return). After a brief interruption by houses, wildness resumes to Amsterdam Bay, 2¼ miles from Otso Point.

Round trip 8 miles, allow 6 hours

More
   The island is of a size that a complete circuit might be done in an energetic day. However, Amsterdam and Oro Bays require detours via inland trails and roads. The trip would total about 15 miles, demanding steady pace, good tides, and much toleration.
   The tempting morsel of Ketron Island was not surveyed, owing to a suspicion that though virtually all wilderness, it's so small that the handful of residents would be less appreciative than usual of invaders. Still, the ferry stops there on some runs and the 3½-mile shore might make several great hours, say for a lone walker on a murky February Tuesday.

Hartstene Island (Map — page 188)

Where Puget Sound fritters away in reaches, passages, inlets, bays, and coves is one of the largest islands in the Sound and the least-known. Though virtually all beaches are private, the location is remote and as of 1978 the population is low, the mood relaxed, the toleration high. There's still a country chumminess here; residents are likely to come out not to chase a walker but to chat about the weather or give a history lecture. The canal-like waterways are intimate, the beaches varied by secret estuaries thrusting deep in wildwoods, spits sticking out in the breezes. The entire 30 miles of shore probably are walkable (for the full survey, see the next edition).

Drive Highway 3 to 8 miles northerly of Shelton, 10½ miles southerly of Allyn, and turn east on the road signed "Hartstene Island." Drive 4 miles, over the bridge that at the end of the 1960s replaced the ferry and park on the shoulder.

Pickering and Peale Passages

The bridge footings give public access to the beach. Surveyed only by eyeball, the shore is mostly wild, with rather few interruptions by houses, south along Pickering Passage and then, beyond where Squaxin Island splits the waters, Peale Passage.

Round trip to Brisco Point 16 miles, allow 10 hours

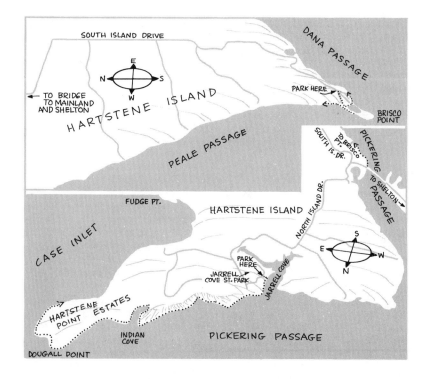

Brisco Point-Peale Passage-Dana Passage

Drive ¼ mile from the bridge to the T and turn right on South Island Drive, which goes 8½ miles down the island to the shore near the south end. Turn right at the water and drive ½ mile more, up the hill, where the public road seems to end in three private drives. Park here, elevation 80 feet, on a shoulder well out of everybody's way.

The righthand drive actually is an unsigned county road that drops steeply to an abrupt end — and that's why the car should be parked up the hill. The public right-of-way continues out into tidelands, so the access is public though the beaches are private.

Here is the island's scenic climax. The spit of Brisco Point juts out in the waves; whatever traffic is headed for Olympia must funnel through narrow Dana Passage, up which can be seen the mouth of Henderson Inlet and Johnson Point at the end of Nisqually Reach. In the other direction are mouths of Budd Inlet (Olympia) and Eld Inlet, and Squaxin and Peale Passages on either side of Squaxin Island. Beyond rise Black Hills and Olympics.

Nice looking. The surveyor was out of time at day's end and so could not do much walking, but an hospitable resident praised the routes along both sides of the island, up Peale Passage to the bridge, and up Dana Passage and Case Inlet to Dougall Point.

Round trip to the bridge 16 miles, allow 10 hours
Round trip to Dougall Point 28 miles, allow days

Jarrell Cove State Park

At the T ¼ mile from the bridge, turn left on North Island Drive and faithfully follow "state park" signs 4 miles to 43-acre Jarrell Cove State Park. Park at the beachside campground.

The estuary fingers of Jarrell Cove halt boots westerly but the other direction is open along the narrows of Pickering Passage. The bluff of iron-stained drift is high enough to guard the beach from scattered houses out of sight in trees. A wonderful mixed forest leans over the beach, making a woodland walk even as the waves lap. Cool ravines break the bluff. In 1½ miles is Indian Cove, with a boat basin and picnic shelters (private). The creek estuary pokes deep in trees, where the green-shadowed creek-aisle can be crossed on a footbridge. (The inland trail system is private; stay off.) After a scant ½ mile of cove-rounding the far tip is attained and in ¾ mile more is the north tip of the island, Dougall Point.

Here the shore rounds to Case Inlet, with views north past Stretch Island to Vaughn and Rocky Bay and North Bay — the end of Puget Sound. For an introductory tour continue ½ mile more, by the dredged basin and picnic areas and whatnot and look south along Case Inlet to Herron Island. The survey proceeded no farther but the beach appears lonesome and open and superb the 2½ miles to Fudge Point. Beyond are more great miles to Brisco Point.

Introductory round trip 6½ miles, allow 4 hours

Moon snail shell

KITSAP PENINSULA

A surprise package, a package of surprises, that's the Kitsap Peninsula. For most of Puget Sound City (saving only the Bremerton and Tacoma neighborhoods, for whom this is the backyard) the walks are well beyond the Two-Hour Circle, and even though much of the travel time can be part of the solution, via Fauntleroy-Southworth, Seattle-Bremerton, Seattle-Winslow, or Edmonds-Kingston ferry, the days grow long. Ah, but the surprises! Worth it!

The Longbranch (Key) Peninsula, for example, between the twin fishhook ends of Puget Sound, Case and Carr Inlets. Thrusting out in Main Street to near views of dense-homed Tacoma-Olympia shores, and within a half-hour's drive of Narrows Bridge, it nevertheless is mostly rural, the beaches largely wild. Amazing. How come? The hiker's faithful friend, the drift bluff, helps. So does the lack of a water supply sufficient to support massive commuter subdivisions. That's one.

The "Narrows Peninsula" and the shores north in the Tacoma-Port Orchard-Bremerton axis have water, and suburbs, and urbs. But also, thanks to noble bluffs, lonesome beaches — one veritably inside Second City. Plus the "battleship trail." Surprise, surprise.

And Hood Canal, holy cow. To be sure, the fishhook from the Great Bend is house piled atop house; from Belfair State Park there is a walk to mudflats of the Canal head, a Momentous Spot but otherwise unappealing except for the peep. And granted, north of the Great Bend the Olympic shore is Highway 101 and that's that. But the Kitsap shore is wow — the longest most purely truly wild beaches of the inland sea. Is there nobody in our society, in our government, who hears the voices of the future, pleading that the opportunity be exploited for the largest, grandest water-and-woods wilderness park of the inland sea?

Final and perhaps most amazing of Kitsap surprises, or bundles of surprises, is the Tahuya Peninsula, named for the long-gone Tahuyas ("oldest people"). On its north are the Green and Gold Mountains, towering over Bremerton as their companion remnant of the "Pre-Olympic Mountains" towers over Seattle, with smashing views up, down, and across the entire **Footsore** world. But that's only the beginning, folks.

The peninsula proper, a plateau up to 600 feet in elevation, scarps plunging to Hood Canal south and west, is something like 120 square miles of second-growth wildland. In the wake of the glaciers the rolling upland is dotted with hundreds of lakes large or small, broad-view or moody-lonesome, ever-birdy, and myriad marshes and peatbogs and swamps and meadows. Also due to the glacier, the gravel soils rapidly flood off the 40-inch annual rainfall, supporting dry-site vegetation. The prevalence of pine — lodgepole, western white, even some Ponderosa — is striking. So are the creekside groves of quaking aspen. Startling are the clumps of Oregon white oak. The understory also is un-Puget-Sound-like, typically dominated by evergreen huckleberry and rhododendron and manzanita. In the meadows during the spring flowering a walker may wonder how he was magically transported to alpine elevations.

The logging that commenced with 19th-century bullteam operations at tidewater progressed via railroad methods over the plateau, finishing before War II, leaving only scattered "long corners" of hard-to-get-at old-growth in ravines and on ridges. The cut-and-get-out loggers let the land go for taxes — and thus the miracle of the peninsula, its last and greatest surprise, the Tahuya Multiple Use Area of 33,000 acres (intermingled with private lands) managed by the state Department of Natural Resources (DNR) under the same statutory guidelines as Capitol Forest (which see). The land is "worked": cleanup clearcutting of old-growth continues even as commercial thinning of second-growth begins; among the charms of a visit is driving through miles and miles of Christmas trees, which grow slow and thus shrubby here on thin-soil sites poor for production of pulp or lumber; everywhere to be seen are commercial brushpickers.

But the use is genuinely multiple with due emphasis on recreation. The DNR has built interpretive signs, vista points, picnic grounds, and 13 campgrounds (good bases for visits by Puget Sounders who live a bit too far for day-tripping); by 1983, using workers from the Mission Creek Youth Center, it will have a trail system of some 53 miles, permitting a walk on continuous trail from saltwater of Hood Canal to the summit of Green Mountain, sure to become a Northwest classic. Ten miles already exist — come in winter for the solitude, in November to watch dog salmon spawning in rivers and creeks, in May and June for the flower show in rhododendron gardens and mountain-like meadows.

Yes, it's DNR land, mandated by the Legislature as giving equal opportunity to razzers. The trails are all-purpose — for boots, hooves, wheels. And there are hundreds of miles of "bootleg" trails built without permission by motorcycle clubs on old rail grades. But walkers must not make the mistake of staying away. As visitation increases and conflict develops the DNR will separate user groups, as in Capitol Forest. But only if there's a demand for it. Don't walk here and the wheelers will take it all. You hold the future in your feet.

USGS maps: Vaughn, Longbranch, Burley, McNeil Island, Fox Island, Gig Harbor, Olalla, Bremerton East, Bremerton West, Duwamish Head, Suquamish, Belfair, Lake Wooten, Holly, Wildcat Lake, Potlatch, The Brothers, Seabeck, Brinnon, Poulsbo

For the free map of Tahuya Multiple Use Area, write Department of Natural Resources, Olympia, WA 98504

Longbranch Peninsula — West Shore (Map — page 193)

A host of South-Sound-typical treats — estuaries, spits, islands. Yet with a North-Sound-like excitement of a weather shore. Much of the distance the views are across Case Inlet to the wild shore of great long Hartstene Island, but farther south are over Nisqually Reach to suburbia of Tacoma-Olympia, a sight that makes the peninsula solitude the more precious. Wilderness! Only a half-hour's drive from the Narrows Bridge, some 11 miles along Case Inlet can be walked with only a few minutes of the total journey spent passing houses. All in all, here are some of the finest beach walks on the Sound. And the area is so empty that toleration is rarely required; when it is (beaches are mainly private) the natives tend to be amiable; the walking is open in any season, any day of the week.

Herron to Dutcher Cove

From Highway 3 or Highway 16 drive Highway 302 to Key Center and there go south on Key Center-Longbranch Road, recognizable by the sign directing to Penrose Point State Park. In 5 miles is the village of Home, a utopian colony founded in 1896; the anarchists and nudists were run out of the country early in this century. Just before the bridge over Von Geldern Cove turn west on Western Home Road, signed "Herron Island." At an unsigned Y in 2¼ miles keep left, descending in ⅔ mile to the shore. The scattering of homes is called Herron. Park on the shoulder by the ferry dock.

Ah yes, the ferry. One longs to ride it the ¾ mile to Herron Island and circle the shores of same, but ferry and island are private. You can look all you want but you mustn't touch.

There's the walk north to console. Cross (not at high tide you don't) the creek-estuary. The several houses atop the bank are left behind and wildness rules between green-jungled slopes and white-splashing waves. Look to boats boats boats, some with pretty white sails, and to Dougall Point on Hartstene Island, up to Stretch Island and beyond to North Bay, end of the Sound. At the turnaround is the peering into little Dutcher Cove.

Round trip 6 miles, allow 4 hours

Joemma Beach to Herron

From the bridge at Home continue south on the highway a scant 1¼ miles and turn right on Whiteman Road, signed "RF Kennedy Recreation Area." At another RFK sign in 2¼ more miles turn right on Bay Road, which leads 1 mile to the Joemma Beach parking lot of Robert F. Kennedy Education and Recreation Area, a DNR site with campground, picnic area, privies, boat ramp, public dock, and a short strip of public beach. No habitations are anywhere near so trespassing off the ends is readily tolerated.

The walk north begins on sandy beach, great swimming, in views south to the mouth of Case Inlet and over to Johnson Point at the mouth of Henderson Inlet. A half-naked iron-brown bluff lifts high, then in ⅔ mile drops to a valley containing an abandoned summer home and a birdy lagoon behind a baymouth bar augmented long ago to form a dam; concrete piers indicate some ancient boat-harbor scheme.

Madrona-overhung bluff resumes, briefly broken by a bulkheaded fill terrace and a dozen cottages. Vertical cliffs are patched by clumps of manzanita, hangings of poison oak. At 1 mile from the first baymouth bar is a second, also enlarged by man, also with a dammed lagoon, herons croaking, but also with a home, a small youth camp, and a bunch of playful dogs. Directly across the inlet are McMicken Island State Park and wild Hartstene shores. Fudge Point catches the eye.

Herron Island is the final feature, its shores paralleled to walk's end at the ferry dock, 4½ miles from Joemma Beach.

Round trip 9 miles, allow 6 hours

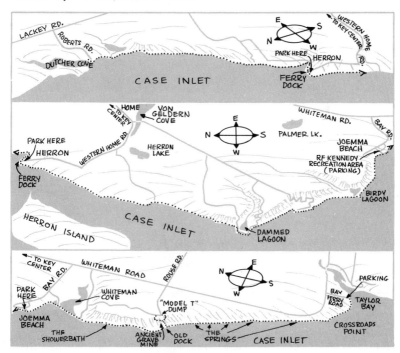

Joemma Beach to Taylor Bay

One of the two Longbranch Peninsula classics. Nearly 3 miles of unbroken solitude would be merit enough but there also are an incredibly ancient gravel mine, two fine estuaries, and a unique phenomenon — The Springs.

Walk south from the parking area at Robert F. Kennedy Recreation Area. Just around the bluff is Whiteman Cove, a lagoon converted to a lake by raising and widening the baymouth bar, a favorite entertainment hereabouts. Forest slopes plunge to secluded waters, swimming float and dock whitely gleam, ducks float. Then jungled bluff commences and the beach continues purely wild for miles beneath the 200-foot guardian wall.

Listen for a waterfall. Duck head under overhanging maples. Ah, The Showerbath! Water pours over a clay cliff, splashes in a basin. Cool, man. And, baby, if it's hot outside, take the shower, there in privacy of the green-lit forest cave hung with maidenhair fern.

At 1½ miles see an odd terrace above the beach, search for the expected kitchen midden, be puzzled by heaps of cobbles, expanses of "moss meadows," and realize the terrace is not natural, this is a gravel mine dating from early in the century. So are explained the stumps of pilings on the beach — the dock. A trail climbs through the mine to a midden featuring rusting car bodies dating to Model T vintage and continues to the bluff top and a woods road from which locals dump their garbage; they also descend to the camps beside the creek under the alders among middens of beer cans and bottles.

Soon beyond, The Springs — finest example of the type encountered anywhere by the surveyor. Some in the open, some under beach-overhanging trees, dozens of creeklets drip and splash down walls of gravel or clay, a continuous series for more than a mile. At a shore bulge where an old road-trail descends a gully to the beach is Best Waterfall; walk up the trail a bit to another showerbath, a 30-foot two-stepper down a clay precipice. The bluff becomes vertical, a garden wall colorful in summer with yellow monkeyflower

Kingfisher at Joemma Beach

around the creeks, and in fall, on drier sites, with pearly everlasting's white and goldenrod's yellow and the evil maroon of poison oak festooning cliffs and entangling the overhanging madronas.

Pause at "Crossroads Point," where the shore bends into the nook of Taylor Bay. Look down Nisqually Reach to the Nisqually delta and beyond to the Bald Hills. Look out Dana Passage past the end of Hartstene Island to the Black Hills. Look back up Case Inlet to the Olympics. As for the water vista, here is the veritable crossroads where Dana, Henderson, and Case Inlets and Nisqually Reach meet. Barges-tugs, and rarely ships, pass en route to Olympia and Shelton; most of the traffic is for pleasure.

Here appear the first houses in the whole walk, and at 3½ miles is the trip end at piling stubs of the dock of the old ferry over Nisqually Reach. To do the hike from here, drive south on Whiteman Road 3 miles from the Bay Road turnoff, turn right on Bay Ferry Road, and park at the deadend.

Round trip 7 miles, allow 5 hours

Longbranch Peninsula — East Shore (Map — page 196)

The lee shore of Longbranch Peninsula is more comfortable than the weather west — not only are winds and waves usually quieter but the bluffs are mostly shorter or absent and cozy bays more numerous. Population thus is greater. Nevertheless, stretches of solitude interrupt civilization and views are superb of waterways and islands and pleasure craft cruising to and from homes and marinas. And on the south tip is one of the peninsula's two greatest walks, a real champion.

Burley Lagoon

Burley Lagoon, at the head of Henderson Bay, at the head of Carr Inlet, has almost as much right as North Bay at the head of Case Inlet to be considered the End of Puget Sound. Thus, as the barb tip of one of the twin fishhooks, it is Momentous. Aside from that it offers an easy and exceedingly popular walk.

Drive Highway 16 from Tacoma or Bremerton to Purdy and turn west on Highway 302. Cross the bridge over the channel of Burley Lagoon and park anywhere on the shoulder of the ¾-mile-long baymouth bar, augmented by riprap to be a causeway.

The lagoon head is 2 miles north; the brush-tangled mudflat shore forbids rational walking. So just look. At old pilings of old booming grounds where hundreds of gulls perch, at paraphernalia of the oyster industry.

On the south side of the causeway walk the pleasant small-pebble beach. Admire the tidal rush through the lagoon mouth. Look down Henderson Bay to the Black Hills.

The west end of the causeway is a put-in for a longer walk. After ½ mile of wall-to-wall bulkheads-houses from Wauna, the good bluff leaps up, man must climb high amid trees to live, and views widen south.

Round trip on causeway 1½ miles, allow 1 hour
Round trip to Minter Bay 6 miles, allow 4 hours

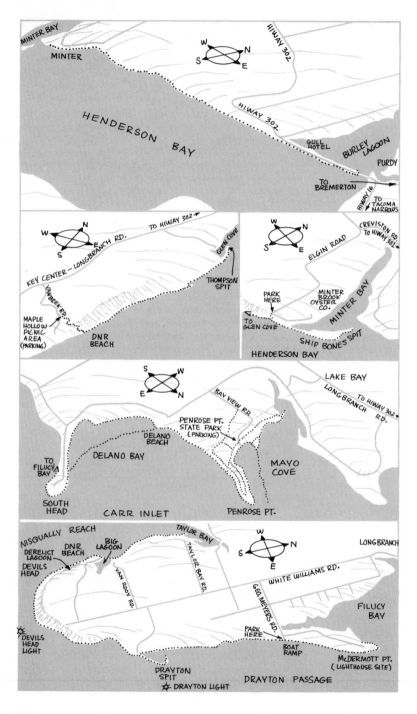

Ship Bones Spit

What became of the mosquito fleet? Here's part of the answer — skeletons of a dozen or more ships, naught left but rusted wrought-iron metalwork and a few bleached timbers, barnacle-encrusted and settling ever deep in sand.

From Highway 16 at Purdy drive Highway 302 for 3 miles and just past a garden shop-fruit stand diverge left on obscurely-signed Creviston Drive. In 2½ miles, shortly after crossing the estuary of Minter Creek, turn left on Elgin South Road. In 1½ miles, where it turns sharp right, park on a shoulder atop a 100-foot bluff.

Solely for times of tolerated trespassing, the walk begins on a private road-become-trail that drops to the beach and is on private beach the whole way — at the end, on oyster grounds where a person wearing a rucksack may be suspected of attempted grand larceny (the rule is, don't bend over).

After ¼ mile of wild bluff two beach-side houses must be passed — or not passed if the owners come out and shoo you away. Then commences the wonderful ½-mile baymouth bar that nearly closes off Minter Bay. Views are splendid into the cute little cove and Minter Brook Oyster Company (which may be visited after the walk to **buy** fresh oysters) and out to Raft and Cutts Islands, north to Burley Lagoon, and far south down Carr Inlet to goshamighty Rainier looming whitely high. The salt flora in the driftwood interest. But the feature is the dead ships. Presumably the stripped hulks were beached here to provide oyster habitat. In any event they form striking patterns of rib cages in the waters, the sands.

For more walking from the same put-in, the beach south is sparsely populated the 1¾ miles to Glen Cove.

Round trip to spit 1½ miles, allow 1 hour
Round trip to Glen Cove 3½ miles, allow 2 hours

Maple Hollow Picnic Area

Bless your heart, DNR! One feels ashamed for ever saying you have no soul. The nature trail on this wildwooded hillside was designed with tender loving care. Worth a trip even if one doesn't visit the beach, of which ⅓ mile is public.

Drive Highway 302 to Key Center and go off on the Longbranch Road, signed "Penrose Point State Park." In 3 miles turn left on Vanbeek Road. In a long ¼ mile turn left at a "Maple Hollow" sign; in a short bit is the parking area, elevation 150 feet.

The trail switchbacks and meanders down the steep hillside to the beach, and even with two sidetrips on loops totals a round trip of only maybe ½ mile. But good, but good. In mystic depths of the green are springboard-notched, monster stumps of long-ago-logged cedars and firs, mingled with old-growth wolf firs, some up to 8 feet in diameter, wow, and canopies of tall, mossy maples, and understory of swordfern and evergreen huckleberry. Stairs lead from picnic ground to beach.

The way south to Home on Von Geldern Cove is quite solidly populated, unattractive. North, though, is mostly wild the 3 miles to Thompson Spit at the mouth of Glen Cove. Look south to Penrose Point and South Head, green pastures of McNeil Island, Fox Island, Steilacoom gravel mines. Look across to Raft Island and cupcake-like Cutts Island.

Round trip to Glen Cove 7 miles, allow 5 hours

Maple Hollow Picnic Area

Penrose Point State Park

Only 146 acres? Impossible! What with inlet dips and peninsula juts, at low tide there are 2 miles of public beach. And the paths that loop around in big-tree virgin forest total golly knows how many miles. A long day is scarcely enough to sample this compact treasure trove.

Drive from Key Center on Longbranch Road, following state park signs that render unnecessary any description of the 8 miles twisting and turning through Home and Lakebay to the park entrance. In ¼ mile, past headquarters and campgrounds (82 sites), the entrance road Ts. For the recommended complete tour turn right ¼ mile to the picnic area parking.

First, Mayo Cove. By the privies find a trail through the mixed forest to one of the campground parking areas and down to the dock. Admire the picturesque estuary and then circle back via either beach or the bank-top path, returning to the start to complete a 1¼-mile loop. (At low tide a miraculous bar emerges in the middle of the cove; the sidetrip out and back amid sands and gulls, ducks and crows, adds nearly 1 mile.)

Now, the point. Round the swimming-beach cove, cross a trickle-creek at the mouth of a tiny lagoon ("ark! ark!" squawk the herons), walk the little spit to the start of low bank topped by madrona and fir — and poison oak, gaudy red in fall, a peril to pickers of the black-fruited evergreen huckleberry. In ¾ mile is the tip of Penrose Point. Look up Carr Inlet, across to Fox Island, down to McNeil Island; between Fox and McNeil see the pulpmill plume at Chambers Bay and gravel mines on the Puget Sound Trail. Continue a scant ½ mile from the point, past a grassy terrace with shells of a kitchen midden, and spot a trail obscurely marked with a sign, "underground cable."

Now, the forest primeval. A network of paths has been tunneled through the peninsula's wildwoods to make it seem enormously larger than it is. Just inland from the beach, turn left on one trail — or a bit beyond, right on another. Either way, loop around and then take the other loop. Often the way is on a bank close above the beach, trenched in head-high salal and huckleberry. Often the way is in cool-shadowed alder-maple-swordfern, or madrona groves, or old-growth Douglas fir up to 6 feet in diameter. A straight shot from the beach to the picnic parking area is only ⅓ mile but wiping out the whole trail system adds 2 miles. Do it.

Complete tour 6 miles, allow 4 hours

South Head

A lovely gooky bay mudflat, a peninsula thrusting far out in the water, and then miles of mostly wild beaches along Pitt Passage, with close views of McNeil Island.

From the trail south of Penrose Point (see above) continue south on the beach. Wildness yields to cottages and grand old houses of Delano Beach. At medium tides the head of Delano Bay must be rounded, crossing a trickling creek to the resumption of tanglewood-guarded beach; at low tide there is an elegant shortcut over the mudflats, squishing along far from land, out amid the clams and gulls and peep. Mainland is regained, and a 100-foot bluff. At 2 miles (or via shortcut 1½ miles) is South Head, with views down to Pitt Island in Pitt Passage, separating the peninsula from McNeil Island.

The surveyor did not proceed farther, being disconcerted by learning from shore folk, at first quite surly, that they had taken him for a convict who had just crawled out of the brush and paddled a driftwood log over Pitt Passage and squished through a mudflat; critics, critics, everywhere critics who don't know high-style beach garb when they see it. In any event, the beach appeared virtually all wild, and fascinating, the 4 miles to Mahnckes Point at the mouth of Filucy Bay.

Round trip to South Head 4½ miles, allow 3 hours
Round trip to Mahnckes Point 12½ miles, allow 8 hours

Filucy Bay

A classic spit, a lighthouse site, a charming bay, and water vistas.

From the bridge at Home (see above) continue on the highway south 4½ miles to old Longbranch on Filucy Bay. Continue 1¼ miles on White Williams Road and turn east on George Myers Road (the sign is easy to miss), which in ¾ mile deadends at a public boat-launch. Park on the shoulder.

Walk north under a rusty-gravel wall from whose top leans a spreading madrona. In fall the fruit of evergreen huckleberry (sweet) and bitter cherry (bitter) tempt, the wine-red leaves of poison oak warn to admire from a distance. The bluff lowers to a cluster of cottages, rises again, and drops to naught at McDermott Point. On the tip of the spit is the concrete octagon foundation of the vanished lighthouse, amid scotchbroom and grass where once grew a kempt Coast Guard lawn.

Views are smashing. Around the corner is many-armed Filucy Bay, to whose green shores cling old houses of Longbranch, whose moored boats dot the bay. Up Pitt Passage, leading to Carr Inlet, is little Pitt Island. The forests and fields and beaches of McNeil Island make the feet itch thinking of the time when the penal colony is terminated. In Balch Passage, the slot between McNeil and Anderson Islands, is tiny Eagle Island; out the slot are Main Street and the Puget Sound Trail.

Round trip 2 miles, allow 1½ hours

Devils Head

Close views of islands, a classic spit, a headland out in Main Street traffic, two lights, two baymouth bars with lagoons, and a charming bay. A busy walk — among the greatest of all beach walks on the Sound.

From the George Myers boat-launch (see above) walk south. In the first 1 mile are trails and bulkheads and the genteel decay of the once-palatial Kraemer Estate, but only a couple of small houses. Wild bluff then rises, maples arching over the beach. The first spectacular is Drayton Spit, hooking north to enclose a lagoon. Out in Drayton Passage is Drayton Light. Across is Anderson Island, whose entire west shore is paralleled on this trip, from Otso Point past Amsterdam Bay to Treble Point. Sidetrip ¼ mile out to the spit tip — the gulls won't like your intrusion but the exercise will do them good. At the base of the spit are a big lawn and private picnic shelter; don't loiter.

In a scant ½ mile are a private boat-launch and the bulkhead and lawns of a development, quickly passed. Now the bluff leaps to over 200 feet and the walls of vertical clay and jungle ensure solitude. In the next 1 mile Devils Head Light is passed and the shore rounds to its apex, wild and bluff-guarded Devils Head, the tip of Longbranch Peninsula.

Don't rush away. It's a Momentous Spot. Drayton Passage has been left for broad seascapes of Nisqually Reach, views extending past Anderson Island to the Nisqually delta and the greenland from which come the booms of Fort Lewis war games, and to Johnson Point at the mouth of Henderson Inlet, and to Case Inlet and Hartstene Island. Here in "The Crossroads" see tugs and barges, fishing boats, pleasure boats, a few sailboats, and, if lucky, that nostalgic anachronism, a rowboat.

Now for the bayshore bars. In ¼ mile is the first, enclosing a lagoon where two derelict houses sag into the forest beside the mud and driftwood. In ½ mile is the next, with an increment of human fill to make it a lake drained by a small creek. Beware of croaking herons, quacking ducks, squealing killdeer. A house atop the bluff warns of impending civilization, but solitude resumes the final ¾ mile to Taylor Bay, where one may ponder pilings of the long-gone ferry dock, memories of the golden age of the Water Road.

Round trip 8 miles, allow 6 hours

Kopachuck State Park (Map — page 201)

Old forest and pretty beach and fine views over Carr Inlet.

Drive Highway 16 from Tacoma Narrows Bridge to the Gig Harbor vicinity. Take either of the two exits signed "Kopachuck State Park" and follow those infallible signs through an intricate route some 6 miles to the entrance. Pass the campground (41 sites) to the parking area, elevation 150 feet.

The 109-acre park is a maze of paths up and down and along the slope, through big firs and spruces and cedars and maples. The ½ mile of public beach gives views past cupcake-cute Cutts Island to Raft Island and over to

Penrose Point and Glen Cove. In good toleration season a person might venture south another mile on private beach into Horsehead Bay — but never on nice sunny weekends.

Round trip 2-4 miles, allow 1-3 hours

The Narrows (Map — page 202)

Incredible. In the very suburbs of Tacoma are 6 miles of beach with but a single solitary house on the shore — located at the single solitary ravine breaching the 200-300-foot cliffs that plummet to the water. And the view is across the skinniest section of Puget Sound's main channel to that brave jungle-bluff wildland extending from Point Defiance to Titlow Beach. Inside the city, and lonesome! Well, not entirely. There are close looks at pleasure boats, fishing boats, tugs and barges, occasionally a ship. And fleets of birds that grab free rides on river-swift tidal currents. The beach is narrow, yet walkable at medium tides.

Drive Highway 16 to the west side of Narrows Bridge and turn off on the road signed "Airport-Wollochet-Point Fosdick." This road loops under the bridge, permitting easy egress from the highway and easy return, from whichever direction you come. Find parking space on shoulders under the bridge or someplace in the vicinity. From the shoulder on the north side of the loop road a trail descends a forest ravine to the beach, which invites walks in both directions.

South to Point Fosdick

Yes, people live atop the bluff, but except for barking dogs and occasional paths you'll never know they're there. The only habitation on the beach is in the ravine at ½ mile. Fir and madrona lean over the beach, decorated with red-in-autumn poison oak; maple and alder arch over. "Ark! Ark!" go the herons, "Splash! Splash!" go the leaping salmon, "Hor-or-or!" go trains on the Puget Sound Trail, a mile away across the water. In 2 miles the bluff drops to a mere bank at Point Fosdick and houses crowd the shore so the heck with it. Enjoy views over Hale Passage to Fox Island, up to the mouth of Wollochet Bay, and turn back, enjoying the graceful arch high above the water.

Round trip 4 miles, allow 3 hours

North to Gig Harbor

Wild all the way — blufftop mansions out of sight, and the city across the way also. Just water and woods and fishing boats ambushing salmon. True, one work of man is evident, indeed dominates — the bridge — but that is in fact a chief glory of the walk.

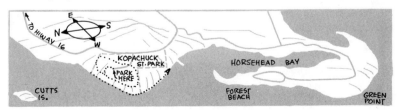

At 1 mile is Point Evans, with a light and a non-drivable woods road down the precipice — probably to become a private beach access for some flossy subdivision above. For nearly 1 mile beyond the point the tidelands are public, the beach is rugged and dramatic; bare cliffs of sand and gravel form precipices and jutting ribs — at "Squeeze Point" narrowing the beach to a mere 10 or 5 feet at medium tides, nothing at high — beware! Clay and gravel ledges outcrop on the beach. And tree clumps slid from above may force brushfights. The view over the waters is distinguished by the mouth of Bennett Tunnel swallowing up and disgorging trains, the ¾-mile strip of Salmon Beach's below-the-bluff cottages, and the wilderness of Point Defiance Park.

The beach smooths, the bluff becomes less vertical, though still a steep jungle, gashed by several ravines (with creeks and trails). At 2¼ miles the protuberance of "Bulge Point" is rounded, fully opening the view to Gig Harbor and Colvos Passage and Vashon Island. Wildness continues another 1¼ miles to houses near the mouth of Gig Harbor.

Round trip 7 miles, allow 5 hours

Colvos Passage (Map — page 204)

From Gig Harbor to Point Southworth the west shore of Colvos Passage extends some 15 miles around bulges and in and out of coves. The many ravines that breach the bluff permit many a shore village, large or small, fancy or modest, but much of the distance is empty, the beach wild for stretches of as much as a mile. Pleasure craft cruise the canal-like passage, and fishing boats and tugs and barges. Views are over a mile of water to Vashon Island, forest-green and mostly bluff-wild the entire length from Dalco Point to Point Vashon. The beach is private but the toleration level is high in the good trespassing season of winter and bad-weather spring and fall days. A number of put-ins permit a varied assortment of walks.

Sunrise Beach
From Highway 16 drive through Gig Harbor and around its estuary to Crescent Valley Drive. Turn left ½ mile, then right on Drummond. In ¾ mile is a T; turn right on Moller ¼ mile, then left on Sunrise Beach Road, and descend a valley ½ mile to just above the water. Spot a driveway on the left obscurely signed "Park" and proceed to the informal parking area, elevation 60 feet. This is a private park on the old Moller homestead; pay the modest fee for use.

The choice trip is south, in fine views to Point Defiance, ASARCO smelter, St. Regis steam plume, and Rainier. After ½ mile of Sunrise Beach homes is ½ mile of wild bluff. Then, past a shorter row of houses, is 1 wild mile under a

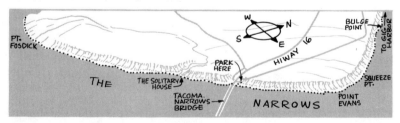

Ruins of Olalla Trading Company

formidable 280-foot bluff. At the end is the baymouth bar of Gig Harbor, the most charming estuary of the region, chockablock with fishing boats and pleasure craft.

North the populated gulches and wild strips alternate the 2¼ miles to Point Richmond.

Round trip to Gig Harbor 4 miles, allow 3 hours
Round trip to Point Richmond 4½ miles, allow 3 hours

Point Richmond

Drive Drummond to the T (see above) and turn left on Hallstrom a long 1¼ miles. Turn right on Point Richmond Road and switchback down ¾ mile to a large quasi-public, maybe public, parking area beside the light.

North is the trip, in views south to Point Defiance, across to Camp Sealth. Past the first ¼ mile of solid homes the way is more wild than otherwise the 3½ miles to Olalla Bay, with only one major valley and several gullies cutting the 100-200-foot bluff.

Round trip to Olalla Bay 7 miles, allow 5 hours

Olalla Bay

The drowned lower length of Olalla Valley, estuary snaking back into muck and trees. The place was anciently inhabited: just south of the baymouth bar are ruins of the Olalla Trading Company, offering (it did) "General Merchandise"; on the hill above is a gracious mansion with cupolas and a widow's walk.

KITSAP PENINSULA

From Gig Harbor drive Crescent Valley Road north to Olalla Bay. Just north of the bridge is a large public parking area.

This is the most dependable (least toleration required) Colvos put-in. Walk south past the Trading Company and immediately onto below-the-bluff lonesome beach.

Round trip to Point Richmond 7 miles, allow 5 hours

Prospect Point

Just north of the Olalla Bay bridge turn right on Banner ½ mile. Turn right on Prospect Point Drive and wind ½ mile down the gulch to a T at the beach. Park here, on the right.

Despite the light (just south of which is a remnant of a mosquito-fleet dock preserved for sentiment, not use) there is no guaranteed access to the beach; the trip is for periods of highest toleration, the most dismal days. Mention is mandatory, though, because the walk north is the best on Colvos. In ¾ lonesome mile is the handsome empty spit of Anderson Point. In a scant 1½ miles more, wild below the 200-foot wall, is Command Point, with the first sizable settlement. A final ½ mile leads to the wide valley of Fragaria Creek,

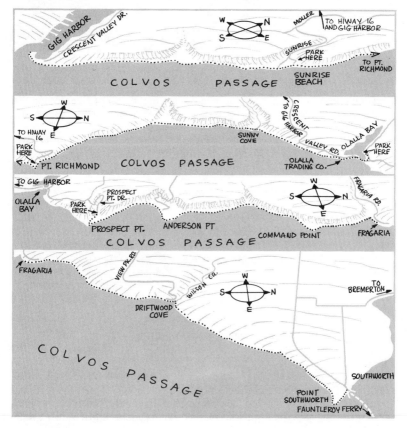

where the old village of Fragaria is built on saltmarsh and pilings, old and distinctly unwealthy.

Round trip to Fragaria 5 miles, allow 3 hours

Southworth Point
Now for something completely different in the way of approach. Park at Fauntleroy in West Seattle and walk on the ferry to Vashon Island and Southworth Point.

Walk off at Southworth, easily gain access from ferry dock to beach, and head south. Around the corner is a fine, grassy spit. Views are north to Blake Island, across to Point Vashon, whence appear ferries. Beyond Main Street is the densely-populated Seattle shore, with the Green Mile of Lincoln Park, Alki Point, the mouth of Elliott Bay.

At 2¼ miles, mostly lonesome, is Driftwood Cove at the mouth of Wilson Creek. Houses. Several more settlements come to or near the water in the next 2 miles to Fragaria.

Round trip to Fragaria 8½ miles, allow 6 hours

Manchester State Park (Map — page 205)

Nobody who has ridden the ferry through Rich Passage, close by rocky-tipped, hill-topped Middle Point, can but wish to visit.

One approach is via Seattle-Bremerton ferry, Port Orchard, Annapolis, along the extravagantly scenic shore of Sinclair Inlet and Rich Passage. Another is via Fauntleroy-Southworth ferry, Harper, Manchester, along the extravagantly scenic shore of Yukon Harbor. Another is via Tacoma Narrows Bridge and Highway 16 to either of these approaches, both of which become Beach Drive. From the north at a long ½ mile from Point Glover on Rich Passage, and from the south about 2 miles from Manchester, turn east on Hilldale Road into the park and through it to the parking area.

Still under construction as of early 1979, the 111-acre park, former part of Fort Ward (which occupied both shores of Rich Passage) is scheduled to be opened by early 1980. A trail system of some 2 miles, unbuilt at time of the survey, will sample the forest interior and the shore.

The shore walk is short but sweet, every step, so take each slowly. The way

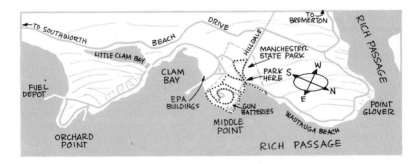

Manchester State Park

partly rounds Middle Point, a 90-foot hillock that was an island when sealevel was a dozen feet higher; in the forest valley that was the cutting-off waterway is Building 63, a handsome brick edifice from military days that will be preserved, converted to a picnic shelter. Underground concrete vaults remain of the gun battery that — with the guns of Fort Ward on Bainbridge Island — prevented foreign navies, the swine, from bombarding Bremerton. A concrete wall on the shore anchored the south side of the anti-submarine nets that impeded ferry traffic during World War II. The sedimentary outcrops (in this area is virtually the only hard rock on Puget Sound) enclose little nook beaches, jut out in picturesque buttresses. Madronas overhang the waters — and poison oak is insidiously everywhere, beware, beware.

The special feature of the views is the big white superferry thrashing past just offshore, but there are also long looks out to Blake Island and the Green Mile of Lincoln Park in Seattle.

Adjoining the park on Clam Bay is a new laboratory constructed by the federal Environmental Protection Agency. Beyond, on the larger, higher former island now Orchard Point, is the Navy's Manchester Fuel Depot — there, when as happens to all warlike arrangements, time renders these obsolete, is the supreme park.

Round trip 4 miles, allow 2½ hours

Bremerton (Map — page 207)

The Edmonds-Port Townsend new serendipity aside, the trip to Bremerton is the longest sea voyage (55 minutes) in the Washington State Highway System south of the San Juans, and the most intricate and entertaining, the behemoth ferry heeling over as it whips around sharp turns in Rich Passage. And Bremerton is the wateriest city of the inland sea — glance at a map and gasp at all those inlets and bays and ports and narrows and coves. Indisputably you need a boat to get to the heart of this matter. However, by boot (or sneaker, or sandal) a visitor can richly sample the essence.

The city Parks Department plans an extensive system of paths; even now residents have a wealth of fine pedestrian exercises available. The trips suggested here are for foreigners arriving from across the waters. The joy of the affair is leaving wheels far across those waters, using the ferry as if it were a bloated survivor of the mosquito fleet. One has a vagabond feeling, slinging rucksack on shoulder and running away to sea. One has a subversive feeling, playing hooky from the automobile.

Park on Alaskan Way in Seattle (or better, arrive by Metro bus), pause to admire the Tsutakawa fountain, and catch the ferry, 85¢ (cheap) each way. The going-and-coming 2-odd hours from the largest city on Puget Sound to the wettest, the busiest harbor to the most warlike, in themselves make the day a success — the two waterfronts, boats and ships of Main Street, long looks up and down the Sound, to Olympics and Cascades. Play your cards right and you can add a sunset over the mountains and the evening light show of downtown Seattle, nova of the Northwest.

Sinclair Inlet and USS Missouri

One of the city's two major inlets. And the only 45,000-ton battleship on a **Footsore** trail.

From the ferry terminal exit left on 1st to a sign, "To **USS Missouri,** Bus 3, 9:45 a.m. to 5:45 p.m., quarter to the hour." The "Mo" visiting hours are: Memorial Day-Labor Day, daily 10 to 8; Labor Day-Memorial Day, noon to 4 weekdays, 10 to 4 weekends.

Subs, destroyers, carriers, and battlewagons are included in the 25 "Naval

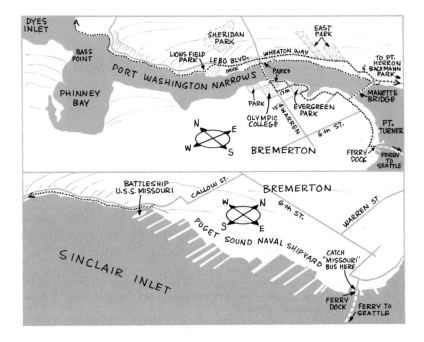

*U.S.S. Missouri, the only 45,000-ton battleship in **Footsore** territory*

Inactive Ships." The star is the "Mighty," mostly mothballed and closed to touring, but offering the surrender site, one of the main batteries of 16-inch guns, secondary batteries, the high-thrusting bow with monster anchor chains, and a museum.

Spend an hour aboard. Then, for perspectives on warship and city, walk a mile or so along the railroad trail down the shore of Sinclair Inlet. Bus back to the ferry. If schedule permits, in the terminal browse the Puget Sound Naval Shipyard Museum (open Wednesday-Sunday afternoons to 4).

Round trip 3 miles, allow 3 hours

Port Washington Narrows and Dyes Inlet

Walk the length of Port Washington Narrows from Dyes Inlet to Port Orchard Bay, crossing the waters on two high-in-the-sky, big-view bridges.

Turn right from the ferry terminal and invariably take the street (names are inconsequential) closest to the water; do this for ½ mile, then stay left and pass the Manette Bridge — the loop return. In ½ mile more enter Evergreen Park; poke along the Narrows shore, looking one way to Manette Bridge, the other to Warren Avenue Bridge. The latter is reached in ½ mile, walking from the park up 17th, then right on Warren. The view from the span 100 feet above the Narrows is superb: one sees that Bremerton, like Seattle, is built on hills of the "Pre-Olympic Range" whose best-known remnants are the Issaquah Alps and the Green and Gold Mountains; the latter are here a foreground for Olympics from Zion to Constance to The Brothers; the other way, see Manette Bridge and downtown Bremerton.

After ⅓ mile of bridge and approach, descend steps to Lebo Boulevard. For a mandatory sidetrip, head left. In a scant ½ mile drop through kempt greens-ward of Lions Field Park to the water; added to Olympic views is the tip of Rainier. In ⅓ mile the park beach ends but the sidetrip should continue another 1¾ miles. Two options: at high tide walk the shore road; at medium tides walk the beach under leaning madronas, past across-Narrows Phinney Bay and Bass Point, the tip of Rocky Point Peninsula, to the opening-out into great wide Dyes Inlet, a fine prospect of bays and peninsulas.

Returned to Warren Avenue Bridge one has two choices: at high tide walk Wheaton Way 1 long mile to Manette Bridge (views of water and mountains from lawns of an apartment-house complex are smashing); at a lowish-medi-um tide descend beneath the bridge to the water and walk skinny beach, with an easy return up to Manette Bridge.

Now, another essential sidetrip. Walk from the one-time separate town of Manette (site of first school in Kitsap County and before that an Indian racetrack), following the nearest-shore street, a long ½ mile to the Narrows mouth at Point Herron and around to tiny Bachmann Park. Here is the spot to watch the ferry tearing through Port Orchard Bay. (In middle tides of toleration season one can sidetrip farther — along private beach 2 miles to Illahee State Park, which see.)

The final 1 mile has a final thrill — views from Manette Bridge, which in the 1920s replaced the Manette ferry.

Loop trip with sidetrips (except Illahee State Park) 9 miles, allow 6 hours

Port Orchard Bay (Map — page 209)

In the north suburbs of Bremerton are two fine walks, a short stroll in a state park combining splendid old forest and a nice beach, and a long lonesome ramble on beneath-the-bluff wild beach.

Illahee State Park
Salt shores are enhanced by big-tree forest, and vice versa. Masses throng the 75-acre park (25 campsites) on fine weekends; try it on a bright spring morning or a moody winter afternoon.

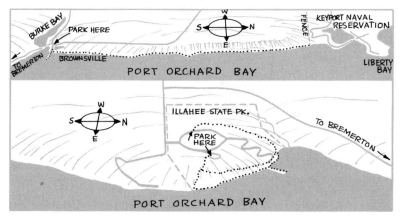

From Burwell, the new name for 6th Street (Highway 304), in Bremerton turn north on Warren Avenue (Highway 303) and follow state park signs infallibly to the entrance. Descend the loop road, passing a parking area with trailhead and a sideroad to the beach parking area. For the best walk continue on the loop to another parking area and trailhead, elevation 260 feet.

Descend a great gulch in gorgeous maples and firs a scant ½ mile to the beach. Lolligag south along the sands, with a sidetrip out on the dock for maximum views up and down Port Orchard Bay, across to Bainbridge Island, and to ferries rocketing through Rich Passage. In ⅓ mile, when a fence bars the beach to public feet, climb the trail high on the precipitous bluff. What seems to be the gully of an ancient logging skidway is passed. And Douglas firs up to 5 feet in diameter, and cedars and maples and ferns — the climax is a fir snag, bark still on, 9 feet in diameter, wow. Return to beachside picnic area and parking and climb back up the great gulch.

Round trip 2 miles, allow 1½ hours
High point 260 feet, elevation gain 400 feet

Burke Bay to Liberty Bay

Most of this vicinity lacks the standard shore-defense (against houses) system and thus the beaches are insufferably populated. Here, though, a drift bluff leaps up a dandy 200 feet, giving the longest lonesome walk hereabouts; trespassing usually is amiably tolerated.

From the turnoff to Illahee State Park continue north on Illahee-Browns-ville-Keyport Road 5½ miles to the bridge over the estuary of Burke Bay. Just across, turn right to spacious parking areas of the large marina; park out of the way of the customers.

This is Brownsville, terminal of the long-ago ferry from Fletcher Bay on Bainbridge that permitted sailors on leave and Navy Yard workers to commute from the island; it is also historic as the end of the Long Swim by the surveyor's father, who while with his girl friend on waters of Fletcher Bay jumped out of the rowboat fully clothed and set out, for the hell of it.

A public fishing dock and float ("Use At Your Own Peril"), reached by a bluff-edge path behind an old boathouse, permit close looks at pretty yachts and long looks north to Liberty Bay, Battle Point, and Agate Pass, and south to University Point. Access is easy to the beach, alder-overhung, little molested by man at the start and less so as the bluff rises to full height. Views of Fletcher Bay yield to views of Manzanita Bay. Liberty Bay grows, and the Navy torpedo installation at Keyport. In 3 miles the fences of that reservation halt progress at the mouth of Liberty Bay, across from Point Bolin.

Round trip 6 miles, allow 4 hours

Gold Mountain (Map — page 211)

The summit view encompasses Edmonds and Seattle and Tacoma and Olympia and Bremerton, and lakes and islands and saltwaterways and two mountain ranges, and that's a lot. However, the unique dazzler is a sight not to be seen from any other vantage point: spread out close below as if on a map are the "triplet fishhooks" — Hood Canal curling north from the Great Bend to

Telephoto of Mt. Rainier rising above Gold Mountain

its end in Lynch Cove, and the two terminal fingers of Puget Sound crooking north, Case Inlet to its end in North Bay, Carr Inlet to Burley Lagoon.

From Highway 3 just north of its junction with Highway 16 turn west on Old Belfair Valley Road 5½ miles and turn north on Minard Road. Drive 2½ miles, dodging myriad lesser sideroads and motorcycle and jeep tracks, the way becoming narrow, twisty, chuckholey, to a gate. Park here, elevation 800 feet.

The walk is entirely on a service road, gated so four-wheelers can't get in but harassed by millions of motorcycles on weekends. But not on Wednesday. In mixed second-growth the way climbs steadily; stick with the main road, avoiding lesser spurs. At 1 mile, 1240 feet, is a switchback; from the end a rut-trail descends to Mission Lake, whence roar multitudes of razzers on

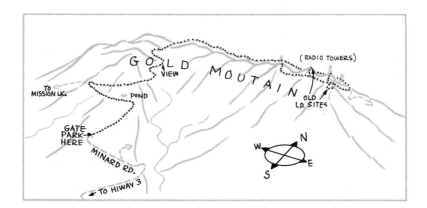

Sunday, but an interesting alternate approach (not surveyed) on Thursday. Windows begin to open, including a big one south from a short spur. Moss and flowers embellish rubbly basalt outcrops, the forest of small conifers is enhanced by rhododendron and copses of manzanita and evergreen huckleberry. At 1¾ miles, 1560 feet, the road crosses the summit ridge and winds along the north side, with windows across the gulf of Gold Creek to Green. In 1½ more miles the road bends around the east end of the ridge and goes west a final ⅓ mile, sprouting sideroads.

Gold is a blabbermouth, sporting four yap-yap facilities; one is worth visiting as the site of an old lookout tower and each of the others offers wide arcs of the round-the-compass panorama, as does the site of a second lookout on the highest summit, 1761 feet. So, there are five knobs to get, all close together; a couple are notable for glacier-polished slabs of vesicular basalt; the spring flower show is glorious.

But not for towers nor flowers did ye come, but lessons in Puget Sound geography. South and southwest are the three fishhooks, and Union River, and lakes and airports and golf courses and forests, and Bald Hills and Black Hills, and the Skokomish valley and southern Olympics. Northwest and north are Hood Canal, Dabob Bay, Walker and Zion, The Brothers and Constance, and Doomsday structures at Bangor. Below, close east, are Dyes and Sinclair Inlets and Port Washington Narrows, the Bremerton Navy Yard and the **USS Missouri.** Trace the ferry route out Rich Passage, between Bainbridge and Blake Islands — and way out there are the shining castles of Seattle. Puget Sound sweeps north past Kingston and Edmonds to Whidbey Island and the pulpmill plumes of Everett, and south past Alki Point and Vashon Island to the pulpmill plume and evil finger of Tacoma and on to Olympia. As a backdrop are Issaquah Alps, companion remnant of the pre-Olympics, and volcanoes from Baker to Glacier to Rainier to St. Helens.

Round trip 8 miles, allow 6 hours
High point 1761 feet, elevation gain 1200 feet
All year

Green Mountain (Map — page 213)

From the mountain range nobody knows, look to the two mountain ranges everybody knows, seen from here in a novel perspective. Also look to virtually every nook of the inland sea from Admiralty Inlet south, and to cities and towns and forests, and to implements of World Wars II and III. In season, sniff the rhododendron blossoms.

Exit from the Bremerton ferry dock and go right on Washington, then left on Burwell, the new name for 6th (Highway 304), continuing on this thoroughfare as it changes name to Kitsap Way. Or, if driving from Tacoma Narrows Bridge, exit from Highway 3 onto Kitsap Way. From the Highway 3 underpass drive Kitsap Way 1½ miles to a Y; go left, signed "Kitsap Lake, Seabeck, Holly." In 1 mile go left, signed "Wildcat Lake, Holly." In 3¼ more miles go left, signed "Wildcat Lake, Holly, Tahuya Lake." In 2½ miles go left on the paved Tahuya Lake Road. Soon a DNR sign announces, "Green Mountain Entrance, Tahuya Multiple Use Area," and in 1 mile the gravel Green Mountain Road (possibly unsigned) diverges left. This is the route.

(However, there is an alternate. Continue on Tahuya Lake Road 2 miles, to just before Gold Creek, and find the new Overland Trail, scheduled for completion in late 1979. Park here, elevation 626 feet. Follow the trail ½ mile along Gold Creek, passing the falls. The way then starts up and at 1½ miles from the start joins the Green Mountain Loop Trail at an elevation of about 1200 feet.)

Drive Green Mountain Road, ignoring lesser sideroads and at one spot crossing the Loop Trail, 3½ miles to a Y. The right is signed "Vista" and leads to the summit; go left, signed "Camp," and proceed a scant 1 mile, passing a trailhead, to Green Mountain Horse Camp. Park at the picnic area, elevation 1150 feet.

For the most esthetic looping, walk back on the camp entry road ⅔ mile, contouring in the forest of fir, hemlock, cedar, madrona, and pine that characterizes the route; mostly it's pretty spindly stuff. In May admire the rhododendron blossoms, in September browse black fruit of the evergreen huckleberry. At the signed trailhead leave the road and follow the upsy-downsy path ¾ mile to the crossing of the road, with a look up to the summit radio tower. The trail now drops gently ⅔ mile, passing a moody stump-and-snag marsh where dragonflies patrol. For the final 1¼ miles the way is steadily and often steeply up, switchbacking above the marsh bowl in larger conifers, and springs, coolwort, maidenhair fern, and (October) chanterelles. On mossy balds of metamorphosed sandstone are gardens of strawberry and alumroot and the first screened views. One feels high. At an unsigned Y of good trails, go right, uphill; the left contours ¼ mile to the summit road. Soon the trail (unsigned, a matter of confusion to loopers from the other direction) emerges on the parking lot just below 1689-foot "Lookout Summit." Total distance, about 3½ miles; elevation gain, about 1000 feet.

Three vista points offer different panoramas. The first is a few steps north of the trailhead by a weathered wood-panel map that once identified the surroundings. Below is Tahuya Lake, west are Hood Canal, with Dabob and Quilcene Bays, and the town of Brinnon, and the peaks of Zion, Walker, Constance, Jupiter, and The Brothers, and the four major river valleys separating them. The second vista is from the rock-knob cliff-edge site of the lookout tower: south over Gold Creek to Gold; north to the end of the world at Bangor; east over waterways of Bremerton to Bainbridge and Blake and

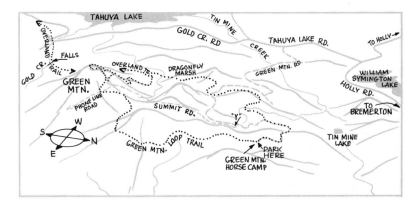

Hood Canal from Green Mountain

Vashon Islands, Seattle towers, and Issaquah Alps and Cascades. Now, the third. Walk from the lookout along its former service road a scant ¼ mile south, by a radio tower, to 1700-foot "Radio Summit." Here on a rock bald amid ocean spray, manzanita, and rhododendron, look across marshy Gold Creek valley to tower-infested Gold and over green-wild, lake-dotted Tahuya Peninsula to the Great Bend of Hood Canal, mill plumes of Shelton, Black Hills and Olympics.

Now, for home. From the lookout parking area descend the main summit road. Pass the old (gated) lookout service road, then a sideroad down right to a small quarry. In ⅓ mile an unsigned trail goes off the road left (to intersect the summit trail in ¼ mile). Here leave the road on the trail right, signed "Green Mountain Camp." In ¼ mile, after crossing the quarry road, the trail hits the unsigned Phone Line Road. A trail sign directs the few steps to where trail (a true one, don't confuse it with a razzer track passed first) takes off left, uphill. The final 1¼ miles are mainly a contour, with minor ups and downs, around the lower north summit of Green, in pleasant forest and wide-view clearcuts. After a total 2 miles from the summit, fairly consistently downhill, an alder swale leads to the trailhead by the red handpump providing well water to the campground. A short bit uphill left is the picnic area.

Loop trip from Green Mountain Camp 6 miles, allow 4 hours
High point 1700 feet, elevation gain 1200 feet
All year

Round trip from Overland Trail 9 miles, allow 6 hours
High point 1700 feet, elevation gain 2200 feet

Tahuya River Trail-Overland Trail (Map — page 216)

Where are we? Surely not in Puget Sound country, scarcely above sea-level? It feels more like a valley 8000 feet up in the wilderness of Montana. The modest river rattles in gravel meanders through meadows dotted with small pines, bright with alpine-like flowers. The trail ascends from its banks the forest plateau, passes silent ponds rimmed with reeds, and at last climbs to the Kitsap Peninsula summit, Green Mountain. No, we're not in Montana after all, but home — yet a part of our home we never suspected.

First of the MVA's system to be built, the Tahuya River Trail is 4½ miles long (surveyor's count; the DNR says 5½). Scheduled for completion in 1979 is the Overland Trail, about 14 miles. Segments of the trails lend themselves to hikes of various lengths from a number of road accesses; these will be described south to north.

Collins Lake Road to Tahuya River Camp, 2¾ miles, elevation gain 300 feet

From Belfair drive Highway 300 west 3¾ miles and just past Belfair State Park turn north on a blacktop road with a bundle of signs, including "Tahuya River." In 2 miles is a major intersection with Elfendahl Pass Road going left and right; go straight on Collins Lake Road. In 3¾ miles, as the road nearly has reached a flat valley bottom, spot a trail on the right, just across from a two-car parking shoulder. (If you cross the Tahuya River you've gone a tad too far.) Elevation, 200 feet.

The way climbs a bit, then goes upsy-downsy along dry-gravel drumlin ridges in rhododendrons and spindly firs and linear-pond bottoms in cool alder, partly on old logging-railroad grade. Razzer trails confuse; stay with the main track, and when there are two "mains," go left, where runs the Tahuya River, your goal.

After 1¾ miles, something different, something wonderful. The trail drops off the plateau scarp to alder bottom, crosses a beaver-dammed slough into copses of spirea, and emerges in broad, big-sky meadowlands dotted with young pines and huckleberry-topped stumps. Sidepaths lead to the river, where ducks swim off, herons cumbersomely flap up and away. The clear stream delights. One wants to choose a gravel bar, take off boots, and wade. In fact, one has a Great Notion of coming here in shorts and tennis shoes on a warm spring day and doing the Long Wade for miles along the Tahuya. It could be done — the stream, scarcely a "river" except in the monsoons when floodwaters roar, has plenty of bars for pausing to let feet thaw. And the Wade is truly wild, for only here and there are banks neared by trail or road. Just you and the birds, and the fish, and the deer, squirrels, and coyote, maybe a bear, even a cat.

But, back to the trail. Through fields it winds, in columbine, meadow rue, fairy bells, blue-eyed Mary, and strawberry, and by hellebore bogs and groves of cottonwood and quaking aspen, sometimes climbing the 20-50-foot valley wall, in pines and twinflower, vanilla leaf, ginger, and coolwort. After 1 enchanting mile the trail enters Tahuya River Camp, elevation 250 feet.

Tahuya River Camp to Kammenga Canyon Camp, 1¾ miles, elevation gain 100 feet

From the intersection where Collins Lake Road goes west, drive north on

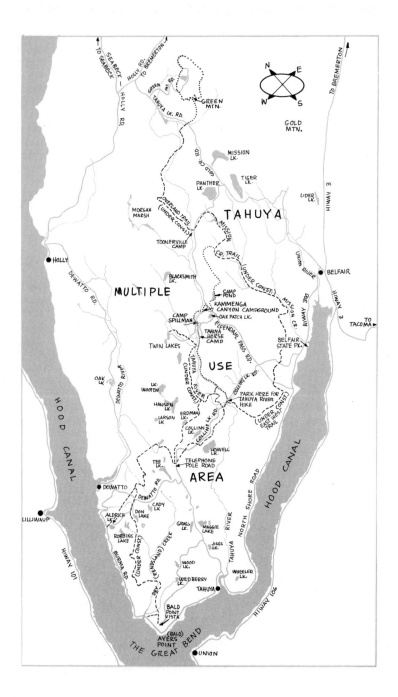

Elfendahl Pass Road 2½ miles and turn west on Goat Ranch Road (commemorating an early homestead, many of whose traces remain hereabouts), signed "Spillman Camp, Tahuya River Camp, Twin Lake." Drive ¾ mile, passing Oak Patch Lake (yes, oaks grow in the vicinity), to Camp Spillman South Entrance (by the river, but no bridge connects to the trail on the far side). Drive a scant ½ mile more to a sideroad right, signed "West Spillman," that crosses the river and the trail and then splits, the left going to Twin Lakes and the right to West Spillman. Continue past this sideroad a short bit and turn right, signed "Tahuya River Camp." In ¾ mile, or 2 miles from Elfendahl Pass Road, switchback down to the campground, largest in the Tahuya and a beauty, in lovely forest beside the delightful river.

The trail upstream climbs to a punily-forested bench above the river's alder bottom and proceeds in ½ mile to the West Spillman-Twin Lake Road. Turn left on this road over the river; the bridge is a great spot to watch discolored, dying dog salmon in the November spawning. On the far side is a junction of three trails. On the left is the north terminus of Howell Lake Trail. To be built in 1981, Twin Lakes Trail will go from here 1½ miles to those pretty waters-in-the-woods. The Tahuya River Trail turns right ½ mile to Camp Spillman, site of a fire camp during War II. All that's left is a garage-become-picnic shelter; a wide gravel bar is great wading. A final ¾ mile, again mostly on bench, in maple-alder forest, with pretty views down to the meandering river, leads to the footbridge to Kammenga Canyon Camp, in pleasant groves of big firs and giant cottonwoods. Elevation, 320 feet. Here ends the Tahuya River Trail.

Kammenga Canyon Camp to Green Mountain Loop Trail, 14 miles

From the turnoff to Camp Spillman continue north on Elfendahl Pass Road ½ mile, turn left on an unsigned road and in a short bit turn right on an unsigned meager track that switchbacks down to primitive Kammenga Canyon Camp. Here starts the Overland Trail, under construction at time of the survey in 1978, scheduled for completion in late 1979. A few clues as to what to expect:

In a scant 1 mile, after crossing Elfendahl Pass Road, is Camp Pond, ecologically amazing. The forest (with primitive camp) ringing the silent waters includes lodgepole pine and oak; unusual in second-growth, here grow calypso orchids. The little meadows of the vicinity are lush with beargrass (really!) and other plants unusual for this elevation. Note old ditches which seem unnatural — they are, having been dug by homesteaders to drain meadow-marshes to make pasture.

In another 1½ miles or so, northern terminus of Mission Creek Trail (which see). Ponds, marshes, creeks, forests. Another crossing of Elfendahl Pass Road, then of Tahuya River. Just before the river, pass Toonerville Camp, named for the famous Trolley; here in the long ago was a logging-railroad reload, the grade later used for the "Lost Highway" that came from tidewater at Dewatto Bay and deadended here for many years, before modern county roads tied it to civilization eastward. Recross river and road. Recross road, cross Gold Creek Road, then Gold Creek — for car approach to here, see Green Mountain. Along Gold Creek past the falls, then up the hill to join the Green Mountain Loop.

One-way trip from Collins Lake Road to Green Mountain Loop 18½ miles
All year

Howell Lake, Mission Creek, East-West, Bypass, and Connection Trails (Map — page 216)

Scheduled for completion between 1979 and 1983 is a batch of trails that will tie the Tahuya country together and liberally sample its pleasures. The accompanying map shows their tentative routes. In subsequent editions they will be surveyed. But why wait? Go now and beat the crowds.

Howell Lake Trail, 1979, 6 miles. From Tahuya River Trail at Twin Lakes Road, parallel Tahuya River downstream and cross several tributaries. Junctions with Bypass Trail. Cross Collins Lake Road and Creek. End at Howell Lake Campground, there meeting Connection Trail.

Mission Creek Trail, 1981, 4 miles. Southern trailhead on entry to Elfendahl Pass Road at 1 mile from Highway 300 near Belfair State Park. Cross Little Mission Creek, follow near Mission Creek upstream. Join Overland Trail about 1½ miles from Camp Pond.

East-West Trail, 1983, 3½ miles. Eastern end at Mission Creek Trailhead. Cross Elfendahl Pass Road and Stimson Creek, turn north to hit the Collins Lake Road at the southern terminus of Tahuya River Trail.

Bypass Trail, 1981, 3 miles. From Tahuya River Trail at about ½ mile north of Collins Lake Road, west over Tahuya River to join Howell Lake Road and follow it north ½ mile. Then go off west to join Connection Trail.

Connection Trail, 1983, 5½ miles. From Howell Lake Campground west. Cross Telephone Line Road, go by Shoe Lake and across creek canyons, to join Aldrich Lake Trail.

Aldrich Lake Trail-Bald Point Trail (Map — page 216)

If much Tahuya country is quiet in mood, here it's bam-boom-pow-zowie. The only argument is over which is the most dramatic, the Aldrich Lake Vista or the Bald Point Vista — both are loud with the exclamations of visitors goggling at panoramas of Hood Canal and Olympics.

According to present plans, by 1983 the two vistas will be linked by the 8½-mile Aldrich Lake Trail, wandering the glaciated upland by marshes and lakes, crossing creeks, including the major valley of Dry (Rendsland) Creek.

Even sooner, by 1981, Bald Point Vista will be linked to waters of Hood Canal by the 1-mile Bald Point Trail dropping to the mouth of Dry Creek.

If there's not much walking to do here as of 1979, there's the looking. Oh boy, is there ever.

First, Aldrich Lake. From Elfendahl Pass junction (see Tahuya River Trail) drive Collins Lake Road about 6½ miles, passing Howell and Collins Lakes, to a line of telephone poles through the wilderness. Here the thoroughfare changes name (but is not so signed) to Telephone Pole Road. In a scant 1½ miles from this point take the sideroad right, signed "Dewatto, Tee Lake." Pass Tee Lake and in about 2½ miles come to a Y. The right leads 1½ miles to Dewatto Bay; go left, signed "Robbins Lake, Aldrich Lake, Public Fishing." In 1 mile is a Y. The left is "Robbins Lake"; go right, signed "Hahobas." In 1 mile is a T. The left is to Hahobas Scout Reservation; go right the short bit to Aldrich Lake picnic area, elevation 560 feet.

The history fascinates. The lake, a pretty pool in the forest, was a log dump in the 1920s and before. From it the logs were sluiced down a flume (its line still

Rhododendrons blooming near Aldrich Lake with Hood Canal and Mt. Washington in distance

evidenced by a gully-like gouge) to tidewater for rafting to mills.

Ah, but the view! From the scarp edge a stone's throw from the lake the forest slope plunges to Hood Canal. Across the waters are Highway 101, the town of Lilliwaup, the peaks of Dow and Washington and Ellinor, the valley of the Skokomish.

Now, Bald Point Vista. From the end of Highway 300 at Belfair State Park drive its continuation, the North Shore Road, to Tahuya. Just past the Tahuya River turn right on the road signed "Dewatto." Where the Tahuya River Road goes off right, stay left. In 2 miles from the shore, spot on the left a little sign, "Vista," marking a single-lane gravel lane striking off over the rolling, shrubby plateau. Lots of luck — there are dozens of forks, some signed "Vista," some not. However, by choosing the obviously most-used alternative, and retreating from new clearcuts when wrong, in 6¼ slow but scenic miles, passing pretty Wood Lake and Wild Berry Lake, you probably will arrive at the picnic area of Bald Point Vista.

Zounds. From the tip of a spur ridge thrusting out from the upland plateau, at an elevation of 500 feet, the slope plummets to Bald (Ayres) Point, jutting into the Great Bend of Hood Canal. For the best looking, descend the slope a bit to an open grassy slope. Amid manzanita and evergreen huckleberry and rhododendron, sit and gaze. To boats stirring white wakes in blue water. To Annas Bay and the wide delta of the Skokomish. To South Mountain and the mill plumes of Shelton. North up the canal to the Tacoma City Light powerhouse at Potlatch, and to Hoodsport, and Dow. Across to Union, sufficiently settled by 1858 to have a postoffice, for many decades reached most easily from civilization by mosquito-fleet steamers. The original Union Cemetery was below, on Bald Point; disruption of funerals by foul weather caused relocation on the town side of the water.

Hood Canal (Map — page 221)

Old country. "Head of Canal" (Belfair, now) was settled in 1859, though not reached by overland road until 1918, despite an 1895 gold strike (fake, fake) on Mission Creek. The water road was about the only way to go in those days, and steamers from Seattle called at the major fishermen-sheltering ports of Holly and Dewatto (where, in the mid-1880s, a boat-building enterprise began) and especially Union, the metropolis. When settlers arrived in the early 1850s the Indians had more than 30 villages from "Head of Canal" to Dewatto Bay; they were moved to reservations, such as Squaxin Island, to make room for loggers — by 1876 there were 50 logging camps on the Canal, bullteam operations, logs flumed down the scarp from the plateau to the water and then rafted to mills. The walker still finds traces of Indians, loggers, mosquito fleet.

Beautiful country. The fjord-like waterway voyaged by fishing boats, pleasure craft. Olympics rising abruptly and high.

Even now, mostly lonesome country. Solid houses extend from "Head of Canal" to the Great Bend and have crept around Bald (Ayres) Point. And Highway 101 on the west side is continuous cars, trucks, resorts, homes. But there's a wild side, the east, where deer nibble seaweed unconcerned by the hiker, and crows harass nesting bald eagles, and little creeks ripple out of deep-forest ravines. It won't last, the end is nigh. But it's a creeping doom, the good past will linger a while. Walk now and weep later.

Or maybe not. Friends of the Earth is proposing that Congress protect the treasure by creating a Hood Canal National Scenic Area to be administered by the National Park Service.

Dry Creek to Dewatto Bay

Drive west from Belfair on Highway 300, which becomes North Shore Road. At 17½ suburbia-slow miles round Bald Point and in 1 long mile more come to suburbia's end in the wide vale of Dry (Rendsland) Creek. Park on the south side of the creek and its splendid delta.

(This is an undeveloped DNR site. Eventually there will be a facility of some sort here. In 1981 there will be a magnificent 1-mile trail up the scarp to Bald Point Vista, which see.)

The shore north was a roaring wilderness until very recently, the only overland access by rude and crude roads, prior to illegal construction of a road from Dry Creek to Dewatto. Though a twisty, tortuous lane winding in and out of gullies along the face of the forested 600-foot cliff, the "Burma Road" has opened up the country. Year by year the realtor frontier pushes north. A gloryland is becoming just another expensive piece of real estate. But not yet, by golly, not yet. As of the survey in May of 1978 there were only a couple dozen houses visible from the beach on the whole route, and most were summer cottages; the surveyor didn't see a soul on his tour and was only twice barked at by beach-watching dogs.

From the creek, the far south of Vancouver's 1792 voyage of discovery, walk the ½ mile to Musqueti Point and its several beachside homes. Passing

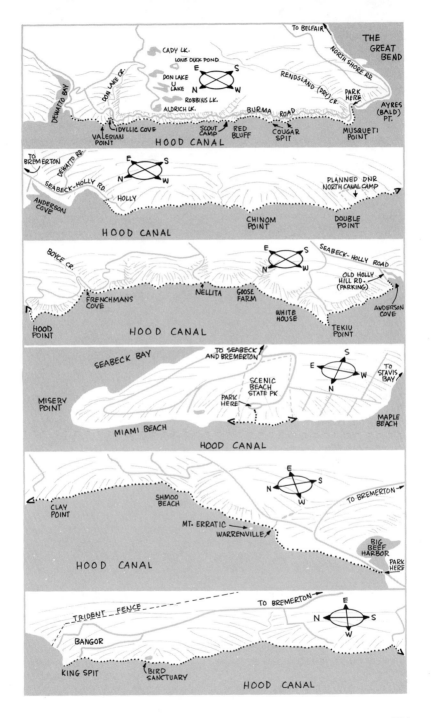

Killdeer

these requires toleration, presently at a high level; should problems arise in future, hikers can drive the Burma Road north past the limit of thick habitation, wherever it happens to be at time of the visit, and find an easy and safe way 100-200 feet down one of the many ravines to the beach. (A major cause of intolerance is the slimy gold on the beaches. As the price of oysters goes higher so do feelings about rustling, virtually a hanging offense. So, leave the shellfish alone. And if chased off by oystermen posses, go away — and find a lonesome put-in from the Burma Road — which also, by the by, serves as a splendid overland return route if cut off by tides.)

Shortly past Musqueti Point the frontier (1978) is reached — telephones and powerlines stop and beyond here only the hardiest folk eke out a primitive existence. Henceforth much of the beach is guarded by drift bluff that always will keep the way wild. But there are pleasant deltas and terraces where Indians once camped and soon the victors will live.

Across the 1½-mile-wide Canal, plied by sailboats and motorboats and oyster dredges, is busy Highway 101. Hoodsport and its valley of Finch Creek stand out, and south of that, Potlatch and the Tacoma City Light Powerhouse. Dennie Ahl Hill and Dow Mountain rise above; above them, Ellinor and Washington.

A long 1 mile from Musqueti Point is charming Cougar Spit, with a pretty creek and a half-dozen cabins weathering on a terrace. In ½ mile more is another nice point with a shack bearing a sign claiming this is the veritable Cougar Spit. In a scant 1 mile more is Red Bluff, with a 120-foot naked wall of iron-stained gravel, an old Scout headquarters building, pilings of the dock where Scouts used to debark onto their Hahobas Reservation; here are the delta-point of a gorgeous creek sparkling out of the alders and a masterpiece of a forest, especially grand in May when rhododendron, madrona, dogwood, and evergreen huckleberry are in bloom.

In ½ mile of wild shore the reservation ends and the shore is crowded (by local standards) — in the next 2¼ miles some seven or eight cabins cling to the bluff. But one never would suspect the Burma Road is above. The shore bulges out, swings in, the forest and waves go on, creeks waterfall to the beach or rush from ferny-green gullies or spread over gravels of delta points. Throughout here, and all the south Canal, the beach gravels are strikingly tawny, unlike the gray gravels typical of the inland sea elsewhere, including the north Canal; the main constituents are sandstone and basalt, iron-stained, from the Skokomish Gravels washed out from the front of an Olympic glacier. This stretch culminates in the gasper of the trip, the bay and estuary-delta of "Don Lake Creek," with a creekside, mudflat-side meadow, an orchard, and an old summer house and two old cabins. What a hideaway! What an idyllic sanctuary! (Before the Burma road.)

In a scant ½ mile from the bay's south point is "Valerian Point," where in May the grassy wall is bright with Scouler's valerian, paintbrush, vetch, and lupine. In the final scant 1 mile are another great creek, a couple more cabins, and the rounding into Dewatto Bay, deepest indentation for miles — and presumably connected by a fault or something with Lilliwaup Bay on the opposite shore.

Admire Lilliwaup town and Washington, The Brothers, and other Olympics, and turn around to begin the 7 miles back, by beach and/or Burma Road.

Round trip 14 miles, allow 10 hours

Dewatto Bay to Holly
Gone from Dewatto Bay is the boat-building industry of 1884. Gone too are the fleets of fishing boats. Old houses and moldering ruins remain — and not much of them.

Dewatto Bay presently is not a hiker's put-in (unless, like the photographer, he has a canoe). Houses block the way south. And to walk north a person would first have to wade the Dewatto River, and that would be easy, but then he'd have to thrash through estuary muck and brush to the outer beach, and that would be madness. A pity, because the beach north of the bay is the wildest on Hood Canal — the wildest on the inland sea. It will not so remain. Aside from residential invasion, the recreationists are coming, the recreationists are coming. At the bay is a public property that will be developed in a few years either by Mason County or the DNR. Presently no public road nears the beach from Dewatto to Holly, but the DNR plans a North Canal Campground some 3 miles north of the bay.

As of 1979, when this stretch of beach is most worth doing, it must be done from the north. From Bremerton drive west by Wildcat Lake (see Green Mountain) and Symington Lake. Just west of Camp Union, at a T, go left on Seabeck-Holly Road. Drop off the plateau to water level at Anderson Cove, pass the Dewatto Road, into old Holly, originally "Happy Valley" and home port of many fishermen, now inhabited by about three dozen families. The problem is ditching the car. There's no provision for invaders — not so much as a road shoulder to park on. This must be done wherever opportunity affords without clogging traffic — maybe 1 mile away at Anderson Cove. However, as of late 1978, where the town entry road intersects Allan King Road, it was possible to turn left, uphill, and find unobtrusive parking in a new subdivision.

In any event, do not park on roadway or in driveways — not only would you mess up the good life for residents but you would bring about an end to the toleration, presently at a high level except in summer. And no toleration of trespassing, no walk.

Once free of the car walk down Allan King Road, by Holly Beach Community Club, to the beach, and turn left. In a scant ½ mile a point is rounded and the last houses passed. The way now is securely wild, guarded by the steep jungle that rises to the plateau at 400-600 feet. At the start the drift bluff has much blue clay and is slidey — in the first stretch the beach is blocked by pants-ripping tangles of seaweed-hung barnacle-encrusted tree clumps. After that the "brown beach" dotted with big erratics is easy open at tides of 8-9 feet or less, often canopied by alder and maple.

The quiet of this shore is underscored by the hum-roar of Highway 101 across the waters. A deer steps out of the evergreen-huckleberry thickets and calmly inspects you. Great blue herons object to your presence — the surveyor saw 20-odd, once four in a gang.

Across the Canal are villages — Mike's Beach Resort and Tree Farm, where the surveyor's father is resident gypo, and Eldon, Jorsted Creek, Aycock Point. The mountain backdrop shifts as the walk progresses, from Jupiter between the Dosewallips and Duckabush valleys, to The Brothers (with Webb Lookout in front) and Bretherton and the Hamma Hamma valley, to Jorsted Point in front of Pershing, Washington, and Ellinor, and at last, past the Lilliwaup valley, to Dow and Dennie Ahl and the Skokomish valley.

The beach curves in to coves, out to points, requiring many foot miles to make any heron miles. The way is enlivened by gulches, ravines, and mini-valleys, most with creeks, some with detlas. Now and then terraces of old beaches are elevated above the tides. At 2¼ miles is the first civilization since Holly, a valley with a couple trailers parked. In another 1½ miles is Chinom Point, most prominent feature of the route, with a valley and delta-spit and filled-in lagoon and a dozen flossy summer homes. Several ancient homes/modern camps are passed in gulches the next 2 miles to "Double Point." By now the bluff has become mainly gravel, drier, with grass slopes and a forest of fir and madrona.

Poignance of a visible past. A pictograph on an enormous erratic. A lonesome apple tree bearing a lush crop of some antique species. Ironware of ancient logging rusted nearly to nothing. A huge stump grooved for a cable, at the mouth of the gully down which bull teams dragged the logs. Remnants of a waterwheel, a primitive hydroelectric plant. Stubs of old pilings, dwellings collapsed to litters of rotten lumber. More people lived here in the 1930s — the 1910s — the 1880s — than now. Met on the survey was an old settler, 77, who told how on his place, a terrace no more than 30 feet wide between beach and bluff, there was in the 1930s a chicken coop 60 feet long — the supplier of eggs and drumsticks to the entire south Canal. Until nearly War II a freight boat ran once a week, down the west side of the Canal in morning, returning up the east side in afternoon, nosing to the beach to load and unload. In earlier decades the Canal was busy with mosquito-fleet traffic and among the settlers on terraces and deltas were many who made livings cutting cordwood for wood-burning steamers.

Just past "Double Point" begin some 2 miles of public tidelands. Here the DNR is planning its North Canal Campground. The survey proceeded only ½ mile past "Double Point" to a camp in a valley, a grand spot to lunch and turn

Hood Canal north of Dewatto Bay. Mt. Washington in distance

around. And so the surveyor did, 3 miles from the mouth of Dewatto Bay, suspecting this was the wildest section of the shore and wanting to save it for leisurely inspection on a walk north from the bay. He ·was foiled. But the photographer, cheating by using a canoe, confirms this is, indeed, the wildest. Better hurry.

Round trip to Turnaround Camp 12½ miles, allow 8 hours
Round trip to Dewatto Bay 19 miles, allow 12 hours

Anderson Cove to Hood Point

South of Holly wilderness is the rule, civilization the exception. Now, north, the balance swings the other way — the bluff relents, lessening in steepness for long stretches, more frequently breached by gully-ramps to the water. However, the mood still is dominantly lonesome, though more frequently interrupted by summer homes and a scattering of year-round residences.

There is only one easy access, at the south end. Drive toward Holly and 1 mile before that, just before crossing Anderson Creek, turn right on Old Holly Hill Road along Anderson Cove. In several hundred feet park in a wide turnout on the right.

The way curves out of the cove around a head. In the first scant 1½ miles to Tekiu Point (including ¾ mile of public tidelands) are several cabins at the

225

start, requiring toleration, then wildwood bluff broken by tanglewood creeks, and one substantial old home. Tekiu Point is a splendid unmolested spit poking out in wind and waves, the views across to Triton Head and up to The Brothers (and Webb Lookout).

The shore turns from a northerly to easterly trend and the route can be seen all the way to the next spit, Hood Point. In a vale is a gracious two-storey two-chimney white house, and in another wide valley with a sizable creek is a comfortable old goose farm where the fowl hiss at beachwalkers. But that's the most of civilization in the 1½ miles to Nellita, a cluster of well-worn summer cottages by the beach.

Herons "grawk!" and kingfishers "ti-ti-ti" and cormorants pose on old pilings. Cedars and firs and madronas overhang the beach. Another cluster of quaint cottages on the hillside, and another picturesque farm — green house amid orchard, big delta of a pretty creek. Wild bluff leaps up again. At 1¾ miles from Nellita is the major valley of the route, Frenchmans Cove, with several houses and, inland, a fine big pasture and barn. Boyce Creek must be lept or waded — or crossed inland on a plank bridge.

The final 1 mile is mostly inhabited. Several cottages are on a bulkhead, a couple more on a bulge, and at the base of the spit of Hood Point are a dozen fancy homes. But go out on the tip and look far south to Holly, and across to Black Point and the Duckabush valley, to Olympics from The Brothers to Jupiter, and north to Scenic Beach and Dabob Bay and the Dosewallips valley.

Though not surveyed, the next 2½ miles to Stavis Bay appear mostly wild.

Round trip 11½ miles, allow 8 hours

Scenic Beach State Park

It sure is. More scenic than beach, but some strolling is to be done. And oh the looking!

Exit from the Bremerton ferry dock and go right on Washington, then left on Burwell, the new name for 6th (Highway 304), and continue on this thoroughfare as it changes name to Kitsap Way. Or, if driving from Tacoma Narrows, exit from Highway 3 onto Kitsap Way. From the Highway 3 underpass drive Kitsap Way 1½ miles to a Y; go left, signed "Kitsap Lake, Seabeck, Holly." In 1 mile go left, signed "Wildcat Lake, Holly." Stick with this highway some 7½ miles to Big Beef Harbor and continue 2½ more miles to Seabeck Landing, whence once the **Lake Constance** ferried Model As and Trapper Nelsons over the Canal to Brinnon. About ¼ mile south of town turn right, following "Scenic Beach" and "State Park" signs here and at the Y (go left) in 1 more mile, in a final ¾ mile entering the park and descending to parking areas near the beach.

An old farmhouse and orchard, a log cabin roofed by moss and swordferns, fine fir forest and ¼ mile of public beach, are the standpoint for the views: Across Hood Canal to Oak Head at the tip of enormous Toandos Peninsula, and into enormous Dabob Bay, within which is smaller Jackson Cove, site of Camp Parsons. Rising above are Walker, Turner, and Buck. Higher are The Brothers, Jupiter, and Constance, the mountain masses cleft by trenches of Duckabush and Dosewallips Rivers. That's scenic.

The 71-acre park is mostly devoted to spacious picnic spots and 50 campsites. In the high-toleration season of lonesome winter the beach walk

The Brothers from Scenic Beach State Park

might be extended in either direction: south 2 miles to Stavis Bay; north 1 mile to Misery Point at the mouth of Seabeck Bay.

Round trip 1-6 miles, allow 1-4 hours

Big Beef Harbor to Bangor

The wild Canal has been left well behind, south. Now the bluffs lower, breaching gullies and valleys are numerous, highways from population centers short and fast, and people cuddling the waves many. Nevertheless, short below-the-bluff stretches are wild. And the valleys themselves, most containing coves-lagoons-marshes cut off by baymouth bars, intrigue, and littoral architecture interests. And Olympic views are continuous and stupendous.

Drive to Big Beef Harbor and park on the shoulder of the causeway that has augmented the baymouth bar. Head what seems north but is actually closer to east.

Beach population is dense at the start, then diminishes. But the time for this walk is dismal winter, not bright summer when toleration is low.

The view is from Seabeck Bay across to Brinnon at the mouth of the Dosewallips and to Dabob Bay, enclosed by the Toandos Peninsula. The mountain front extends from The Brothers (and Webb Lookout) over the Duckabush valley to Jupiter, over the Dose valley to Constance, Turner, Buck, and Walker, and over the Quilcene valley to Townsend and Zion.

Continuous bulkhead quickly ends and a bulge is rounded to the creek, valley, baymouth bar, lagoon-marsh of Warrenville. The offshore mass of "Mount Erratic" is passed, then the concretions of "Shmoo Beach" and slidey "Clay Point" leading to the cove, creek, and valley of Anderson Creek. Fancy homes of Sunset Farm are left behind at 2 miles and henceforth there is more solitude than population. Here the shore, passing the end of Toandos Peninsula, bends sharply due north.

In the next 4 miles a half-dozen gulches-valleys break the bluff, most with a few houses, though one has a wild lagoon signed "Private Bird Sanctuary." Down the 100-foot bluff come paths, even electric trams, to camps or boathouses.

At 6 miles is the trip end, on the tip of King Spit amid driftwood and gulls. Look north to past and future. Past: Old pilings of the mosquito fleet's Bangor Landing, where Bangor Boats on a pier and the mercantile house of H. W. Goodwin on the shore are being restored. Future: The fence, and the home of Trident, and cold-eyed fence-patroling troops who glower at bearded old ragged old surveyors carrying rucksacks and umbrellas, suspecting them of being peace freaks.

Round trip 12 miles, allow 8 hours

Mt. Constance across Hood Canal from Bangor

SOUTH OLYMPIC PENINSULA

Having driven so far from Puget Sound City, will not any sensible pedestrian proceed onward into Olympic National Forest, Olympic National Park, for trails in virgin forests along wild rivers?

Usually, yes. And therefore the survey went light on woods and waters, focused on views. Here in the last chapter of the four-book series is finished the journey along the mountain front ringing the Puget Basin: From Chuckanut south along the Cascades to Stahl, west through Bald and Black Hills. In **Footsore 3,** south along the Olympics from Zion to Jupiter. In following pages the gap is filled, the circle completed.

USGS maps: Mt. Tebo, Potlatch, The Brothers, Brinnon, Holly, Mason Lake, Lake Wooten

Twanoh State Park (Map — page 229)

Yes, you'll want to stroll the park shore and absorb the calm beauty of this quintessential sea-in-the-forest stretch of Hood Canal. But cheek-by-jowl bulkheads-houses prevent long beach tours. However, there's walking to be done — in a wild, green gorge, a grand big-tree forest, on trails that climb the gorge walls and meander plateau-top woods.

Drive Highway 3 to just south of Belfair and turn south on Highway 106 to the park. Park in any of the lots, elevation 10 feet.

On the island side of the highway, on the west bank of Twanoh Creek, find the wide trail upstream into the canyon. Ignore lesser sidepaths up the slope and walk the gorge in large firs and cedars and hemlocks, moss-swollen maples sprouting high-in-the-air ferns. In ½ mile a good trail switchbacks uphill right, signed "Tent Camping Area." Continue by the creek; on a winter day the dripping, hushed valley, treetops misty, has a rainforest feel. Shortly before a major fork in the valley note a footlog over the creek, leading to a lesser trail (not surveyed) climbing the opposite wall. Past the forks the trail climbs steeper and in 1 mile from the highway switchbacks. (Off the end a meager path proceeds straight, to unsurveyed wildwoods.)

Ascending to a plateau-ridge at 400 feet, the trail enters drier woods of small firs, evergreen huckleberries, madrona, salal, and the occasional rhododendron, and Ts with an old fire road become trail. To the left the road goes an unsurveyed distance, out of the park and on and on. To the right it loops back

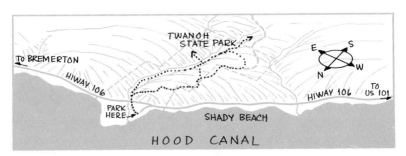

northward past the Tent Camping Area and steeply descends to the highway.

That's a good introduction. But the 175-acre park has more trails. And there are adjoining wildwoods. A walker could keep busy all day.

In midwinter a feature of the trip is the litter of spawned-out salmon carcasses in the creek, filling the valley with a ripe aroma — and with gulls that surprise the woods walker, flying far into the green gorge seeking tasty bites.

Introductory loop 2 miles, allow 1½ hours
High point 400 feet, elevation gain 400 feet
All year

Skokomish Delta (Map — page 230)

The largest delta of the Hood Canal side of the Olympics also is the most scenic. It's additionally the wildest, the lonesomest — a preserve of solitude nearly 3 miles wide and up to 2 miles deep from saltwater to civilization, not counting a couple square miles of low-tide mudflats. Except for occasional cows and oysterpickers, a walker communes undisturbed with plovers and herons and clams. Beach and mudflats can be alternated with saltmeadows that in spring are fields of flowers. Just be sure to pick a tide on the low side of medium or you won't get far.

Drive Highway 101 to Potlatch State Park, 3¼ miles south of Hoodsport, and park.

The first ½ mile is on beach close by the highway; this section can be skipped by parking at a wide turnout. Hop a nice little creek rushing over pebbles into Annas Bay and diverge from the highway into peace and quiet (except for squealing killdeer) onto the delta. Views are grand over the bay to the Great Bend, Bald Point jutting into the angle, and to Union, also on a jut. Close above the shores where lie Potlatch and Hoodsport rises mighty Dow, with Ellinor and Washington higher and mightier behind.

Tidal channels finger the delta; at low water the mud can be walked and trickle creeks hopped over. (Please don't step on the oysters and for golly sake don't pick them up.) Alternate by walking above the beach in fields of saltwort and sea blite and, in May, rosy-lovely masses of seablush.

Views evolve — the Tacoma City Light powerhouse grows prominent, and Dennie Ahl Hill. Cows panic at your approach and hightail for the barn. After a last mudflat squish, at 3 miles from the state park the route ends where the Skokomish River also does, rolling green waters into the bay.

Round trip 6 miles, allow 4 hours

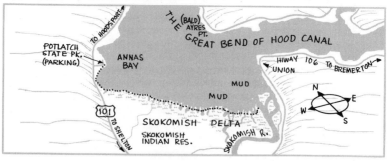

Hood Canal

South Mountain (Map — page 231)

On the crystal-air November day of the survey, five volcanoes were seen and one ocean, plus a Canal and a Sound and Three Fingers, Index, Phelps, Daniels, Chimney Rock, Goat Rocks, Green and Gold, Issaquah Alps, Doty and Bald and Black and Willapa Hills. Yes, and Olympics too. Rising abruptly from lowlands where the Puget Glacier petered out, South is the absolute southernmost peak of the Olympics, a unique viewpoint giving novel perspectives on the full length and width of the Puget Trough.

Drive Highway 101 to ⅔ mile south of the Skokomish River and turn east on Skokomish Valley Road. At a Y in 6 miles go right on road 2260, signed "Camp Govey" and "Seed Orchard." In 2¼ miles, where road 2202 turns right, continue straight on 2260. In ¼ mile turn left on road 2199. Round a promontory (look down to pastures at the upper limit of the Skokomish floodplain), drop to cross Vance Creek (look up to a bridge in the sky — the railroad from Fir Creek Reload). Road 2254 (but signed 5860) joins from the right, as also does the Simpson log-haul railroad, whose cheery old-timey whistle enlivens weekday hiking in all this area. Follow signs, "Bingham Transfer 2, Matlock 8." At 4½ miles from road 2260 is a T at Bingham Creek with no signs; go right and stay on the main road (still 2199), a wide mainline. Pass Bingham Creek Reload (where log trucks transfer loads to rail cars). At 2 miles from Bingham Creek is a sideroad right, signed "South Mountain Lookout 4." Turn up it,

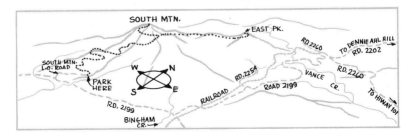

immediately starting to climb. In ½ mile is a big switchback. Park here, elevation 950 feet.

The road is perfectly drivable beyond — all the way to the summits — but the views from the near-naked slopes start almost immediately and demand constant attention. On an early-melting south slope, the route makes an excellent snowline-prober, the views richly rewarding long before the summit. Winding into valleys, out on spurs, crossing saddles, cutting through walls of rubbly basalt and harder pillow lava, the busy, entertaining way ascends in panoramas uninterrupted by the shrub plantation. Flower gardens on lava walls and in creeklets compete for attention — fields of lupine and beargrass especially striking. In 3 miles, at 2750 feet, is a saddle in the summit ridge, adding views north. Left ½ mile is West Peak, 3125 feet, formerly with a lookout tower, now bare and lonesome. Right an up-and-down ridgecrest 1¼ miles is radio-towered East Peak, 3000 feet. Both are essential.

Here on the scarp that without prelude leaps up 2500 feet are views that demand large-area maps and long hours. Close at hand, of course, are Olympics: a foreground of ridges and valleys being totally denuded of trees, one of the most awesome and in a gaudy surrealistic way beautiful scenes of clearcutting in all the Northwest; footstool peaks, Dennie Ahl and Dow; and the rugged heights, The Brothers, Washington, Ellinor, Pershing, Copper, and Cruiser. The East Peak (this is the one you see while driving up the Skokomish) gives the classic look down to the pastured floodplain of the valley curving around to join Hood Canal at the Great Bend. The West Peak (whose basalt surprisingly is capped with conglomerate) gives the dramatic vista to Grays Harbor. Below south is the forest plateau where the Puget Glacier terminated. Beyond this gulf where the meltwater streams flowed, including the Pretty Big River of ice-dammed rivers from the east side of the Olympics, rise the Black Hills, beyond which rolled the Really Big River from the Cascades; beyond that valley (now the Chehalis) are the Doty and Willapa Hills. Close enough below to see the house the Spring twins grew up in is Shelton, mills pluming. Then, saltwaterways, cities, Cascades. The Spring twins spent the night on the summit, viewing lights from Aberdeen to Olympia to Everett, and hasn't spoken a rational word since.

Round trip (both peaks) 9½ miles, allow 7 hours
High point 3125 feet, elevation gain 2800 feet
February-December

Dennie Ahl Hill (Map — page 233)

The prime time for this easy-to-get mountain-edge viewpoint is winter, when snow or the chance of same discourages the tourist trade, and on a crispy-clear day you can see three volcanoes and half-a-dozen cities and towns, plus ice-chiseled crags of high mountains and sparkling waves of low waterways. But then, in June the strawberries are ripe.

Drive road 2260 (see South Mountain) to road 2202 and turn right on the latter, signed "Steel Bridge 3, Dennie Ahl Seed Orchard 4." It's more like 2½ miles to the bridge — be sure to pause for it. Park at the far end and walk back on the airy-scary span over the chasm, the river thundering between rock walls an appalling 400 feet below. Across from the parking spot a good, wide,

Mt. Washington from Dennie Ahl Hill

unmarked trail leads ⅛ mile downstream along the gorge lip to a spectacular promontory viewpoint.

Carry on. Drive ¾ mile to a signless Y and stay left on the main road (the lesser right is to the seed orchard). In 1⅓ more miles, where the main road bends right, go left on lesser, unsigned road 2301. (Elevation, 700 feet — a good place to park on a snowline-prober.) The old logging-railroad grade made forest-management road is easy driving — but also pleasant green-tunnel walking in the quiet season. In 1½ miles suddenly there are signs: the road one has come on proceeds straight, revealed to be 2301011. The summit route is the right, road 2301, signed "Dennie Ahl Lookout 4." In that good old wintertime, park here, elevation 984 feet.

Yes, the road is drivable to the summit, mostly on old rail grades. In the sport season one likely will prefer to drive. Get the views and go someplace else for exercise. Yes, winter is best.

Railroad-logged in the War II era and "planted 1947," the way is lined with second-growth firs that permit few glimpses out from the road, which circles

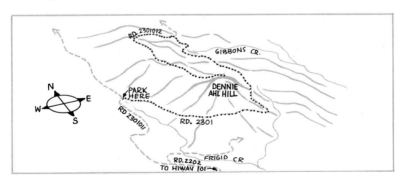

the peak. A tributary valley of Frigid Creek is entered and a saddle crossed to Gibbons Creek, which is crossed. In 3 miles, at 1550 feet, is a T and an alternate parking spot. The left, road 2301012, is signed "Dennie Ahl Lookout 1." It's really 1½ miles, views beginning shortly before the summit, 2004 feet.

Whizbang! The island peak, cut off on one side by the valley of the South Fork Skokomish, and on the other by a wind gap where once a river flowed, sits far out in front of the range. The lookout tower is long gone but the summit is well-pruned. Wander strawberry fields from one edge to another. See up the valley to such peaks as Prospect, Capitol, Tebo, Timber, and Lightning. Across is scalped South. Everywhere are green slopes motheaten by brown clearcuts. North are a bit of Lake Cushman, Dow, a piece of Ellinor, all of snowy-cragged Washington, and the top of The Brothers. Below is Dennie Ahl Seed Orchard and beyond are Annas Bay, Skokomish Delta, Great Bend of Hood Canal, Bald Point, Union, Dewatto Bay. Green and Gold. Black Hills. Mill plumes of Shelton. Olympia, Tacoma, Seattle. Rainier, Adams, St. Helens.

Round trip from road 2301011 9 miles, allow 6 hours
High point 2004 feet, elevation gain 1100 feet
All year

Dow Mountain (Map — page 234)

Cut off from neighbors by two deep valleys, the North Fork Skokomish drowned by Cushman Reservoir, and a wind gap used in the long ago by ice and water, Dow is another island mountain, sensationally located close above Hood Canal and just by the craggy mass of Washington. Unfortunately, as of 1978 the whiskery summit is badly in need of a shave; there is no single mind-blowing panorama, rather a series of nice windows. Also, folks, do this walk in winter as a snowline-prober or in spring before blood stirs in the sports. Dow has become the premier motorcycle heck of the south Olympics, with a slurbful of basket cases at the peak's foot to ensure an abundance of Sunday racket on the mount.

Drive Highway 101 to Hoodsport and turn west on the "Staircase highway." In 4 miles, at the great big gaudy-flagged sales headquarters of great big Lake Cushman City, turn right on Dow Mountain Road, signed "4 wheel drive recommended." To skip the dreary bit, drive ½ mile to the end of houses, up the bottom of the mountain, to a large turnout on the left. Park here, elevation 920 feet.

Park because only a sport could enjoy this steep, narrow lane and ordinary passenger cars eventually would come to grief. But it's a superb footroad when free of wheels. Sideroads branch off left to expanding suburbia and to tree-farming activity but the main track generally is obvious; if you do go wrong

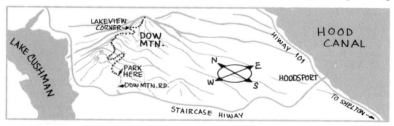

you'll quickly deadend. Below right is loud Dow Creek, to which two sideroads contour to nice spots to sit by the splashing. The road then switchbacks left, out of the valley, to windows down to green Skokomish pastures and blue Hood Canal waters. The only confusing part of the route is at the second switchback, 1700 feet, where one of the many thinning roads in the spindly second-growth goes straight ahead uphill by a road cut in pillow lava; be sure to take the sharp switchback right. After more Canal windows the road, steadily worse for wheels, better for feet, tops the summit ridge and flattens along the viewless crest in 30-foot firs. Then climbing resumes, and Canal views — to the pastoral Skokomish valley, joined by the forest slot of the North Fork, to Stevens and Rose Lakes, the Skokomish Delta in Annas Bay, and the Great Bend into which juts Bald Point. Hear roosters crow, trucks rumble. See Rainier, and towns and cities of the lowlands.

At 2300 feet, 2 miles, is a switchback on a promontory, "Lakeview Corner." An excellent window opens down to blue waters and brown mudflats of the reservoir that drowned the primeval Lake Cushman and miles of the river, and over to Cushman Hill and Prospect Ridge, and most notably to brown crags and white snows of Ellinor and Washington, anchor peaks of the Olympic's south skyline. Rhododendron adds foreground color in June. In ½ mile more is the summit, 2600 feet, the old lookout bulldozed aside to flatten a helispot. Until some maniac runs amok with a chainsaw the screen of puny trees will prevent any better looks around than were had below at Lakeview Corner.

Round trip 5 miles, allow 3 hours
High point 2600 feet, elevation gain 1700 feet
All year

Jorsted Point (Map — page 235)

Climb by flower-brilliant walls of pillow lava to a high viewpoint. Look up and down Hood Canal from the Hamma Hamma to the Lilliwaup to the Skokomish. Look east over Green and Gold Mountains on the Kitsap Peninsula to Puget Sound and towers of downtown Seattle and volcanoes of the Cascades.

Drive Highway 101 north of Hoodsport to Jorsted Creek and on the north side turn west on the unsigned road, at first blacktop, then gravel. At a Y in 1¼

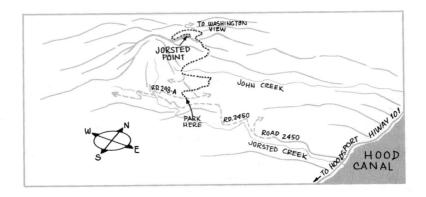

Hood Canal and Green and Gold Mountains from Jorsted Point

miles keep left on road 2450 (perhaps not so signed, but maybe signed "Heliport, Pumpsite"). In 2¼ more miles, at 700 feet, turn right on lesser and perhaps unsigned road 248A, which passes a gated waterworks and twists and turns up and out of the Jorsted valley. In a scant 1 mile road 248A levels out at 997 feet and an obscure sideroad reverse-turns left. Park here.

Bushes nearly hide the old sign, "Jorsted Point." A newer sign announces "service road — not maintained for public travel," and the narrow, steep track is a pleasant footroad rarely molested by wheels of any kind. The way switchbacks and passes through an interesting cleft between the mountainside and a high knoll, then bends around a corner into the valley of John Creek. Now begins the rock-garden walk, vertical walls of pillow lava colorful in season with alumroot, stonecrop, Scouler's bluebells, pearly everlasting, St. John's wort, starflower, penstemon, currant. Now, too, there are windows over the John valley to saltwater.

In 1¼ miles a lesser sideroad switchbacks left; proceed straight ahead, soon crossing a lovely splash of John Creek. Now the scene shifts from deep, cool second-growth to dry woods, scrubby scrawny trees, of a burn. More basalt rubble, more windows, and more flowers — rhododendron (gorgeous in June) and beargrass. At 2¾ miles the rude track switchbacks to the ridge crest at 2100 feet.

Here is a Y. For a sidetrip take the right, contouring about 1 mile above Washington Creek to a saddle with views of Washington, Pershing, Stone, and the Skokomish valley.

For the top continue left, straight, on "Heliport" road, and in a final scant 1 mile switchback twice to the small, little-used heliport atop brushy-open Jorsted Point, 2300 feet.

Though not the highest spot around, this is the best viewpoint. Burned and cleared, the crest has only small trees amid goldenrod, fireweed, rhododendron, silverleaf, salal, and beargrass. The panorama east is grand. Boats speed and sail up and down Hood Canal. Just below north is the hamlet of Eldon on the Hamma Hamma delta. South are valleys of Jorsted and Eagle Creeks, Lilliwaup Bay and River, and, far south at the Great Bend, the wide delta of the Skokomish. The wildwooded far shore of the Canal extends from Bald Point to Dewatto Bay and north to Holly, Seabeck. Dominated by Green and Gold, the Kitsap Peninsula sprawls, all the wildland of its Tahuya Peninsula near and clear. Beyond, silvery waterways of Puget Sound. Seattle, Issaquah Alps, Cascades. The mill plumes mark Shelton. Another identifies Tacoma.

Round trip (with sidetrip) 9½ miles, allow 6 hours
High point 2300 feet, elevation gain 1300 feet
All year

Webb Lookout (Map — page 237)

In a straight line with Green and Gold on the Kitsap Peninsula and the Issaquah Alps east of Seattle, both prominent in its panorama, this peak can be imagined to be a companion remnant of the "Pre-Olympic Mountains" now incorporated in the Olympics. The view is to everywhere. In addition, here is the most intimate straight-down look-from-on-high to Hood Canal, where myriad boats draw white lines over blue waters.

Drive Highway 101 to 15 miles north of Lilliwaup. Just ¼ mile north of Fulton Creek turn off west on a subdivision road signed "Webb Lookout Road" and/or "Seamount Estates, Recreational Paradise." Stick with the obvious main road as it climbs through the subdivision to its end, and then, after crossing a powerline swath, the end of habitation. The narrow, steep, but solid forest road climbs second-growth to a T at 2 miles from Highway 101.

When to stop driving, start walking? The most satisfying trip is from beach to summit, the nearly unique opportunity presented by this route. For a shorter day, though, turn left at the T and drive 2½ more miles, crossing Fulton Creek (pretty), to the crossing of South Fork Fulton Creek (also). The suggested compromise starts here, elevation 1250 feet.

Since the T the route has been on old logging railroad sliced in the steep Olympic scarp; watch for ghosts of old trestles. It's a lovely footroad tunneling in spindly trees, a 1938 Forest Service plantation after a forest fire whose silver snags are everywhere still. Traffic is rare, walkers practically never bothered by razzers. Woods pleasures are sweet, the more so in the season

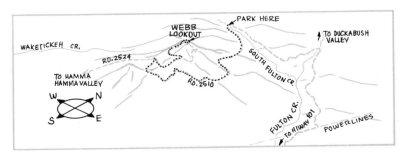

Mt. Washington from Webb Lookout

of forest flowers. But views are the feature and at 1¾ miles, 1700 feet, the first window gives promise of what awaits on high. More windows maintain the interest, as do rhododendrons, and gardens on rubbly basalt walls. At 3¼ miles, just after the road (2510) passes through a 2000-foot saddle in a spur ridge, is a junction with better road 2524 (a bore to walk) up from the Hamma Hamma. Switchback right on it and swing around the corner into nearly continuous whoopee views. In ¾ mile, at 2400 feet, this good new (logging) road continues straight; switchback left on a little old road.

In the final ½ mile to the summit a sideroad left a short bit gives the best look down Waketickeh Creek to the Hamma Hamma, and to Washington and Pershing. Above looms the bald knob of East Rock, 4269 feet, blocking the view of nearby The Brothers.

And then the 2775-foot summit. Here came the surveyor late in the fall of 1978, nearly 2 years to the day since the start of his **Footsore** journeys. He looked up and down the Olympic front from South to Jupiter. And up and down the Canal from the Great Bend to Dewatto Bay, Holly, and Bangor. And over the Kitsap Peninsula to peaks ringing the Puget Basin from Black Hills to Rainier to his home-base Issaquah Alps to Index to Glacier to Baker. Now ending his travels which he had made in the **Footsore** world, he saw nearly everywhere he had been in the 2 years, and behold, it was very good.

Round trip 9½ miles, allow 7 hours
High point 2775 feet, elevation gain 1600 feet
February-December

INDEX

INDEX